MIDSHIPMAN RNR

Midshipman RNR

by

F.N. GOODWIN

The Memoir Club

© F.N. Goodwin 2001

First published in 2001 by
The Memoir Club
Whitworth Hall
Spennymoor
County Durham

British Library Cataloguing in
Publication Data.
A catalogue record for this book
is available from the
British Library.

ISBN: 1 84104 033 9

Typeset by George Wishart & Associates, Whitley Bay.
Printed by Bookcraft (Bath) Ltd.

Dedication

This book is dedicated to my son Timothy. It was he who set the ball rolling by asking me to put down a few notes about what I had done during the war. It is also dedicated to all of his generation; for it is they who now have the responsibility for ensuring that the circumstances for writing such a book will never occur again.

Contents

List of Illustrations

Foreword

by Sir Robert Atkinson DSC (two bars) RD BSc (Eng) Fr Eng
Fi Mech E Fi MARE

I am sensible of the compliment, and indeed somewhat flattered, to be invited to write the foreword to this splendid publication.

It is rare for a midshipman to have had so much experience and to have served in so many ships of different types and sizes; also to have been deeply involved in so many incidents in different theatres of the war at sea.

He is clearly blessed with keen powers of observation and self-expression, as his diaries constantly reveal.

His attention to detail made him a precise and reliable navigator which he practised successfully in many parts of this globe; sometimes under the most appalling conditions where sound and rapid judgement was necessary.

The author deserves success with his book which, in my view, is totally accurate, and equally objective throughout. It gives a most interesting, and sometimes fascinating, account of his wide experience in several theatres of the war at sea in World War Two.

It is also well written with a penetrating sense of humour and, typically for him, flashes of human kindness and ever present humility.

Robert Atkinson

CHAPTER 1

Early Training. HM Training Ship *Conway*

First Impressions

MY FIRST SIGHT OF THE *Conway* must have been during the summer of 1937. She was moored in the Mersey several hundred yards up stream off the Rock Ferry Pier. Her traditional 19th-Century warship black-and-white livery stood out in marked contrast to the murky waters of that tidal river and one-time gateway to the sea routes of the World. Further upstream from the *Conway*, in traditional battleship grey, lay the Boys Training Ship HM Training Ship *Indefatigable*. The *Conway* trained officers for the Merchant Navy, the *Indefatigable*, boys destined for either the Merchant Navy or the Royal Navy. Although the two training ships lay so close to each other, there was virtually no contact between them. Even though the duty boats from both ships used the Rock Ferry Pier, their boy crews made little contact.

Mother and I had driven up to Birkenhead to visit the *Conway* with a view to my joining during the following year. This was the first time that I had been to the industrial North West. The dirt and squalor made a deep impression. At one point we passed a pond where even the swans were grey. At Birkenhead, on the way to the ferry that would take us to Rock Ferry, we passed a gaunt man. To me his hollow cheeks and bent stature spelled only one thing: the man was starving. I pointed this out to Mother, who hurried me along. Later in the day, after our visit to the *Conway*, we passed a youth whose face was a running sore; adolescent spots and impetigo had gone wild. One had heard of the depressed areas. This was seeing it in reality.

The actual visit to the *Conway* made far less of an impression. All that springs to mind is the sense of warmth and comfort in the Captain's sunlit quarters in the sterncastle. It was holiday time, so the ship was empty of cadets. I don't think that we went anywhere else except to the Captain's quarters.

Joining Ship

I joined the *Conway* at the start of the summer term in 1938.

Because I had done quite well in the entrance exam, I joined the 2nd term class instead of the beginner's class. The effect of this was that I was always in a different class from those of my intake. It also meant that I would do two

1. HM Training Ship Conway.

terms in the top and final class and thus have two shots at the passing out
examination. The major snag, as far as I was concerned, was that in the
signalling class I was a whole term behind. Semaphore I knew well enough
from scouts at prep school, but I had never learnt Morse and never did master
it. This was really critical when it came to the final passing out exam. To get
an 'Extra Leaving Certificate', claimed to be equivalent to a 'Higher School
Certificate', one had to get over 60 per cent marks in every subject. In my
final exam I scraped through with 61 or 62 per cent in signalling! Not good
enough to read a signal, but enough to get me my Extra Leaving Certificate.

Life Aboard a Training Ship in the Late Thirties

Life on board was very busy. As far as I know, we did as many schoolroom
hours as in any normal school. On top of that we did all the necessary ship's
work. The ship's company was divided into six divisions, one for each class in
the two-year training course. Except for the Senior Cadet Captains, we all
lived on the orlop deck, three decks below the upper deck. There each cadet
had his chest, in which he kept all his possessions. We kept the chests locked.
It was the school ethic that you didn't even sit on someone else's without
invitation. The chest was the only space in the ship that you could call your
own.

Each Division was responsible for a certain part of the ship. The whole ship was swept and, where necessary, scrubbed before morning divisions. The Captain inspected the ship on Sunday mornings. Before Sunday Divisions every deck was scrubbed and dried, every steel pillar polished, every spot of paint washed, every piece of brass polished to perfection. All done in about two hours. There was considerable rivalry between the divisions to make their part of the ship immaculate and therefore in the acquisition of the resources to do so. This meant the accumulation of cleaning gear: buckets, hand-scrubbers and soap. The only available source of these was the gear belonging to the other divisions. To leave a bucket or a scrubbing brush unattended for even a minute was to lose it. During my two years on board, the apparent official endorsement of stealing was gradually withdrawn.

All meals and most of the classes were taken on B Deck. Screens swung down from the deckhead divided the deck into classrooms. The cadets got the classrooms, tables and benches ready for class and meals. They also did all the clearing up afterwards. Everyone slept in a hammock. These occupied two decks. In the mornings, the standard time for lashing up and stowing away one's hammock was three minutes. During the first week of one's first term, one was allowed a generous five. A hammock was much more comfortable to sleep in if it was spread out by means of 'spreaders' placed between the lanyards of the hammock; up to four were allowed. The use of spreaders was a privilege that had to be earned. How this was done, I forget. The spreaders were made from notched lengths of broomhandle. These were not easy to come by. Perhaps this was why deck brooms tended to vanish.

The most unpopular task was coaling. This consisted in transferring coal from the hold to the bunker on the foc'sle for the ship's boiler, that supplied central heating and domestic hot water. The task fell to the junior cadets, who formed the coal-heaving team in the hold. More senior ones handled the coal in the boiler house. You had to be 'well in' to be the tally boy or the winch operator. The former kept a record of the number of bags hoisted and relayed the winch orders to the winch operator. He stood above the hatch to the hold and shouted orders up the winch hoist trunking to the boiler room above. His was the cleanest job of the lot, being almost free from the coal dust. In the hold there was little light and minimum ventilation. Oddly enough, a spell in the coal hold was an excellent cure for a cold. The dust mopped up all the mucous and perhaps the chemicals in the coal were too much for the cold virus.

The schoolmasters lived ashore and came aboard every morning by ship's launch. Most of the ships' officers slept on board. Their cabins were off the main deck, except for two warrant officers who had cabins at the after end of

2. HM Training Ship Conway, *Speech Day; looking for'ard from the quarterdeck. The cadet band is assembled on the roof of the physics lab. and classroom. Note the safety net spread below the mainmast. By courtesy of Wm. Cull.*

the Orlop Deck. Between them they provided 24 hours' supervision of the cadets. One, a much respected and, to us, elderly man was an ex-RN PT instructor who continued his calling on the ship. The other, a much younger man with a sarcastic disposition, was a Thames Waterman and the ship's rowing instructor. He was commonly known as 'Snarky'.

During the summer holidays of 1938 the ship underwent a major refit. One alteration made a great difference: the removal of the old open-fronted primitive lavatory cubicles. Gone were the series of public seats poised above an open channel. Down this every one's contribution was slowly propelled by a sluggish stream of Mersey water. Now there were enclosed cubicles with flush toilets supplemented by proper urinals. This probably did more to improve the morale of the cadets than any other single improvement. At last there was one place at least on the ship where one had some privacy.

Education and Training
At the start of the autumn term we joined the ship in a dock at Birkenhead. The next day tugs manoeuvred us out of the dock and upstream to our

moorings off the Rock Ferry Pier. There was, of course, only cadet power to move the rudder or to handle the mooring ropes and chains. Throughout the voyage up river most of us were below decks. At first there was the setting out of a confusing array of blocks and tackles, the function of which was only briefly explained to us. This was followed by hectic and strenuous activity as we heaved on or released various tackles. I was with a group of 15 to 20 or so of the youngest and lightest, and therefore the least strong, of the cadets. Our job was to snatch back one of the blocks of heavy tackle hauling in the mooring gear. There was little room below decks for the heavy tackle to run, so it would be heaved in for about thirty feet. The cable would then be secured and the block run out again to be secured further up the cable. Because of the weight of the blocks and thickness of the ropes, we had a light three-fold purchase to haul the block out with. All this was done at a run. Other groups of cadets were attached to tackles operating the steering gear. Possibly some of the senior classes had it all explained to them afterwards, but in my group there was little comprehension of how we fitted in with the complete operation.

The curriculum was centred on seamanship and navigation. We went through all that was required for the Board of Trade Master's Certificate and touched on some aspects required for the Extra Master's Certificate. These latter centred on the theory and practice of correcting magnetic compasses and certain aspects of marine engineering.

We had playing fields ashore. If you were so inclined, you could play rugger, hockey or cricket in season. There was no compulsion to play games. On board, in our free time, we had to find our own amusements. If the weather was good, you could climb the rigging of the main mast. But once you had overcome the initial nerves of going up the rigging and out on to the yard arms, this pastime palled. You had proved the point, at least to yourself if not to the other cadets.

Promotion

During my final year I was promoted to Junior Cadet Captain. Firstly, I think, as Ship's Postman. This was a good job. It meant that you were the only cadet that went ashore every day. In fact the Postman went ashore twice a day: in the morning to collect the ship's mail from the post office at Rock ferry and again in the evening to collect the officers' evening papers. It was in the evening that one also bought their tobacco and cigarettes for them. This gave the Postman an excuse for carrying cigarettes in the post bag. Thus he was also able to collect illicit cigarettes for the cadets. Smoking was, of course, forbidden. But naturally it was done in the heads and other 'secret' places. So although being a Junior Cadet Captain was no great thing in itself, being Postman gave one a certain amount of influence.

The other post I had was being in charge of the charthouse. The charthouse was situated on the upper deck just below the raised quarterdeck. It contained many of the features that would be found on a ship's bridge and wheel house, and was used for teaching purposes. My job was to keep the place immaculate. I was also required to keep the ship's weather log and to maintain the meteorological equipment on board. Thus began a lifetime's interest in this branch of science. The charthouse was to be kept locked at all times except when in use. Thus I had a key. I also had a large private place of my own. No one could enter without my permission. In the crowded public conditions on board, this was a wonderful escape and privilege.

On the practical side, we were taught how to row, how to sail a dinghy and a cutter, how to sew canvas, do rope work, and signalling.

On the whole it was a pleasant time. 'Happy' might be too strong a word. We were all doing what we wanted to do, namely to be trained to become the best ships' officers in the world. It was accepted that to do that properly we had to be capable of doing all the things that ships' crews had to do. We were even taught how to feed and trim a coal-fired boiler.

The Outbreak of War and the Great Freeze of 1940

The spring term of 1940 was very cold. There was heavy snow followed by a hard and prolonged frost. The water bowser at Rock Ferry froze, so our fresh water barge had to be towed down to Birkenhead to be filled. This was an all-day job. It was not long before fresh water supplies became critical and no water was available for personal washing. There was plenty of snow on the upper deck. 'If you want to wash,' we were told, 'melt some snow in a bucket in the boiler room.' When the thaw came, large snow floes drifted up and down with the tide. At this time a whale factory ship with a full cargo of whale oil was in collision and a whale oil tank was holed. Whale oil leaked out into the Mersey and mingled with the snow floes. It was not long before the down-haul ropes to our ship's boats moored out on a boom became smeared with the oil, as did the gangway. The sickly butyric smell of whale oil drifted through the ship and clung to one's clothing. It still lingered long after the oil and snow floes had been washed out to sea.

The outbreak of war made little difference. In case of an air raid, we all had to lie on the deck with our heads inboard. We practised abandoning ship – an unpopular exercise because of the effort required to hoist all the lifeboats back into their derricks at the end. For lack of use, the pulleys on the boats' falls had become stiff, if not rusty. Furthermore, the boats' derricks were much higher up than those of the daily duty boats that were hoisted out of the water every evening, so they all took far more hauling.

Cadets on all the main Merchant Navy Officer training ships, *Conway*, *Pangbourne* and *Worcester*, were automatically given honorary rank of Cadet, Royal Naval Reserve (RNR). When war broke out all cadets successfully passing out were offered commissions as Midshipman RNR. As far as I was concerned, acceptance was automatic. My father had been in the Territorial Army, as was my eldest brother. The next one up was already a Sub in the Navy. Thus it was that on the 5th May 1940, while I had still not completed the first half of my seventeenth year, I stood on the pier at Greenock in my brand-new uniform with duffle bag at my side, waiting for the launch from HMS *Canton*.

CHAPTER 2

HMS *Canton*

THE *CANTON* WAS ONE OF P&O's newest liners, launched in 1938 and now converted to an Armed Merchant Cruiser.[1] She was fitted with eight six-inch guns dating from the 1914/18 War, four on each side. Above the bridge, on the monkey island, was fitted a rangefinder and a primitive gun control system. The ship could fire a broadside of four guns. Her armament was completed by two single-barrel three-inch high-angle guns mounted on A deck abaft the single funnel. She had twin screws, each driven by three steam turbines (high, medium and low pressure). Steam was provided by oil-fired boilers giving 18,500 s.h.p. She had a service speed of 18 knots.

All the crew had cabins. Most of the officers' ones were on A or B deck. The midshipmen were allocated two-berth cabins near the main entry port on C deck. Petty Officers and ratings had cabins on C and D decks. These were shared between either two or four men per cabin. The Wardroom was what had been the first class dining room on D. deck. The Midshipmen's Gunroom, also on D deck, had been the second class dining room.

Our new ship

On arrival, the other midshipmen and I, who had joined straight from the *Conway*, were officially enrolled as Temporary Probationary Midshipmen, Royal Naval Reserve. The probationary period was, I think, three months. The 'Temporary' part was to span the duration of the War. There were eight midshipmen on board, all but one from the *Conway*. The odd one was ex-*Worcester*. The two eldest midshipmen included the man from *Worcester* and the cadet who had been the Chief Cadet Captain (i.e., head of School) on the *Conway* in the preceding year. They had both been at sea together as apprentices on a Blue Funnel Line ship. The rest of us were straight from the *Conway*. After the end of the next *Conway* summer term, we were joined by two more and I ceased to be the youngest member of the ship's company.

---

1. As a condition for a Government construction subsidy of passenger liners, it was required that during building, certain parts of the ship were to be strengthened to take naval guns.

3. HMS Canton. *By courtesy of P&O.*

Probationary Midshipman

The *Canton*, after conversion to an AMC, had been doing anti-raider patrols in the Denmark Strait. In January 1940, when on her way back from patrol in heavy weather, she struck the rocks off Barra Head on Lewis in the Outer Hebrides. The ship had been on dead reckoning for many days while on patrol and when homeward bound. It turned out that the navigator was some fifty miles out in his dead reckoning. She was lucky to get off the rocks and home without foundering. The other midshipmen and I joined her when repairs had been completed.

The ship returned to a shipyard up the Clyde for a few days. This must have been when the lower holds were loaded with empty forty-gallon oil drums. Some said that the drums had been filled with ping pong balls. The purpose was to provide greater buoyancy in the event of the ship being torpedoed. Knowing how inflammable ping pong balls were, I had hoped that that part of the story was not true. As I listened to the dockyard mateys talking to each other, I found them quite incomprehensible. From there, we went back down the Clyde to the Degaussing Range off Greenock. This was to test the equipment that would protect us from magnetic mines. It seemed to consist of a thick band of solid copper fixed all round the outside of the hull, midway between the upper deck and the waterline. After that we swung the compasses and then sailed south to Freetown.

Early Interest in Navigation

For the first month or so I shared a cabin with the senior Midshipman, none other than the ex-chief Senior Cadet Captain. On the *Conway* and later, he had been a role model. He was the navigating officer's assistant and ran the navigation plot during Action Stations. In every subsequent ship, I too became the navigating officer's assistant or 'Tanky', until I became a navigating officer or pilot myself.

When the new intake of Midshipmen arrived, the youngest berthed with me. Thus the two youngest members of the ship's company shared a cabin.

Training in Gunnery

During the first voyage all of us new midshipmen were put through the basic recruits' drills by the senior gunnery Petty Officer or Gunner's Mate. We had already learnt some parade ground drill on the *Conway*. Now we learnt to 'form threes' (instead of fours). We were also trained in rifle drill and gun drill. For the latter there was a mock six-inch gun, dummy shells and cordite bags.

Personally I found the 100-pound shells too heavy to handle easily and was always bruising my fingers in trying to get the shells into the breech. You only dropped the shell once at this game. We were all taught the drill and duties of each member of the gun team. By the time we reached Freetown, we were considered to be a competent gun's crew and a well-drilled squad.

Training however continued. We stood bridge watches under the eye of the Officer of the Watch. We were taught the rudiments of Naval Gunnery and all of us did spells in the engine room and boiler rooms. In harbour we stood four-hour gangway watches with the duty Quartermaster and gangway messenger, being responsible to the Officer of the Day.

Our First Voyage. Impressions of Freetown, South Africa

Our first port of call was Freetown where we anchored in the river. The ship was regularly surrounded by native canoes, their crews anxious to sell us fruit, coconuts, monkeys and general tourist gifts. When they talked amongst each other, it strongly reminded me of what I had heard at the ship repair yard at Glasgow.

Among the canoe owners was one we knew as King Kong. He was a remarkable mimic and was adept at copying the bo'sun's whistle and calls. No doubt egged on by the crew, he would mimic the bo'sun's call for 'Stand Easy', thereby bringing all work on the upper deck to a standstill. One day, when on gangway watch, word had come down that the Captain was going ashore at a certain time and that he did not wish to be piped over the side. As

Midshipman of the Watch, I warned the duty Quarter Master and Bo'sun's Mate. In spite of that, to my horror and the fury of the Captain, the Bo'sun's whistle shrilled out the moment the Captain stepped onto the gangway. He glared at me in protest and anger. While still saluting and before he could say anything, I nodded my head towards King Kong's canoe lying just for'ard of the gangway. The Captain followed my eye and, with a nod of exasperation, continued his way down to the launch.

The Commanding Officer (Captain G.D. Belben DSC AM) and the Commander (Cmdr(G) C.H.Lingard-Gutherie) were both RN Officers. The Commander had been pulled out from retirement and possibly also the Captain. The Commander was the first hard-drinking officer that I had ever met. When on the harbour 8pm-to-midnight gangway watch, it was not unusual, in the late hours of the watch, to see the Commander pulling himself up the stairway from the wardroom. As he reached deck level, he then had to negotiate twenty feet or so of open deck to reach the handrail of the next flight of stairs up to the next deck level. He would pull himself upright, fix his eyes on to the bottom of the next stairway, and with great concentration make it to the next handrail. Although he may have consumed a commanding proportion of gin in harbour, I am not aware that he ever drank at sea.

All the other deck officers were RNR. Most had been serving on the *Canton* in peacetime. The same applied to the Engineering Officers. Many of the lower deck were also ex-P&O. The Gunroom steward was one of them. Apart from being a steward, he had also been in the ship's band and played the accordion. Occasionally he could be persuaded to give us a tune or two. Probably all the Petty Officers (POs) and senior ratings were RN, with a smattering of Reserve and Hostilities Only (HO) personnel. All the signalmen were RN. The Merchant Navy was never renowned for expertise in signalling.

Escort Duties

When escorting a convoy, the *Canton* was usually stationed somewhere in the centre of the convoy as a precaution against a submarine torpedo attack. Our function was to protect the convoy from surface attack by raiders. We had virtually no anti-submarine capability. Orders to the convoy were conveyed to the ships by signal flags. Each ship, including ourselves, would repeat the signal hoists so that they could be clearly seen by other ships down the columns. This gave us midshipmen a chance to show off our signalling abilities.

A duty of the Midshipman of the Watch was to keep an eye on the

Commodore for signals. There were usually two midshipmen on watch at a time. Mike and I, certainly on one voyage, shared the watch. We commandeered a very large telescope that was intended to be used by the signalmen, though they preferred to use their own. The large telescope was mounted on a stand. The extra magnification allowed us to distinguish the flags hoisted by the Commodore even when they were being blown end on to us.

It was not long before a competition developed between us and the signalmen about who could first read the messages. With the better telescope, we usually won. In time we found that if we shifted the telescope's stand a little, we could keep the Commodore's flag deck and his flag locker in full view. We watched the signalmen bending the flags on to the halyards as they made up a signal. Knowing the storage place for each flag, we could read the signal before it was hoisted. At first the Chief Yeoman was very sceptical, but in time he realised that we were accurate. Soon co-operation replaced rivalry. As the flags were pulled from the Commodore's flag locker, we sang them out and our signalmen made up the halyard. A quick confirmation of the signal as it was being hoisted, and our repeat signal was up almost before the signal halyards were secured on the Commodore ship.

The ship's main task was anti-raider patrol in the South Atlantic. We would sail out from Freetown and go westwards into the South Atlantic until we reached close to the 300-mile South American exclusion zone. We stayed at sea for about three weeks before going to Simonstown to refuel. From there we would go out on patrol and then fuel at Freetown. There were long spells without mail because when we got to Simonstown, the mail would be waiting for us at Freetown. By the time we got back to Freetown, the mail would have been sent to wait for us at Simonstown.

Gunnery Practice
The tedium of patrol was broken by gunnery practice. This was always a very long-drawn-out affair. Even by 1940 standards, the system of gunnery control was quite primitive. Each gun layer and gun trainer had a repeater dial that indicated the bearing of the gun and its elevation. The repeaters on the guns had two sets of pointers. One operated from the gunnery control position and the other from the gun. By winding their gun elevation and training handles, the gun layer and gun trainer had to keep the two pointers in line. The gun layers' repeaters were dominated by the range to the target and the roll of the ship. The longer the range, the more the gun barrel had to be cocked up into the air to throw the shell the required distance. Each time the guns were closed up, the repeaters had to be checked for accuracy. This is where the trouble lay. Some of the repeaters were invariably out. It took ages

to get them right. The repeaters were electrically operated by Direct Current (DC) circuits. These were very vulnerable to spontaneous earthing, especially in a salt-laden atmosphere.

To save on ammunition, we would fire a .303-rifle bullet instead of a six-inch shell. Fitting rifles into the breach of each gun and getting them properly lined up and calibrated also took a long time. At last everything would be ready. The target would be thrown overboard. This would be a wooden crate with a canvas sail fitted to it to give greater visibility. Then away we would go.

'Target bearing green 040, Range 0700, Load! load! load!'

When each gun came onto bearing and was loaded, the layer would press the 'Gun ready' button. The moment all the ready buttons were lit, the order would be 'Salvos!' This meant that only one gun from each battery would fire the moment the target was centred on the gunlayer's cross wires. Corrections would be left or right until the splashes from the 'shells' were in line with the target. Then we could see if we were shooting short of or over the target. Once the fall of shot was seen to straddle the target, the order 'broadsides!' would be given. Then all guns that could bear on the target would fire. When at Freetown we would sometimes go out and fire full-sized rounds at a towed target. This was much more exciting than popping off .303 cartridges and spelt a busy time for the carpenters and electricians. The cabin doors were not solid. They consisted of wooden-louvred slats. The concussion from a broadside of the four six-inch guns could be felt throughout the ship. Between broadsides one could hear the clatter of the loosened louvres falling to the deck. The concussion also loosened the overhead conduits carrying the electrical cables along the gangway deck heads and they hung in sad twisted loops after each exercise.

I never saw how well or badly we did. My action station was in the 'Aft Transmission Station'. This was a small back-up unit designed to relay the orders to the guns should the main Transmission Station, or TS, be put out of action. It was located in what had originally been a store-room within the superstructure and close to the after starboard-side battery. The room was completely enclosed with a steel door. No windows or portholes, just forced draught for ventilation. The crew consisted of three: myself, ostensibly in charge, a one-badge leading seaman gunner and a three-badge able seaman. Apart from headphones for communication with the gunnery officer and the guns, we had two 1914 hand-held mechanical devices on which we kept tally of the various traverse and range corrections that had been made. This tally was necessary because, when at a normal fighting range of several miles, there would be one or more salvos or broadsides in the air on their way to the enemy when our shells splashed down. Any corrections to be made on the result of that fall of shot had to take into account the settings on the guns when they had last fired.

Putting me in charge of the TS is a typical example of the way that the Navy encouraged junior officers to accept responsibilities. There was I, the youngest member of the ship's company, placed in charge of two men, one of whom was at least ten years older than I and the other twice my age. If the worst came to the worst, I was expected to go out on deck and take charge of whichever after battery was being engaged. The strangest thing of all was that the ratings seemed to accept the situation.

Patrol Duties

Patrolling was a very routine affair. Only a few instances have stuck in my mind. On one such occasion a solitary ship had been sighted at night. We went to action stations and all was made ready to open fire before the ship was challenged. The ship turned out to be a Dutchman. We must have given her an awful fright because she immediately broadcast an emergency report. Having satisfied ourselves that the ship was what she said she was, she was allowed to proceed. We broadcast a message to counter the Dutchman's report. Later on I was astonished to learn from the Senior Telegraphist that our message to the Admiralty from the South Atlantic had been acknowledged by the RN Station at Hong Kong. The Dutchman had been identified partially with the aid of a book containing a photograph or a silhouette and description of practically every merchant vessel of any significance in the world.

One of the ex-P&O officers told me that he had earned extra money by taking photographs of foreign vessels including warships and sending them to the Admiralty. Possibly to embellish the story, he claimed that so as not be seen to be taking photographs of ships, he took the photographs through an empty rivet hole from inside a ship's ventilator.

The swimming pool on the upper deck was enjoyed by all the ship's company. Different hours of the day were allocated to separate sections of the crew. Diving into the surge of water as the ship pitched in the sea-way was fun, but discouraged after somebody nearly came a cropper when he mis-timed his dive. At the deep end, the water was deep enough to make diving for pennies a bit of a challenge. Crossing the Line ceremonies were of course centred on the pool. On our first voyage the new entry of midshipmen gave Neptune's assistants a satisfying bunch of initiates. The ordeal was not as tough and rough as we had been led to believe.

4. Statue in Simonstown in memory of 'Just Nuisance'.

South African Experiences

Simonstown was our preferred southern port. It was a short electric train journey from Cape Town, where there were bars, restaurants and cinemas for our enjoyment. At that time there lived near the Simonstown dockyard a Great Dane called Just Nuisance. He was already famous in Naval circles. He travelled with the first of the day's libertymen on the train to Cape Town. He also accompanied them back and was reputed to look after anyone who was in trouble or the worse for drink. He frequently slept on board and made up his own mind whom he was going to honour with his company. You don't dictate to a dog that size. A statue of Just Nuisance overlooks Simonstown harbour.

There was only one snag with the Simonstown – Cape Town train. There was no loo on board. Now this was an essential facility on a half-hour journey from the bars of Cape Town. However the guard had an understanding nature. A queue would form in his van to take advantage of a loose section of plank that he raised from the floor. This too was something of an adventure. What, one wondered, would happen if one's stream contacted the numerous sparks that flashed out from the darkness below the carriage?

We spent several days in the drydock at the naval yard. During this period another midshipman and I spent a wonderful weekend with a family out at Bloemfontein. It was a whole day's car drive from Cape Town. I remember little about that drive. It was long, dusty and hot, but well worth it. I can't even recall the name of our hosts, but their house was sheer pleasure. My main memory was the delight of cool white sheets in a large bed, the early morning sun shining through the window and the sound of strange birds outside. Lying in bed I looked across a wide green lawn. There in the middle was a large tree with dark green leaves. From the spreading boughs dangled the largest lemons that I had ever seen.

'Now that,' I thought, 'is wonderful. To have a lemon tree growing in the centre of one's garden and all that that implied. What could be better than that?'

How that trip was organized I do not know. It was all part of the wonderful hospitality that was bestowed on us throughout South Africa.

At the time of Dunkirk, we were down Freetown way. To us in the Gunroom, it sounded as though the UK would be invaded and occupied at any time. There was much speculation on what we should do. There were only two alternatives: one was somehow to continue the fight from South Africa, but this did not seem very viable. The other, and the one decided upon, was that the ship should be taken to Canada and the War continued from there. How that was to be done was never seriously debated. We just did not know. But somehow the fight would continue and eventually we would win.

It was some time after that, when on patrol, that I heard on the radio a report of Churchill speaking to Parliament on events leading up to the surrender of France. He told how he had offered some form of common citizenship between France and the UK if only France would continue the fight. If that had been thought of years ago, I thought, maybe this War would never have started. My brother David would be alive and I would be a cadet on a Union Castle ship heading for the delights of Cape Town.

The War. Leave in the UK

Some time after this we were back in the UK and I went home on my first leave. Fears of invasion were still current. We had to take with us our tin hat and gas mask. We were also issued with a .45 revolver and 20 or so rounds of ammunition. Our orders were that if an invasion took place while on leave, we should report to the nearest LDV (the 'Dad's Army') and offer our assistance. We were only to return to the ship if we were not needed and if transport back to Greenock was available. It was a sad home-coming. Mother had already written to me to tell me that my eldest brother David had been killed in Belgium. My last sight of him had been in September '39, when I had ridden on my bike to Stourport to watch him and the Seventh Worcesters march out of barracks on their way to France. A few days earlier I had gone up to his room, where I had found him packing away his things. I had never seen him so quiet. He told me that he had seen how effective bren guns were. Anyway, Subalterns had a low level of life expectancy. He didn't expect to come back.

We had expected to be in the UK for Christmas 1940. However the *Canton's* large oil bunkers and long range played against us. We were to escort a convoy from Freetown to Glasgow and took on board as passengers several Colonial Service civil servants from the Gambia and Ivory Coast. They were over-due for leave and were thrilled at the chance to take passage home. Towards the end of the voyage, word came through that our oppo ship, the *Carnarvon Castle* had encountered the surface raider *Thor* (Captain Otto Kahler) and had not come off too well. As we neared the Western Approaches, we were ordered to leave the convoy and return to Freetown at our best speed. The patrol gap in the South Atlantic had to be plugged. Our poor passengers! They had actually had a sight of the UK before we turned round and headed south.

We were back in the South Atlantic both for Christmas and the New Year and were at sea for Christmas. Although there was no wind, there was a big swell running. The morning watch was ending and most of the ship's company were enjoying their Christmas dinner. For some reason we had to alter course. To do this would mean that we would have to swing broadside on to the swell. The ship was already rolling quite violently so word was sent down below to warn everybody that this was going to get worse as we changed course. The two officers of the watch discussed the problem of when in the rolling cycle would be the best time to put the helm over. The decision made, they waited. 'Port fifteen.' The ship hesitated as she started to turn, and away she rolled to port, further and further. The inclinometer went past the fifteen degrees mark, past twenty and still she rolled. We were too far above the mess decks to hear the clattering of the plates as they slid off the tables. I believe she just about touched 30 degrees before we slid down the other side of the swell and came back on to an even keel. After that, the motion was much better as we headed more directly into the sea. Shortly afterwards the watch changed and I went down to the Gunroom. It was only then that I realised what chaos had resulted when we rolled. In the Gunroom we lost about a third of our large plates and few of my messmates could complete their Christmas Dinner. Too much had slid onto the deck. There was not much left for me either. So that was my first Christmas at sea. We made up for it on New Year's Eve because we were back in port by then. A few months earlier we had had another intake of midshipmen from the *Conway*. I was no longer the youngest on board, so it was the boy that I now shared a cabin with who had the honour of ringing in the New Year with 16 bells on the Ship's bell at midnight.

Back to Escort Duty from Freetown

Early in the New Year we escorted a convoy to the UK, leaving from Freetown. Shortly before, Fleet Orders had announced that the wearing of pith sun helmets by officers on formal occasions in the tropics was no longer required. The Gunroom greeted this with much joy. Shortly before we sailed on the ebb tide, we ceremoniously launched our pith helmets into the estuary.

This time we went to Liverpool instead of Glasgow and tied up opposite the Liver Buildings. Soon after we arrived, I was given a signal ordering me home on leave to await a new posting. By that time I had already had a wooden chest made by the ship's carpenter for stowing all my possessions. This was well made and secured together by long brass screws. It lasted me until well after the War. I packed my 'sea chest' and bag and spent that night at the Central Station Hotel. Business there was slack. The dining room was almost empty and I felt intimidated by the three elderly waiters who hovered behind me, anticipating my every need.

CHAPTER 3

HMS *Abdiel*

Joining Ship

I DON'T REMEMBER HOW LONG I was on leave – probably not much more than a week. I was ordered to report to an office at or near Portsmouth for instructions for HMS *Abdiel*. I had no idea what sort of ship the *Abdiel* might be. The person I reported to was not forthcoming, except to say that she was not in the Solent. After a telephone call, he suggested I should report to the Senior Naval Officer (SNO) at Gourock on the Clyde. I was issued the necessary warrants and caught a train heading north. It dumped me, in the middle of the night, at Hereford. There I was told that my best bet was to catch the milk train to Warrington leaving at about five in the morning. In the meantime I was welcome to doss down in a carriage standing in a siding. The ticket collector promised to wake me in good time. It was not a very comfortable night but the hot sweet tea that he awoke me with was most welcome.

The *Abdiel*

It took me most of that day to get to Gourock. Enquiries at the pier directed me to a tall RN Lieut-Commander with a trim ginger beard. When I introduced myself, he said that he was going to the *Abdiel* and that the launch was already on its way. I asked what sort of ship she was. 'Oh a fast Minelayer!' was the response, but all that I registered was the word 'Minelayer'. There was nothing out there that looked anything like my conception of a minelayer. I imagined that she would look more like a merchant ship than a warship. I felt a little disappointed. Mine-laying sounded rather a dull occupation. All the way across in the launch, I kept wondering which ship we were going to. It was something of a shock when I realized that we were going alongside a grey three-funnelled ship, too big for a destroyer, too small for a cruiser.

This was the first of a brand-new class of warship, the *Abdiel*-Class Fast Minelayers. They were designed for offensive minelaying operations. Speed was a major operational requirement, because most operations would be conducted close to enemy shores. A rapid approach and departure under cover of darkness was the assumed operational method. With a capacity of

5. HMS Abdiel *on trials in March 1941.*
By courtesy of the Imperial War Museum. Neg. 4388.

150 mines in one mining deck, a design speed of just under 40 knots and
adequate gun armament, the ships were well equipped for this role. These
attributes also made them useful for the carriage of stores and personnel,
where speed and evasion were of the essence. The *Abdiel* was used in all these
tasks.

She had a displacement of 2,650 tons, an overall length of 418ft with a
beam of 40ft. She was equipped with three twin 4in-HA/LA guns, two
for'ard and one aft; also one four-barrelled pom-pom and two 4-barrelled
0.5in machine guns. Machinery comprised geared turbines developing
72,000hp at 350 revolutions, driving two shafts and supplied with
superheated steam from four boilers situated in two boiler rooms. These
would give a speed of 39.75 knots in standard conditions and 36 knots in
deep draught. She had a complement of 240.

I quickly realized two things. Firstly that this was a unique ship. All the
officers, except the Doctor (MO) and myself, were regular RN, as were all
the senior and most of the junior ratings. I had joined an exclusive and elite
club. Secondly, it was soon apparent that no one knew quite what to do with
a midshipman. There was no accommodation for one. As a temporary
measure, I was bunked down with the MO, who had the only two-berth

6. HMS Abdiel, *Ship's Officers, 1941. Left to right: Lieut. McHarry;
Lieut. Lapage; Lieut. Baxter; Lieut. Pearce; Sub-Lieut. Rockford; Lieut. Commander
(E) Brown; Capt. The Hon. Pleydell Bouverie; Lieut. Commander (T) Chavasse;
Mr Millham, Gunner; Pay Lieut. Cmdr. Allen; Pay Sub-Lieut. Bristow;
Mr Mullins, Gunner (T); Pay Mid. Henton.*

cabin. Later I was given a camp bed on the mining deck. For my clothes, I
had a chest of drawers located in the lower cabin flat.

The ship was commanded by Capt: E.P. De-Bouverie RN. The other
ship's officers included a Lieut Cmdr RN specialist mining officer (usually
referred to as 'Torps'); the Pilot (Navigating Officer) was a Lieut, RN.
Subsequently, I was told, he did some sterling cloak-and-dagger work on the
Sicilian beaches in preparation for the landings there. The Paymaster was a
Lieut, RN, with a rather tense disposition. No doubt it was a legacy from the
trauma of being on the *Exeter* during the Battle of the River Plate. The
gunnery officer was a Sub-Lieut, RN, a pugnacious young man, who,
unusually for those days, had come up from the lower deck. He had started
his career as a boy seaman, ex-one of the Arethusa training ships. There were
two Warrant Officers, one gunnery and the other torpedo (in this case a
mine specialist). The engine room department was very strong, being headed
by a Commander (E) RN assisted by a Lieut-Cmdr (E) RN. The MO was
an R.N.V.R. officer ex-Guy's Hospital.

When I joined, the ship was still undergoing acceptance trials. Several of the builder's officials were on board.

Minelaying off Brest

In the very early hours of March 22nd orders from the Admiralty resulted in immediate preparations for sea. We sailed at five in the morning, proceeding at 36 knots towards Milford Haven. We arrived there early that afternoon, having had to reduce speed to 30 knots because of problems with one of the turbines. This dash down the west coast at speeds equivalent to over 40 mph, in misty, variable visibility, was quite a strain on the watch keepers. Although we had RDF (now known as RADAR) it was of a fixed-bearing type and anyway, very rarely worked. Trawlers and small craft would emerge out of the gloom, often at quite close range, giving little time for either of us to get out of each other's way. Discussion in the wardroom afterwards resulted in the decision, under those sort of conditions, to cut down the watch to two-hour stretches and to ensure that there were always two experienced officers on the bridge.

As soon as we arrived at Milford Haven, we went alongside the mine-loading jetty. We anticipated that we would start loading mines immediately. The official report said we did so. However, my recollection was that things did not start all that quickly. It was a Sunday afternoon when we arrived and the jetty was deserted. The Squadron Torpedo Officer (Torps) went ashore to chivvy things up and it was several hours before the civilian personnel of the mine depot could be roused out from their houses and start the mines rolling down the track to the ship. I think we used our own hoists for loading the mines. These consisted of an electric crane at the after loading hatch and the paravane derrick at the for'ard hatch. Once started, loading continued at a fair pace until 19.00. From then on it became slower and slower. Finally we sailed at 22.00 with 15 mines short of complement. We had to arrive at Plymouth in daylight and it was considered inappropriate to steam round the coast at high speed during the night. Even so, we arrived at Plymouth at 08.30 the next morning, having steamed at 28 knots once clear of the land. We sailed again at 13.00 escorted by the *Kashmir* and *Kipling* and carried out a minelaying operation off Brest against a possible break-out of the German heavy ships, *Scharnhorst* and *Gneisenau*.

In a report on the operation, Capt. Bouverie commented: 'The ship had only been in commission 15 days and had done no high speed steaming whatever. A great number of the Ship's Company are extremely inexperienced and the ship herself has not been accepted from the builders.' An Admiralty minute on the report reads:

'This is undoubtedly a most creditable performance. It is extremely gratifying to those who have advocated for many years the building of minelayers with the characteristics which the *Abdiel* alone possesses, that the maiden voyage of the first of the class should have been so outstandingly successful.' The Admiralty sent the ship a congratulatory signal.

A Brief Farm Leave

The ship returned to the builder's yard on the Isle of White for repairs and I obtained permission to visit my old school friend Dennis Whidborne at his father's farm in Hampshire. Before the War Dennis's father had run a small dairy farm on water meadows outside Winchester. The family had lived at Twyford and Dennis's mother took in paying guests to supplement the farm income. Even so, Dennis and his sister were put through private education. Dennis's father had an arrangement to collect all the playing field mowings from Winchester College. He used a small trailer towed behind his car. The mowings were used for making silage in a 'tower' silo made from wooden slats and craft paper. Dennis and I spent many a time treading the cuttings in the silo to compact them whilst watering on a dilute solution of molasses to help the silage to cure. The new farm was a much larger arable affair. It had been sorely neglected in the depressed years before the War. They had taken on the tenancy and were already getting reasonable yields. Unfortunately for them, some years later, when the farm was a really good going concern, the landlord decided to take the place in hand himself. The Whidbornes had to leave. Dennis's father then took on the management of two farms on the edge of Dartmoor. I learnt to plough on one of those farms.

It was a pleasant interlude. It must have been nearly two years since I had seen Dennis. He was now working full time on the farm and was just getting used to the idea of being in a reserved occupation. He had hoped to join the Navy.

I crossed the Solent to Southampton, which had recently been heavily bombed. I found a car hirer. Business must have been pretty low. I recall his startled expression when he saw that my licence was a very recent probationary one. He reluctantly let me go. Enquiring about the smell close to the garage, I was told that an air raid shelter had recently received a direct hit. It was now just a pile of rubble and it was likely that the bodies would remain there.

Passage to the Eastern Med.

We went back to the Clyde to resume the programme of acceptance trials. These were finally abandoned in mid-April, when we were loaded with

guns, torpedoes and other military equipment. They were to be delivered to
Malta. The ship would then carry on to the Eastern Mediterranean. We
travelled with six J.- and K.-Class Destroyers under the command of the
Captain D (Lord Louis Mountbatten?).[1] Before leaving the UK our anti-
aircraft armoury was augmented by placing two 35mm-oerlikons on the
foc'sle and a new anti-aircraft 3in-rocket launcher on the superstructure abaft
No 3 funnel. We encountered heavy weather in the Bay of Biscay and sought
permission to slow down. The flotilla had been pressing south at a fairly high
cruising speed. *Abdiel* was making heavy weather of it into the incoming
seas. Eventually the flotilla moderated speed. By that time the gun shields on
the oerlikons had been flattened back by the seas coming in over the bow.

Being so new, the rest of the fleet knew little of the capabilities of the
Abdiel Class. This was demonstrated when, in calm weather, we approached
the western entrance to the Straits of Gibraltar. Captain D, wishing to
get into harbour as quickly as possible, ordered his destroyers to form line
ahead formation and increase speed to 30 knots. *Abdiel* was told to act
independently, presumably on the assumption that she would soon be left
behind. I was fortunate to be on the bridge at the time to see and hear what
transpired. As soon as the signal was received, the Captain called the Chief
Engineer to him. After a brief discussion concerning the state of the engines
and the remaining fuel, speed was increased. As we steamed past the Flotilla
Leader we sent the signal 'Will this do?' We were already tied up and taking
in fuel by the time the destroyers came in.

I do not recall much of the passage to Malta, or of the onward voyage to
Alexandria. My main memories are of watching the torpedoes being secured
and lifted up through the mining hatches. The torpedoes were for the
remaining submarine(s?) still operating from Malta. There must have been an
opportunity to go ashore. I recall clambering over large limestone building
blocks that had fallen into the street from the bombed buildings. Once
leaving Malta, which I think we did at nightfall, there was a high-speed dash
to distance ourselves from the Island before daybreak. We were closed up at
action stations for a long time and when not actually at action stations, we
were at the next stage of readiness. I also recall watching the firing of our
new anti-aircraft rockets. This, I think, must have been a practice run because
my action station was in the Transmission Station (TS) well below decks.

Operations with Destroyers

Because of our anti-aircraft capability and speed, we operated as a destroyer

---

1. *Kelley, Kipling, Kelvin, Kashmir, Jackal & Jersey:* Cunningham; *A Sailor's Odyssey*, p. 360.

whenever we were at sea with the main battlefleet. During air attacks, we generally put up an anti-aircraft barrage over one of the capital ships as a deterrent to the dive bombers. To be effective, it was necessary that we worked well with the destroyer flotillas. Towards this end we spent a lot of time on exercise off Alexandria with the destroyers. These usually took the form of 'equal speed manoeuvres'. They can be likened to army parade drill. The ships would go through a variety of formation changes. From line ahead to line abreast, for example, all carried out at high, but constant speed. At times officers of the watch and other junior officers were required to take charge of the ship. Even I was allowed, under the watchful eye of Torps, to give the helm orders. This was a great thrill. There was something immensely satisfying in having successfully followed exactly in the wake of the ship ahead through a 90° turn. This was not as easy as it sounds. We were operating with destroyers, whereas the *Abdiel*'s steering characteristics were nearer those of a cruiser.

On one of these exercises we were detached to search for the pilot of a downed Hurricane. He was said to have parachuted down close to the coast. We never found him. The odds against doing so were very heavy. There was a bit of a sea running at the time, so the chance of spotting the pilot's head during the brief moment when he rode over a wave crest was very, very small.

Shortly after we arrived at Alexandria, we were involved in a major fleet operation in support of bringing a handful of merchant ships to and from Malta, which had become desperately short of military supplies. The fleet was also being reinforced by the battleship *Queen Elizabeth* and the cruisers *Naiad* and *Fiji*. This introduced me to the intricacies of destroyer screen work and to the problems involved when moving at high speed from one position on the screen to another. This was probably the last occasion on which we operated with the battle fleet. After that we were fully engaged in moving troops and stores, either in conjunction with destroyers or on our own. However we did lay one minefield before being fully committed to other duties. This was in the early hours of 21st May, in the western approaches to the Gulf of Patras. The minefield was laid between the islands of Cephalonia and Levkas This proved to have been most successful. In a few hours the minefield accounted for two large German transports from a convoy carrying part of an armoured division on its way from Greece to the Russian front. Two escorts, the destroyer *Mirabella* and the gunboat *Matteucci*, were also sunk.[2]

---

2. Burton; *Profile Warship, Abdiel Class Fast Minelayers*; p. 30: Nov. 1973.

The Battle for Crete

The battle for Greece had recently come to a sticky end, with the fleet evacuating a large proportion of the British Army that had been engaged there. The battle for Crete started on May 20th, a little over a month after our arrival in the Eastern Med. On the 24th we embarked troops and 50 tons of stores of the Layforce (Special Service Troops) and accompanied by two destroyers similarly burdened, landed these at Suda Bay on the night of the 26th-27th. At Suda we embarked some 50 wounded soldiers, four Greek cabinet Ministers and several POWs including a young Luftwaffe pilot. I met him briefly as he was being taken below. He was very blond and about my age, although he looked younger. We heard that the POWs were extremely nervous for their safety. They knew that we would have to pass very close to the German dive bomber base. They were convinced that we would be sunk. They had some justification for this, because already the fleet had suffered several ships sunk or badly damaged. There had been several air attacks both outward and homeward bound. These attacks were difficult to follow from the TS. We were lucky not to be hit and received several near misses. Some had been close enough for us in the TS to hear bomb splinters striking the hull.

> At 6 a.m. on May 31st Rear-Admiral King in the cruiser *Phoebe* with the minelayer *Abdiel* and the destroyers *Kimberley*, *Hotspur* and *Jackal* sailed from Alexandria to carry out the final evacuation from Sphakia, a small fishing village on the south coast of the island. The village and the shingle beach, no more than 200 yards of which could be used by ships' boats, was hemmed in by a rugged cliff 500 feet high. At first it was thought that not more than 2,000 troops could be lifted off. Later the force was authorised to embark a maximum of 3,500 troops.[3]

Subsequently we were ordered to fill to capacity. Between 11.20 p.m. of May 31st and 3 a.m. on June 1st, 4,000 men were embarked. but many had to be left behind. We returned to Alexandria without incident, but the *Calcutta* which together with the *Coventry* had sailed to provide additional air defence, was dive-bombed and sunk.

It was pitch dark when we arrived off the beach. We were at full action stations because it was not known whether the beach was still in our hands. After a few tense moments, we heard very English voices coming over the water and in a moment the first of the landing craft came alongside. I have no clear memory of the actual embarkation of the troops. They were mostly New Zealanders, including Maoris. Their mood was generally one of resentment at having to give up the fight. They reckoned that they had been

---

3. Cunningham, *A Sailor's Odyssey*, p. 387.

doing very well. In proof, some of the Maoris had strange things fixed to their belts. On enquiry and closer examination, these proved to be ears. It was a Maori custom to collect an ear of any enemy killed in combat. By the time we left, the ship was jam packed. The troops were not allowed on the upper deck or anywhere else other than the mining deck or mess decks. It was essential to keep the working and fighting parts of the ship clear of any passengers. The rule was relaxed once we reached the approaches to Alexandria. Many of the troops came up on to the upper deck out of the stench below decks. With so many on board, the normal sanitary arrangements were overwhelmed. Many had to relieve themselves where they were. The mining deck had not been entirely cleared of stores before the evacuation started. The troops, many of whom had been without food for some time, fell on the store crates, opening them and the tins they contained with their bayonets. Many of the crates were of tomato puree and there is only so much of that that one can eat at a time. It took a lot of hosing down afterwards to get rid of the mess and the smell.

Once we knew which side we were going to at the landing wharf, all troops were cleared to the other side. This gave us quite a list to port, which quickly prompted an anxious signal from the C. in C., Cunningham, asking if we had suffered any damage. No doubt he was very relieved to receive the assurance that there was none, since, to quote his own words:-

> 'The Mediterranean Fleet suffered severe losses in the battle for Crete. The *Gloucester*, *Fiji*, and *Calcutta* sunk along with the destroyers *Juno*, *Greyhound*, *Kashmir*, *Kelly*, *Hereward* and *Imperial*. The battleships *Warspite* and *Barham*, the aircraft carrier *Formidable* along with the *Orion*, *Dido*, *Kelvin* and *Nubian* were damaged beyond repair on the spot. The *Perth*, *Naiad*, *Carlisle*, *Napier*, *Kipling* and *Decoy* would be under repair for several weeks and the *Havock*, *Kingston* and *Nizan* for a fortnight. Over 2,000 men of the fleet had died. Losses such as these would normally only occur during a major fleet action, in which the enemy might be expected to suffer greater losses than our own.'[4]

As it was, these heavy losses were caused by enemy aircraft, mostly by Junkers 88 dive bombers.

At Alexandria our normal berth was on the outer mole. From there we were in a good position to provide effective anti-aircraft fire against any enemy aircraft approaching from the sea. After Crete there were frequent air raids, usually at night. One evening we had a very lucky escape in the form of a near-miss from a bomb which landed right alongside but just on the seaward side of the mole.

---

4. Cunningham, *A Sailor's Odyssey*, p. 389.

These air raids and the general activity against aircraft at sea caused the Gunnery Warrant Officer a great deal of trouble. It was his responsibility to account for all the ammunition used. Admiralty accounting requirements had not really been adjusted to war conditions. They were still immersed in the days of the depression, when every round and every empty cartridge had to be accounted for. These niceties were not compatible when the highest possible rates of fire, which were often the order of the day. Under those conditions, the guns crews had little interest in keeping empty 4" cartridges around so that they could be counted and stowed away at the end of the action. The most common reaction was to kick any empty cartridges that got in the way off the gun platform. From there, many rolled overboard. The Gunner's problem was that he could not match up empty cartridges with missing rounds. He had many a sleepless night over his account books and magazine records. By the time we left the Med, sense had prevailed and accounting procedures had been made more realistic.

Reinforcement of Cyprus

After Crete, our time in the Eastern Med was occupied with moving troops and military stores to Cyprus and Tobruk. The Cyprus operation started soon after the battle for Crete. We operated with a group of destroyers, at first loading at Haifa and later on at Port Said. The destination each time was Famagusta, a castellated walled harbour on the east coast. Often, as we approached, the first sign of the island would be a sweet, almost sickly, scent, from some flowering tree or shrub. I imagined these as being lotus trees. The harbour itself was fascinating, being obviously very old. Huge stone blocks formed the sea walls and jetty, with castle-like towers defending the harbour. None of us ever went ashore. It was a case of unloading the troops and their equipment as quickly as possible and getting away out to sea again.

At base the army had a red-faced major in charge of loading. He was dubbed by us the 'Mad Major'. This was chiefly because he always wanted things loaded in a different order to that which we had decided upon. He would shout and rage and get very red in the face when we insisted on having things done our way. Poor man! He took himself so seriously and we treated him, safely from the kingdom of our ship, as an object of fun. On one occasion the troops brought with them their goat mascot. There was a great fuss when it was disembarked. The Government vet refused it permission to land, while we refused to have it back on board. We sailed before the matter was resolved, but I expect the goat joined the next curry.

We likened ourselves to carriers and furniture removers. Each ship designed its own 'Firm's' pennant, which we flew at the masthead. Ours was based on the famous firm of Pickfords.

By this time my normal sleeping quarter was on a camp bed on the mining deck. This got pretty hot, so I moved my bed to a cosy spot abaft the third funnel. Although cooler than down below, the fumes from the funnel would waft down to me and the bedding required frequent washing from the smuts.

The *Latona* joins us in the Med

Towards the end of June we were joined by the second of the fast minelayers to be completed, the *Latona*. Like us, she did not complete her acceptance trials and her work-up-cruise was her passage to the Mediterranean via the Cape.

She too had a single midshipman in her complement. We soon made friends and went ashore together whenever we had the opportunity. Together we went through the adolescent stage of finding out how much we could drink without getting completely pie-eyed. We would only patronize those bars that provided lots of canapés. In that way we did not have to interfere with drinking time by having a meal. At times we were wholly irresponsible. We found a delightful bar in Alexandria which was on the first floor. From the window overlooking the street, we dropped empty bottles. We liked it partly because they whistled a bit like a bomb as they went down, and partly because of the satisfying crash as they hit the street below. By good fortune we never hurt anybody. Another prank was to take a gari to the landing pier when it was time to catch the liberty boat back to the ship. We would threaten the gari driver that we would not pay his fare unless we had a go at driving the poor gari horse at a gallop.

During the dark periods of the month, both ships would be on the Tobruk run, taking alternate runs. We had an arrangement whereby each of us kept a suitcase of the other's best possessions on board as an insurance against being sunk. This worked most of the time, but it broke down in October when the *Latona* was sunk on her way to Tobruk. Colin lost everything. Even so, he was quite lucky. He was posted to the cruiser *Galatea*. She was sunk some five weeks later by two torpedoes when entering the swept channel to Alexandria. Colin's description was that he was walking for'ard on the upper deck when the first torpedo struck behind him. He started to run for'ard and again a torpedo exploded behind him. The ship sank very quickly. Only 150 officers and men were rescued.

I am taken in hand

Once Crete was over and life became a little quieter, it was decided that, for his own good, the Snotty should have some training. Possibly at my request, I was designated the Pilot's assistant. In addition to being the ship's navigating officer, he was also in charge of communications and thus confidential books. Most of these were signal code books and ciphers. However I was encouraged to read the confidential reports on the Middle East countries and was fascinated by the detailed political and economic background that was given, not only about the countries generally but also about individuals.

It was also decided that I should learn something about the ship's machinery. The best way to do this was to do watches in the engine room and boiler rooms. Thus for a time, whenever we were on passage, I would stand watches at first in the engine room and later on in the boiler room. There is no doubt that this was a very useful exercise. One learnt the problems and steps required to keep the engines at a given number of revs per minute; the need to keep a high vacuum at the exhaust end of the LP turbine; the importance of the efficient working of the condensers to achieve this. So when there was talk of condenseritis, the most common ailment of steam-powered ships, one had an appreciation of what was entailed. Making smoke is a cardinal sin in wartime. A plume of smoke will give a ship away to a sharp-eyed lookout even when the ship is well below the horizon. To avoid making smoke requires, amongst other things, a delicate balance of air pressure and fuel oil pressure to the boiler. I learnt how to start the auxiliary diesel generators and how to switch from them to the steam-driven generators in the engine room without a) interrupting the electricity supply, and b) getting the diesel generator driven by the far more powerful steam one.

There was also some concern as to whether or not I was too young to drink spirits. The Cmdr E took a very fatherly interest in this side of my upbringing and was of the view that I was too young and should not be allowed gin and other obnoxious spirits. Torps, as President of the Mess, took a similar view but had no real counter to my argument that if I was old enough to be on active service, I was old enough to decide what I drank and how much.

The Lieut.-Cmdr. E was a wonderful instructor in the engine room and I really enjoyed my time with him there. In the boiler rooms I was left to the mercy of the P.O.s i/c of the watch. With them, I found that it was I that had to ask the questions, rather than they who were instructing me.

At one time, when we were going through a quiet period in harbour, I and a visiting midshipman from one of the battleships were given the task of renewing mast running and signalling rigging. We thoroughly enjoyed ourselves up in the rigging. The other midshipman was also RNR, so we both knew Merchant Navy wire rope splices but not the RN system. The Chief Bosun had not realised this until we had almost finished the job. He decided that it would be too much bother to try and make us re-do all the splices, especially as he would have to teach us the Navy splice.

Boat running

Traditionally, midshipmen ran the ships' boats. Our normal berth at Alexandria was alongside the outer mole, where we were able fully to deploy our twin four-inch AA guns. All our communications with the shore, in terms of postmen, landing liberty men and so on, was done by boat. The boat I usually had was a fast launch. Up for'ard there was a cockpit with the helm wheel, reverse gear and throttle, all under the control of the helmsman – me. Immediately aft was a covered cockpit and aft of that, in the well, was located the boat's engine with a stoker in charge of it. There was no means of communication between the helmsman and the stoker. Normally this did not matter. However, on this particular craft the throttle had a habit of jamming wide open, which could be very embarrassing when coming alongside a ship's gangway. Usually the stoker would realise what had gone wrong and manually cut the engine. On one particular occasion I had a relief stoker and was taking the Captain on an official visit to the Fleet Repair Ship. As always, the usual crowd of local faluccas were plying for custom around the gangway. I made my approach in the usual dashing high speed manner, thrust the throttle shut at the critical moment and the launch sped on. I was now frantically trying to tell the stoker to shut down the engine, avoid smashing into the gangway and avoid colliding with any of the feluccas. At the same time we were sweeping round ready to make another approach to the gangway. The Gangway watch were busy piping on board a rapidly retreating and by now irate Commanding Officer, who was banging on top of the cabin casing demanding to know what that idiot of a snotty was doing. Matters were not improved when at the second attempt to come alongside, the engine again failed to slow down. By the third attempt the stoker and I had got our act together. We made a moderately fast approach. The stoker responded to my slow-down signal and the Captain was safely delivered. Luckily for me, he had by that time realized what my problem was, and re-gained his composure. Thereafter strenuous efforts were made by the engine-room artificer to fix the throttle cable for good.

One surprising boat that we were equipped with was a 14ft dinghy, a heavy, clinker-built boat fitted with a tall gaff rig. This I pretty well considered as my own boat. There was a period of almost complete bliss when all the ship's power boats were out of action. I and 'my' dinghy became the sole link with the shore. Special launches were provided as liberty boats. Otherwise I had a complete monopoly of all duty runs. This was certainly the happiest time I had on the ship. And I was being paid for it!

A less pleasant duty was night-time anti-midget submarine patrols. These were done with the launch described above. We were provided with a series of dynamite charges, which were suspended below a small light wooden raft. A Pickfords fuse connected the charges to the raft. They were meant to go off some thirty seconds after the fuse was lit. The charges were dropped overboard at about twenty-minute intervals. As soon as a charge had gone off, the raft would be recovered and a new charge made up. If the charge did not go off, it too had to be recovered. Since I was never able to persuade anybody else on the launch to haul up the unexploded charges, I had to do that myself. While on the *Canton* I had bought myself a pocket watch, of which I was very proud. I can still see that watch sinking out of sight to the bottom of the harbour as I was leaning right over the side, almost upside down, hauling in one of those charges. For arms we had rifles. Some of the merchant ships in the harbour were a bit trigger happy and were liable to mistake us for a midget submarine and open fire. Fortunately they were rotten shots and we always managed to identify ourselves before we were hit.

Supplying Tobruk

Our major operation was running supplies and troops to Tobruk. This would be done each month during the no-moon period. Two groups of destroyers, each with a fast minelayer, would run in under cover of darkness more or less every night when there was no moon. Because this was a regular and well rehearsed event, the loading of stores and troops was well organized and rapidly effected. So was the unloading. On the *Abdiel* we had three discharge points for stores and ammunition. These were the two mining doors in the stern, two midship mine-loading cranes and the two paravane derricks working the for'ard mining hatches. Troops were discharged and taken aboard from the gangway from the upper deck on the starboard side. Although on the destroyers all stores were carried as deck cargo, most of the stuff that we carried was stowed on the mining deck. Fuses for hand grenades, however, were stowed between coir rope fenders on the searchlight deck. These fuses were considered to be very delicate and vulnerable. A premature explosion on the searchlight deck was unlikely to cause any serious damage to the ship. Discharging had to be done as rapidly as possible. My own part in this was to be in charge of the port-side deck party working the mineloading crane. We discharged into landing craft manned by troops using cargo nets. The full cargo net would be lowered to the deck of the landing craft and all but one of the four corner-strops unhooked. The net would then be hoisted up, spilling out its cargo as it was hoisted up. In theory this gave the landing craft crew enough time to stow away the cargo net load before the next one came down. It was often a battle to get the troops to move the stores quickly enough. The Germans of course knew perfectly well what was going on and would sometimes bomb and/or shell the harbour during unloading operations. The soldiers, understandably, were reluctant to carry on unloading under these conditions. Our view was that having got the stuff to them, it was up to them to take it away as fast as possible. However, I can recall only one occasion when the troops broke off unloading during an attack. In order to be out of dive bomber range by daylight, we had a very definite time set for departure. We carried troops of diverse regiments and nations. From our point of view, the tight discipline of the Polish troops made them excellent passengers. The least welcome were the Australians. Individually they were excellent and good company. En masse they appeared truculent and slow to respond to orders. An additional annoyance was that an individual Aussy took up much more room than any other soldier. They all carried very large packs, pyramidal in shape, culminating at the extreme end with a metal mug.

En route to Tobruk we rarely encountered any enemy aircraft until teatime. On most trips, promptly at 4.00 p.m., a stick of bombs would fall nearby from Italian high-level bombers. We rarely saw the aircraft and I don't think that they ever hit anybody. This generally opened up the afternoon performance and spasmodic aircraft attacks would continue until dusk. usually by only three or so aircraft at a time.

Following the experience of air attacks off Crete, it was decided that an additional pair of eyes was required in the control tower. So my action station was transferred to that point. My job was to perch behind the gunnery control officer and keep a lookout for aircraft that were about to start an attack. This implied that I was not to watch the attacking aeroplanes, but to search the skies for others. This I found to be extremely difficult to do. The tactic against dive bombers was to make a big alteration of course when the bomb was seen to be released. From my vantage point, I could see the Pilot, who always had the helm during action stations, watching the oncoming aircraft through binoculars, waiting to see the critical moment

7. Operation NBG.

when the bomb was released. With low-level attacks by torpedo carriers we would turn towards the attacking aircraft to provide a fairly narrow profile, but not too end on, so that we could bring all guns to bear. We had got rid of the anti-aircraft rockets soon after we first arrived at Alex. They had proved to be somewhat dangerous. The light-sensitive fuses tended to explode the rockets the moment they got into the shadow of a cloud. This could be uncomfortably soon after launch. We had also got rid of the oerlikons on the foc'sle. They were difficult to control so far forward and the crews had an uncomfortable time if the A 'turret' was firing forward. I think that we had persuaded the army to take the rockets and one of the inshore ships was glad to have the oerlikons. In exchange we acquired a variety of light anti-aircraft weapons, mostly Italian. Some were light enough to be hand-held. However they were soon banned from the bridge. Without a mounting. they were directionally unstable, especially when being handled like a twelve-bore shot gun.

The four-barrelled machine guns were disappointing. One could see the tracers entering the aircraft, but they had no visible effect. It was assumed that the heavy armour piercing bullets just went straight through the aircraft, it being pure luck if they struck a vital part.

Tobruk was finally relieved on December 11th 1941. It had been besieged since April 12th, a period of 242 days. During that time the Navy carried:-[5]

Personnel out of Tobruk	34,115
Wounded " " "	7,516
Prisoners of war "	7,097
Personnel into Tobruk	32,667
Guns " "	92
Stores " "	33,946 tons
Tanks " "	72
Sheep	108
Naval Casualties:	
Killed and missing	469
Wounded	186
Merchant Navy Casualties:	
Killed and missing	70
Wounded	55

5. Cunningham; *A Sailor's Odyssey*, p. 427/8.

HM Ships sunk: Destroyers 2, sloops 3, Anti-Submarine vessels and minesweepers 7, HM Store Carriers and schooners 7, 'A' lighters 6, Gunboat 1, fast Minelayer 1.[6]

Total 27

HM Ships damaged: Destroyers 7, Sloop 1, Anti-submarine and minesweepers 11, 'A' lighters 3, Gunboats 3, Schooners 1, HMS *Glenroy*

Total 27

Merchant vessels sunk: 6 and 1 schooner
Merchant vessels damaged: 6

Extra-Mural duties

At that time all ship's mail had to be censored. This was a daily chore carried out by everyone in the wardroom, usually during the second dog watch. Anything considered a security risk had to be cut out from the letters. This did not leave much for the writers to write about. I was surprised how distressed many of the men were at being away from home. This was something I had long been used to. I was also surprised over the intimate family details that some men discussed with their brothers or close friends. I suppose that there was not much else to write about. I learnt about things that I had never imagined happened.

Reading these letters reinforced and contributed to my decision not to get emotionally involved with anybody whilst the War lasted, either ashore or on board. At that time I had two main objectives. To do my job as best I knew how and to do my utmost to survive. If, for example, to save the ship I had to flood a compartment and my best friend was down there, would I be able to open the flood cocks? Surely it was better not to have too many very close friends.

Wardroom Parties

Social life mainly comprised going ashore in the evening with the objective of absorbing a fair amount of alcohol. There were the occasional wardroom parties. These were robust occasions, usually involving a fair amount of horseplay. They would start in a decorous manner, with drinks before dinner, usually sherry or gin and tonics. Everyone would be in formal attire. Wine with the well cooked and served food would be followed by port and the

6. The *Latona* had been sunk on the evening of October 25th. After a number of unsuccessful attacks, she was hit by a bomb in the engine room at about 20.00, when outward bound, on her last scheduled run.

loyal toast would always be proposed by the most junior officer – me. After that things would start to liven up as the liquors and harder drinks were absorbed. In spite of the War, we were well supplied with liquor. A lot, of course, we had brought out with us, but there was a local rep. of Saccone & Speed who kept the liquor store topped up.

A favourite game was a competition to see who could go the furthest around the perimeter of the wardroom without touching the deck. This required considerable agility and balance, the latter becoming more difficult to maintain as the evening wore on. Although there was some pretty hard drinking in port, there was a complete taboo on drinking at sea. The Lower Deck, on the other hand, had their tots of rum every day no matter whether we were at sea or in harbour.

The most famous party was the one at Christmas 1941. We had been in Haifa for some time. One day a Russian icebreaker entered harbour. Judging by the holes in her superstructure, she had been shot up on the way. Out of curiosity and to further the entente.cordial between allies, the wardroom decided to pay the ship a visit and to take with them a case of whisky. Suitable approaches were made and the party was on. I was promptly voted Duty Officer for the rest of the day, and so had to remain on board and took no further part in the proceedings.

As far as I can remember, the Turks had taken exception to the passage of a Russian icebreaker through the Dardanelles and had shot her up, whether by shore batteries or aircraft, I do not remember. Neither do I recall the reason for the ship being in the Black Sea in the first place. Does the Black Sea freeze up in the winter? Or why did she come into the Med? Anyway, the party had obviously gone well and the next day a case of vodka was sent over by the Russian officers. It was decided that this would be kept for Christmas.

The main Christmas party was to be held in the evening. Traditionally the wardroom helped out the lower deck with their Christmas dinner at midday. Anyway, I don't remember being involved in the mess deck celebrations. However I do recall that pre-lunch drinks started pretty early in the day – say around 11.00. Drinking and feasting carried on throughout the afternoon and evening. Christmas dinner was, I think, a little disorganized. By then the vodka had been broken out and party games were in full swing. Feeling oblivion coming on, I retired to my camp bed before the party broke up. It was a sorry lot of officers that slowly drifted in for breakfast the next morning. The MO was surprised to see the Torpedo Warrant Officer appear with a bandaged head. The MO had no recollection of stitching up the WO's forehead after he had launched himself off the wardroom fender straight into the whirring overhead fan. The MO claimed that it was the best stitched wound that he had ever seen. By 11.00 all were assembled in the wardroom. With a mixture of strong black coffee and other hangover remedies, a most solemn and binding oath was sworn that never, never again, would vodka be allowed into the mess.

Haifa: Tankers and a Fouled Propeller

We were in Haifa Harbour on several occasions. One particular day I remember was the occasion when we approached the harbour in daylight with Mount Carmel conspicuous in the sunshine. The Senior RDF operator, a court hairdresser in peacetime, poked his head out of the RDF hut, peered at the land ahead and popped back into the hut. Out of curiosity, I followed him in. He was disconsolately twiddling dials in a vain attempt to obtain at least an echo off the land ahead. We had two systems. Type 286 (surface/air warning) and type 285 (fire control). Type 286 in particular was a great disappointment to us. Rarely did it work. The system 285 was better and was known sometimes to register the range of approaching aircraft.

It may have been the same occasion on which we moored close to a burnt-out oil tanker, there being another anchored outside the harbour. One of the Navy ships (a destroyer) had secured the tanker and had been towing her out of the harbour when the tow rope burnt through. The burning tanker drifted onto the one secured along the jetty and set it too on fire. The first tanker was re-captured and towed out of the harbour. The second tanker burned itself out. The entire superstructure was a burnt-out shell. The hull had no paint on it and bore all the signs of great heat. The tanks were still full of petrol! The first tanker had caught alight whilst loading, so some tanks were only partially full or contained fumes. The second had completed loading and was full to the brim. No oxygen in the tanks, so no fire. At least that is how it was explained to me.

When in Haifa Harbour, we usually moored stern on to one of the seaward wharves. On this particular day we were due to go to sea. As was the usual practice, the engine room had rung through to the quarterdeck seeking permission to warm engines. The engines were warmed by turning them at very slow revolutions until no steam condensed in the turbines. This time something went wrong with the communication system. Whilst the engines were being warmed, a deck party was at work 'shortening up'. That is, they were taking inboard all but the essential mooring ropes. The engine room was not told. We didn't even need Murphy's help. Sure enough, one of the stern mooring ropes, whilst being hauled inboard, was caught by the starboard propeller. Luckily it was not a wire rope. Reversing the engine failed to unwind the rope. The only quick way to free the propeller shaft would be send a diver down to cut the rope free. We had neither diver nor diving gear. Neither did the port authorities. At this juncture, one of the senior engine room artificers (ERA), the Chief ERA I think, volunteered to go overboard using a firefighting smoke mask. This he did. He could not stay submerged for very long, but after several attempts he was able to cut the rope away. By this time the ERA was in a state of near collapse. This very early example of aqua-lunging was to me a remarkable example of courage and determination. It was shortly after this, and following hard on the heels of Pearl Harbour, that we were ordered to pick up a full load of mines and proceed to the East Indies Station. We sailed from Alexandria on 29th December 1941.

Passage to Colombo

The Captain was determined to make the fastest-ever passage of the Suez Canal. This would be done by steaming at high speed through the Bitter Lakes, there being strict speed limits through the actual narrow canal cuts. On entering the Bitter Lakes, high revs were ordered. The ship seemed to settle down by the stern and the stern wash was unduly turbulent. The strangest thing was that water was drawn in towards the ship, leaving the banks on either side of the dredged channel bare. There was more vibration than usual and the ship's speed not as high as expected. At lower revs we achieved the same speed but without the turbulence or vibrations. It was explained to me that this was because of the shallowness of the channel. However, in spite of this unexpected setback, I believe that we did achieve a record passage.

The mining deck ran alongside the boiler room casings and in the Red Sea became very hot, to the extent that fears were expressed for the integrity of the mines' explosives. All the mining hatches were opened to improve the ventilation of the mining deck and the temperature of the mines and the air was monitored. Subsequent events demonstrated that the mines' efficiency was not impaired by these high temperatures.

We called in at Aden for fuel and orders. For some reason, probably adolescent b-mindlessness, I was feeling pretty fed up with life. 'Chocker,' we called it. I had been made Officer of the Watch and told to get the only launch we had working alongside the gangway as soon as possible. I was to tell the Captain when it was ready so that he could go ashore and make his courtesy calls and so on. The launch was hoisted out on the port side and came round to the starboard-side gangway. In the meantime I had been indolently leaning up against X turret with my cap nearly on the back of my head. I failed to notice that the launch had arrived. The Captain came up on to the Quarter deck annoyed over the delay. His irritation rose when he realized that he had not been told that the boat was alongside. His anger boiled over when halfway down the gangway his white gloves came into contact with some fuel oil that had contaminated it. I was called over and in a voice that could have been heard all over the harbour, my competence, my dress style, and my general attitude was called into question. Finally I was ordered personally to scrub the gangway clean. This was indeed a humiliating episode, but one which, I had to admit, was not wholly unjustified. The necessary gear was obtained and I started my task. The seamen around were pretty sympathetic. They refrained from staring at my humiliation and one at least commented that the Captain had no business to speak to me like that in public, a sentiment with which I wholly concurred. For my part I was determined to make the best of it. After all, scrubbing decks was not new to me. I had done that often enough on the *Conway*. I resolved to make as good a job as I could of the task. When it was done, it was done. Certainly nobody ever referred to it again in my hearing. As far as I can remember, none of the other officers ever made any remark to me about it.

The passage to Colombo was unremarkable except for one incident. It was during the first watch (20.00 – midnight). I was on watch with Torps. Suddenly the whole sky and sea was lit up by a bright light streaking downwards to the horizon from left to right, trailing large sparks as it went. We were both sure that it was a very large meteorite. However we were just out from the Eastern Med and our reactions were well tuned. The Action Station Alarm button had already been pressed before the meteorite light had died away. It could so easily have been an enemy starshell or a flare dropped from above. There was much grumbling amongst the men as action stations were almost immediately closed down. Those about to take the middle watch were particularly incensed, because it was hardly worth their while to go back to their hammocks.

We entered Colombo Harbour during the forenoon, and we could hardly believe our eyes. There lay the Eastern Fleet with smart white awnings set and guns smartly laid fore and aft. Nothing wrong with that, you might say. But the guns had brightly polished tampons in place and all the brass work on the quarter deck and gangways was brightly polished. Our gun muzzles were protected by round pieces of cardboard stuck on to the muzzles with thick grease. Our brass work had long ago been varnished over so as not to reflect any light. Here was a peacetime fleet!

Our stay in Colombo lasted about two weeks. During that time I called on the family of a one-time girl friend of Ian's (my surviving brother). She was the daughter of the Harbour Master. Ian had met her when he was out that way on a training cruiser (?) at the time when he first joined the Navy. Somehow I had her address. I took a rickshaw to get to their bungalow. This was the first time that I had had a ride in one. I felt uncomfortable at the experience of being bicycled along and never went in one again. I must have been driven back to the landing jetty at the end of the visit.

The Paymaster organized a beach picnic for the ship's crew some way up the coast. My main memory of that occasion was my dislike of the numerous land crabs that were running about. They seemed alien. Crabs in the sea – yes, but on land, definitely no. Quite out of place there.

Defensive Minelaying. We Touch Bottom

From Colombo we laid the mines that we had brought from the Med in sheltered bays and safe anchorages in the Andaman Islands, returning to Trincomalee for replacements. The Andaman Islands are some 800 miles from Ceylon. We were operating near the limits of our fuel range. After one mine-laying trip, we almost lost power for lack of oil as we tied up alongside the mining pier at Trinco.

The Andaman Islands were fascinating. Thick rain forest jungle coming almost right down to the sea's edge; wonderful clean sand beaches edged by clear blue water; a tropical paradise until you looked at the jungle reaching dark and dense to the sea. I well believed that even if somebody got away from the penal settlement at Port Blair in the southern island, no one ever escaped from the islands. How could one survive for long in that jungle?. Furthermore, the islands were said to be inhabited by fierce pygmies armed with poisoned darts, which they released silently from blow pipes.

In the final day of operations we were laying mines at the northern island. The Pilot was a bit worried because there had been no chart corrections in that area for decades. Meanwhile there had been some volcanic activity. As we approached the last anchorage to be mined, I was sent up to the crow's nest to look out for shoal water. This was the first time that I had done anything like that. Certainly the sea around was all of different colours, mostly blue, but sometimes white. Just as I was making up my mind which was deep water and which was not, the ship gave three shudders and the engines stopped. Our starboard propeller had touched a sand bank. We were stopped at the mouth of the bay. On the shore close by, surely well within blow dart range, emerged a group of pygmies, about a dozen in all with a mangy looking pie dog. They just stood and stared as we, gingerly on one engine, felt our way out to deeper water. This was not as easy as it sounds because a certain amount of haste was in order. We had touched bottom just as the last of the mines had gone overboard. We had then been stopped for a while to assess the damage. There was but a thirty-minute interval between the mines being laid and them becoming armed. If we were not quick enough, we could mine ourselves into the bay.

We returned to Colombo. We did not exactly limp back, because we could still do quite a turn of speed even with one engine braked on. On the approach to Colombo, it was decided to test our smoke-laying equipment. This consisted of a cylinder of smoke-making chemicals right aft on the quarter deck. We soon had a dense wall of white smoke streaming astern of us. Atmospheric conditions were excellent. The smoke hung in a great curtain behind us. After a while, a patrolling aircraft called us up, enquiring if we were in need of assistance. We assured him no help was required and soon after completed the trial.

R&R at Nuwara Eliya

We had to wait a short while in Colombo before we could enter the floating drydock for the damage to be assessed and the propeller removed. Because we were no longer operational, the opportunity was taken to send the crew on rest and recreation (R&R) to the rest camp at Nuwara Eliya. Half the ship's company went at one time and I went with the second lot. We boarded the train in the evening and were due at Nuwara Eliya early the next day. The train had to climb to 6,500 ft, part of the way on a rack-and-pinion track. In the carriage in which I travelled there were four hard-bottomed bunks, each supplied with a cotton sheet. This seemed perfectly adequate at the start, but as we climbed higher during the night, the thin sheet proved woefully inadequate. We spent 5 or 6 days at the rest camp. There was not a lot to do there and no one of my age to do it with – except for one. There was a Singhalese lad working at the camp. We played a lot of tennis together until it was stopped by the manager of the camp. I was taking the lad too much away from his duties. I also got the message that it was not considered quite right that I should be so friendly with a Singhalese.

Passage to Durban

Soon after we got back from Nuwara, we slipped out of the drydock and loaded a deck cargo of high-octane petrol in four-gallon tins. In the mining deck no doubt we carried other stores, but I do not remember what. We were heading for the secret RAF staging post, Port X.[7] Standing orders were that any petrol tin seen to be leaking was to be thrown overboard at once.

---

7. This was, I think, Gan in the southern Maldives.

Several went that way. Port X proved to be a coral island with a lot of miserable RAF personnel there. There was nothing to do on the island except swim. But if you went swimming you were liable to get ulcers in the legs. Several of those that we saw had very nasty legs to prove it.

It was a relief to get rid of the petrol. We turned west heading for Mombasa and thence to Durban. The slightly damaged starboard propeller was lashed to the quarter-deck. We could still make a quick passage, managing up to 25 knots on one screw. Once again *Abdiel* was lucky. It was only a day or so out from Colombo when the Japanese bombed Colombo from an aircraft carrier. Amongst the havoc caused was serious damage to the ship then lying in the floating dock.

Torps and I were on the middle watch. The Pilot had gone below an hour or so earlier asking us to keep a lookout for a lighthouse that should come up on the starboard bow in about an hour. We were all concentrating hard on looking for the lighthouse out to starboard. Suddenly there were two shouts from the port lookouts, one 'Breakers Ahead'! The other 'Flashing light Red 030!'. Suddenly the light coloured cloud on the horizon turned into a low cliff and breaking seas. 'Hard a-port' and we swung clear, with possibly only a mile to spare, from serious trouble. Somehow we had been two or three degrees off course. This is a perfect example of how the brain will often make you see what you expect to see. We had all been looking at the coast for maybe twenty minutes, and had not recognized it as such. We never expected to see the coast. What we saw was a low white-to-grey cloud on the horizon, which was what we could reasonably expect to see.

We called at Mombasa for fuel, tying up at a dirty, oily timber pier. Running along the timbers, just clear of the foul harbour water, were the largest cockroaches that I have ever seen before or since. Somehow this seemed to epitomize Mombasa.

The Governor invited two officers for afternoon tea. Before we left the Med. we had acquired a Paymaster Midshipman RN. The two of us were detailed off to partake of tea. We arrived at the impressive Government House. We were shown into a large reception room by a uniformed servant and in due course afternoon tea arrived. We saw neither the Governor, his wife nor any of his staff – only a pet monkey. I was astonished to find how cold the monkey's hands were. So we had our tea, talked to the monkey and went back to the ship.

Durban and South Africa

The entrance to Durban was uneventful. I don't remember if we were serenaded by Durban's Lady in White but I expect we were. We went into drydock within a day or two. The propeller shaft was withdrawn and then began the long process of straightening the A frame through which the shaft went. The precision for this had to be of a high order. One of the problems was that the ship moved in response to changes in day and night temperatures. We were in drydock for about three weeks.

Durban was a wonderful experience. The white South Africans could not do enough for us. We were constantly invited out to people's homes. The other midshipman and I were invited out to stay at a farm some fifty miles south of Pietermaritzburg, where we spent about ten days. The farm was primarily a dairy farm. The farmer had been with the South African forces in North Africa. Having done his stint for a year or so, he had been demobbed. Whilst he was away, his wife had run the farm. The farmhouse was comparatively small and of wood-frame construction. In the morning two ponies were made available for us, on which we roamed the immediate surroundings. Not far away was a wattle plantation that provided some good shaded rides. We would canter or gallop through these, ducking under the low, hanging branches. My companion was not very good at this and usually fell off. On the open veldt, the grass was eighteen inches or so high and dry. One could not see the ground and I was concerned about the ponies stepping into a hole or stumbling on rock. It was a wonderfully pleasant time and most restful. There were two children in the family, and a young girl of whom I became quite fond. I even thought that maybe after the war I would come back with a view to marriage. She had a brother who was at boarding school at Pietermaritzburg. I don't really remember him although we all went out to his school one weekend to take him out for the day. I kept up a desultory correspondence with the family for several years. I think that I stopped writing after learning that the daughter had become engaged to be married.

I thoroughly enjoyed my time in South Africa, both from the *Canton* and from the *Abdiel*. The white South Africans were most hospitable. At Durban several of the ship's crew told me that they had been put under pressure to return to South Africa. They needed more Europeans there, preferably from the UK. One or two even said that they had been given the nod to go to bed with the daughter with a view to marriage. As for myself, I noted that there was still a certain amount of tension between the ex-UK South Africans and the Boers. Both in Cape Town and in Natal there were occasions when I know that I was being paraded in the presence of Boers to make a point.

Although I was well imbued with the European attitude towards Africans prevalent at that time, I felt, certainly in Natal, that the Europeans, be they

Boers or ex-UK, were, in effect, sitting on the top of a kettle. Keeping the Africans down to the extent that they were was bound to lead to an explosion sooner or later. The argument that the Africans did not know how to run things or carry out simple jobs, I accepted. The tales my farmer host told of damaged farm equipment and what I observed for myself in the dockyard tended to confirm this belief in their incompetence.

In due course the A frame was lined up, the propeller shaft in place and the propeller bolted back on again. However, before we actually left drydock, the city threw a party for the whole ship's company with a dinner dance. It was a very good, friendly, relaxed party with an excellent live band. Thank God they did not have discos in those days!

Once out of drydock, we went alongside to complete some minor repairs and take in stores. In the middle of this we were rushed out to sea. A Japanese raider had sunk a merchant ship north of Madagascar and we were sent out to find her. This raider was said to have six-inch guns with a much longer range and punch than our 4-inch ones. With no larger supporting ships around, we would have to engage to sink her should we find her. There would be no chance of shadowing her just out of range in the classic cruiser function.

After an hour or so we went to 'stand by' action stations. Then for the first time in its life and shortly before dusk, the RDF picked up an echo. It was not a very strong echo. Even so we approached cautiously. It was a lifeboat of Lascar crewmen from the sunken merchant ship. They were hauled aboard and we continued our search during the night. In the meantime the Paymaster had a large meal of rice prepared for the survivors and was most incensed when they refused to eat it, even though they had had no food for over a day. It was the rice that was wrong. It had not been parboiled or something. During the night there was a minor alarm when we encountered a merchant ship. However she was a friendly one, and had picked up most of the rest of the crew of the sunken ship. The following morning, at dawn, we were back where we had left the lifeboat. We sank it by ramming and returned to Durban.

At Durban it was announced that we were definitely on our way back to the UK for a refit. It was not long before we were once again serenaded out of the harbour by that wonderful singer, Perla Siedle Gibson, who made it her task to sing in or out of port every naval ship. She is commemorated by a plaque mounted on a stone cairn at the end of the North Pier in Durban Harbour, near where she used to stand to welcome and say farewell to ships. The passage to Cape Town was fast and uneventful. Once again that wonderful South African hospitality swung into action. Both of us midshipmen were whisked away for the weekend to a fruit farm some seventy miles out from Cape Town.

Passage to the UK with Bullion

Back on board we were preparing to leave. The mining deck had been cleared, ready for its prestigious cargo of gold bullion. All of a sudden police cars drove on to the quay followed by several black vans. The vans' back doors opened and out leapt several armed police, who took up defensive positions around the vans. Our working party went ashore and the task of loading the gold bars started. One gold bar per wooden box, one box per man. The steady procession of men coming laden up one gangway and going back down to the quay empty handed continued until almost the whole of the mining deck was covered by gold bar boxes one layer thick.

Almost immediately an armed sentry started his patrol marching over the boxes. The details of the cargo I forget, but it was something in the region of 600 boxes, worth about six million pounds.

The Captain was determined to make the fastest passage back to the UK. This he did in spite of condenser problems that troubled us all the way. We stopped to refuel at Point Noire, just north of the mouth of the Congo. There we took on fuel and the ailing condenser was nursed back to health. In the far distance from our anchorage was the *Queen Mary* with an oil lighter alongside. After a while the lighter cast off and slowly approached us. She got bigger and bigger as she came closer. It was not long before I realized that this lighter was an oil tanker considerably bigger than ourselves and coming alongside to refuel us. Such was the contrast in size between the *Queen Mary* and other ships. We noticed that many of the ships at anchor were streaming lines astern. These, they told us, were shark lines baited with meat. This port was used for flying fighter aircraft reinforcements to the Eastern Mediterranean front.

From there we made a fast passage to Gibraltar. Here I was within a ship's fender-width of missing my ship. On entering port, I realised that the aircraft carrier HMS *Eagle* was in. I asked the Captain for permission to visit my brother, who was serving on board her as Captain's Secretary. A signal was sent across to the Eagle to clear the matter from her end and I was allowed ashore with strict instructions to be back by noon, when we would be sailing.

I met Ian, whom I had not seen since before the War started. The time, as is usual, went far too quickly and I suddenly realised that I had to hurry back to the *Abdiel*. As I approached her, I saw to my horror that she was already casting off. I broke into a run and yelled to the quarter deck working party to throw me a heaving line. This I caught and leapt from the dockside to land on top of the quarter fender and was hauled on board. This incident certainly put me in my place. It had never occurred to me that the ship would actually sail without me. I don't remember being reprimanded about this but I would have been in very big trouble if I had missed the ship.

We made a fast passage to the Clyde and anchored off Greenock. In due course a support drifter came alongside to take off our passengers and the bullion. This was in complete contrast to the operation at Capetown. The bullion boxes were handled into cargo nets, hoisted out to the drifter by the electric mine cranes and just dumped any old how on the drifter's foc'sle. In a few hours we were off to our final destination, Newcastle upon Tyne. As we steamed down the broad expanse of the Firth of Clyde, we noticed a cruiser exercising some miles away. Suddenly the lookouts reported three aircraft approaching fast. They were coming in very low on the port bow – a typical torpedo attack position. The duty watch immediately closed up all weapons and we went to action stations. Just as we were about to open fire, they were recognized as British. They were – to us – new torpedo aircraft (Barracuda?). It was a close call. The leader of the aircraft apologized. They should have been doing a dummy torpedo attack on the cruiser.

We made a fast passage to Newcastle, passing through the Pentland Firth in the early hours of the morning. This was the first time that I had seen the northern sky at night in summer. During the middle watch it was fascinating to watch the faint red glow of the sun slowly pass from the west via the north to the east. The Pentland Firth itself was full of tide rips as we passed through. I was on the bridge again as we approached Newcastle. The Captain had determined on a spectacular entry. We approached the mouth of the estuary at high speed, cutting our speed from 30 knots to the regulation 10 knots at the last minute. We even put the brakes on a bit by actually stopping the engines We had left Durban on June 7th, arriving at Greenock on July 1st, where we had discharged £6,000,000 worth of gold bullion. We reached Newcastle the next day and berthed alongside the *Sheffield*. We reckoned that we had made the fastest passage ever from East Africa to Newcastle. Soon after docking, we were allowed to phone home. My mother was up in no time, and we had a reunion at Uncle Willy's house in Windsor Crescent. It was only a matter of days before the ship's first commission came to an end and we all dispersed home on leave.

So ended one of the most significant periods in my life. In many ways the *Canton* had been just an extension or continuation of the *Conway*. On the *Abdiel* I was on my own for the first time. I had been an insignificant part of an elite ship's company. In the 16 months or so that I had served on her, we had taken part in some momentous episodes of the War in the Mediterranean. I had had more responsibilities thrust on to me than is usual for a boy of my age. I had learnt much about the sea and sea warfare. Following on from the *Abdiel*, I served on two much larger vessels and at first, resented not being given the responsibilities that had been taken for granted on the *Abdiel*. She was a much smaller ship and had the air of the destroyer syndrome about her. I was very fond of her and was really sad at leaving her. Years later I saw her on the way to Taranto, where she was sunk. It so happened that the ship's photographer took a shot of her as she passed. I kept a copy of that photograph for years in my pocket book – in fact until the photograph broke up.

CHAPTER 4

HMS *Sheffield*

AFTER A WEEK OR TWO'S LEAVE, I was appointed to the *Sheffield*, a six-inch gun Town-Class cruiser, and instructed to join her at Scapa Flow. I had to change trains at York. The town had recently been bombed, as the burnt-out roof of the station platform bore witness. Walking up and down the platform whilst waiting for the train, I suddenly heard a rapidly approaching low-flying aeroplane. Instantly I flung myself face down on the platform, my small suitcase skittering across it. Looking upward as the plane passed overhead, I recognised it as a Hurricane. Somewhat shamefacedly I got to my feet and gathered up my scattered belongings under the astonished stare of the other waiting passengers. To my relief, no one said anything. It was a long slow train journey to Thurso, where I had to stay overnight at the only (?) hotel. There was time for an excellent breakfast of porridge and fried herrings garnished with oats, before catching the ferry to Stromness. The *Sheffield* was out in the Flow and in due course a boat came out to pick me up.

The Gunroom

There were fourteen in the Gunroom, eleven midshipmen, of whom five were regular Navy, three RNR, one ex-*Pangbourne*, one a South African and one ex-*Worcester*. He, Lowein, was just a day or so senior to me and there was always a certain amount of hostility and competition between us. Bossing us about were three Sub-Lieuts: Sub-Lt. Farquar RN being the most senior and in charge of the Gunroom. Next to him was Sub-Lt. Tibbs RNVR followed by Pay Sub-Lt. Stephens RN. The brightest spark, the one that constantly kept us cheerful and rarely lost the grin off his face, was Mid. Honeywell RN.

Watch Keeping and Boat Running

On a big ship in harbour, there are basically only two jobs for midshipmen. The one where one was seen most by one's senior officers and so favoured by those wishing to be in the 'Establishment' was watch-keeping on the quarter deck. The other, favoured by the more rebellious ones, was to be in charge of the duty boats. I plumped for the boats. I also found that the

8. HMS Sheffield, *the Gunroom. Back row, left to right: Rees; McKinnon; Lowein;
Manson; Gerrad-Pearse; Reid; Goodwin; Erskine; Front row: Petrie; Tibbs;
Farquhar; Stephens; London; Honeywell.*

position of Navigator's 'tanky'[1] was free and I managed to get that job too. At
sea, on this ship, there was no room for a midshipman of the watch on the
bridge. This I resented because I considered that as midshipmen, we should
be being trained to be seamen officers. I had no desire to be trained as a
gunnery officer. I had already set my sights on specializing as a Navigating
Officer as a first step to serving on survey ships and eventually being the
Hydrographer of the Navy. However, instead – at least to begin with – I kept
watch at the Torpedo Firing Position. There was one of these on each side,
just abaft the bridge. Almost near enough to hear the sound of commands,
but too far away to know what was going on. Venturing on to the edge of
the bridge was discouraged.

The torpedo firing controls were pretty primitive affairs, consisting of an
open sight with three points on it (to give a spread of firing angle) and three
firing buttons to press. The sight transmitted the bearing down to the

---

1. Assistant to the Navigating Officer. This gave access to the Chart Room and sometimes the Bridge.

relevant torpedo tubes. As far as I recall, there was no plot to allow for the speed and inclination of the enemy ship. Later on, my surface action station was changed to the after gun control tower, where I was the 'Rate Officer'. My job was to estimate the speed and inclination of the target ship. My air action station was i/c of the group of oerlikons situated immediately below the after control tower. A major advantage of this change was that I then kept watch in the main gunnery control tower, one of the warmest and snuggest places to be, with a fine view thrown in as well.

The *Sheffield*, being a big ship, had an education officer in her complement. He was, presumably, an ex–teacher. He taught those with reading difficulties. He coached ratings studying for their next rung up the ladder. He, together with the senior Sub-Lt., the 'Snotties' Nurse', was responsible, under the supervision of a Lt. Cmdr., for arranging training classes/lectures for the midshipmen. One of these discovered that I had not been keeping a Midshipman's Log. In this we were meant to record the daily happenings and operations of the ship, together with comments/essays on the local and general political and strategic situations. To my disgust, I was made to keep a log. Typical adolescent bloody-mindedness! I still have the log and have drawn on it for this account of my time in the *Sheffield* and the *KGV*.

Being a boat midshipman, I was free of the protocol of the quarter deck and had a good excuse for being a bit scruffy. It was satisfying to have one's own command, even it was somewhat on the small side. Each boat had its own duty crew, headed by a coxswain, usually a Leading Seaman. There would be either one or two other seaman ratings, depending on the size of the boat, and a stoker, who was in charge of the engine. The relationship between the midshipman and the coxswain was never really defined. Officially the midshipman was in charge, but the older more experienced leading seaman was there to provide guidance and to take over if necessary. He was also responsible for keeping the boat clean and for its general maintenance. Often when it came to hoisting the boats in or out, the boat's crew would be in the boat whilst the midshipman would be supervizing the hoisting procedures.

However, being a boat midshipman was not all fun. Two extracts illustrate this. The first is from the log dated 6/10/42.

> Left the ship in the Motor Cutter (MC) at 1045 this morning with orders to deliver a hand message to the *Argonaut*, who was down at Barray Range. We did a good time as there was a strong breeze astern. When we approached her, I saw that she was underway, so I signalled that I had an important message for her. My signalling was poor at the best of times. A small MC bouncing in the waves is not the best of platforms to semaphore from. However they

understood me and hove to. When I had delivered the message, the Commander of the *Argonaut* told me that as they were going up to the anchorage, they would steam at seven knots so that I could come under their quarter for a lee. When I had got into position we started off. What an odd sight we must have looked! I found that with the engine going full ahead, I was just forging ahead of station. When we were half way up, the Commander came on to the quarterdeck with a tin in his hand. He shouted something and gesticulated with hands, indicating that he wanted to throw the tin into the boat. I closed in as close as I dared and he threw. The tin was caught by the wind and blown aft. I turned the boat round and picked it up and found it contained the receipt for the message. The *Argonaut* had by this time drawn well ahead so the effect of her lee was greatly reduced. However, we made good speed and was close up to her when she reached the Baffles. This was as far as she was going. After a word of thanks, I altered course and steered for the *Sheffield*. Came alongside at 1215 and was hoisted immediately.

The other is an extract of a letter home dated 18/10/42:

I despair of ever getting this finished today. I was in the boat all morning and afternoon, then for half an hour after tea. When I got back, I had just settled down and had written the first paragraph when they called me away again. That was an hour and a half ago. A very unpleasant hour and a half it was too. It was cold and rained the whole time and my shoes leak . . .

Winter in Scapa Flow can be quite wild, as indicated by this extract from the log.

At about 11.30 the wind suddenly freshened, reaching gale force. A second anchor was let go immediately. Orders were given to hoist all boats. It was considered unsafe to get into the 1st M.C so it had to remain bouncing about on the boom.

The M.B's crew managed to get into their boat and rigged the slings. The seas were running pretty high now. The motorboat was being tossed about like a cork. Getting the lines to the boat was the first difficulty. the wind just swept the line aft. The first line across parted as soon as it was made fast. The second line got across was a good 1½" and held well.

The antics the MB put up were amazing. At one time she rose nearly vertical up a wave and was swept aft 10ft or more by it. When they at last got hooked on, it was found that the after sling had been jerked off. Whilst they were hooking on again, the crane came unhooked. The crane was again hooked up and the order 'slow hoist' given. Luckily the men in the boat managed to keep the crane hooked on. When the boat was in the air, the force of the wind on the boat was so strong that the forward steadying line parted. The wind abated during the afternoon so the MC (Motor Cutter) was hoisted without incident.

9. Spitzbergen.

A Visit to Spitzbergen

When I joined her, the *Sheffield* had only recently returned to service after a refit in Newcastle (we had come alongside her in the *Abdiel* when we arrived home from the Far East). She was about to embark on a widespread operation with the major objective of safely delivering a convoy of 40 ships to Archangel and to escort a smaller convoy home. This would involve the 18th Cruiser Squadron: Vice Admiral S.S. Bonham-Carter, flying his flag on the *Norfolk* together with the cruisers, *Sheffield*, *Suffolk*, *Cumberland* and *London* and four destroyers, *Eclipse*, *Bulldog*, *Echo* and *Amazon*. The convoy would be escorted by 30 destroyers. The Cruiser Squadron would be deployed in a supporting role against the threat of the *Tirpitz*, by cruising between Iceland and Spitzbergen. The *Cumberland* and *Sheffield* would also deliver stores to the garrison at Barenstberg on Gronfjord on the south western peninsula of Spitzbergen.

In company with *Cumberland* and *Eclipse*, we left Scapa at 0900 on 6th September, arriving at Greenock at 0600 the next day. Loading of the stores from lighters started immediately. This consisted of three bofors guns, with necessary spares and ammunition, a large amount of petrol and oil, skiing equipment, husky dogs, bundles of warm clothing and food. In all it amounted to some 110 tons. The bofors were stowed in the port hanger along with their spare barrels, wheels and other equipment. The petrol and oil were stored in the starboard hanger. The ammunition and some of the more robust equipment were put midships in the well. All the food was stored in the Admiral's Cabin. What would not fit in there went into the cabin and wardroom flats. The huskies were secured on the hanger deck. Later on in the voyage, these became much endeared to the crew because it was said one had cocked his leg at the moment when the Commander walked beneath. All the stores were embarked and stowed before dark. The following morning we sailed with the *Cumberland* (also with stores) and the *Eclipse*.

The next day (9th) heavy seas caused us to roll violently, resulting in the bofors guns shifting and seas coming inboard at the port well. The port whaler was smashed on it's davits. The ship hove too whilst the bofors guns were secured. We arrived at Hvalfjord, near Reykjavik (Iceland) in the afternoon of the 10th. The next three days were spent exercising in loading the cutters with stores by skates rigged up on the top of accommodation ladders. Eventually the loading time for a cutter was reduced to six minutes. We joined the Cruiser Force on the 14th.[2]

On the 17th the *Cumberland* left the fleet under a deeply overcast sky and entered Gronfjord to deliver her stores. The weather was in our favour. The heavy overcast would make it difficult for enemy aircraft from their base in Norway only 400 miles away to spot what was going on. The fjord is very narrow and there would be little room for a ship to take evasive action in the case of an air attack. The following day it was the *Sheffield's* turn. It was still overcast as we approached Spitzbergen with only a very light wind – ideal conditions. However, once inside the fjord, the sky cleared with a few white fleecy clouds. The tables were turned. Just the weather for German aircraft.

Sheffield dropped anchor two cables off the jetty at Barenstberg, bows to sea, ready to run if attacked.

The coal mine, oil storage tanks and most of the facilities had been destroyed by an army force that had landed there in August the previous year in order to deny the Germans these facilities had they invaded the Island. Subsequently the town had been occupied by a small Norwegian group who had been engaged in sending out weather reports.

Landing the stores proceeded without a hitch. It was speeded up by the Norwegians providing two dories, which could carry twice the load of our cutters. Unloading took just under six and a half hours. We weighed anchor at 2140 and rejoined the fleet that night.

---

2. Speed had to be reduced because the destroyers were having a hard time from the weather, at times disappearing from sight, except for their mast tops, between the waves.

10. Sheffield discharging stores at Spitzbergen.

The next day we heard that the convoy had reached Kola Inlet with the loss of only 13 ships and one escort either damaged or sunk. This in spite of having been subjected to heavy bombing and torpedo attacks. On receipt of this news, the Cruiser Squadron turned for Hvalfjord. On arrival there, the CS18 signalled his intention to transfer his flag to *Sheffield*. As a big sea was running, getting the Admiral, his staff and their baggage on board had some exciting moments. The exercise was completed at 2225. The gale delayed our departure from Iceland for 24 hours. There was still a big swell running, making *Sheffield* roll. However by the afternoon the sea had moderated giving quite comfortable conditions and we had a calm passage to Scapa Flow.

Fire Fighting Training
On one occasion all the midshipmen and a party of stokers were landed at North Pier, Lyness, to attend a lecture on fire fighting. No one knew where the fire fighting school was located. After enquiries at the drifter office, it was

found that the school was at Rennigall. Whereupon two schools of thought arose. One was in favour of waiting for a ferry or attempting to get a lorry. The other, to which I belonged, was all for getting transport, but if that failed, to walk there. There seemed little chance of getting a lorry so we set off up the road to walk round to the other side. Because the road takes a very roundabout route, it was decided to cut off across country. The way was wet and muddy and there were two streams to cross. Forty minutes later we arrived at the school well before the other party which did not turn up until late in the afternoon, whereupon the lecture started. The major theme was that an oil fire could be put out by spraying it with a fine spray of water. The theory was that the fine spray was turned immediately into copious quantities of steam, denying the fire a supply of oxygen. The next day we were dropped off at the right place and proceeded to put into practice what we had learned the day before. We had a lot of fun putting out oil fires, using oxygen masks to pass through a smoke-filled obstacle course, using the thin, high pressure spray to put out a fire as well as to protect ourselves from the heat of the flames. The final piece was an oil fire lit between two bulkheads

11. Sir Stafford Cripps aboard Sheffield. *Nearest the camera: Captain of the* Sheffield, *talking to Sir Stafford, Rear Admiral Harcourt (F.O. Cruiser Squadron); looking at his watch, Vice Admiral Sir Bruce Fraser (C. in C. Home Fleet?); behind the Captain, Sheffield's Commander and beyond, Sub-Lieutenant Farquhar.*

that projected into the fire school chamber. We waited outside until the bulkheads were red hot, then we opened the door and went in with a 'firex' nozzle. This is a branch pipe that can be turned to either a jet or a spray. In no time we had cooled down the bulkheads. Although there were changing rooms and wash basins, we still returned to the ship a pretty sooty, cheerful crowd.

Prelude to Operation Torch

A few days later Vice Admiral Bonham Carter announced that he was hauling down his flag. He would be replaced by Rear Admiral Harcourt, who would fly the flag of the 10th Cruiser Squadron, which would be formed from all the 6-inch gun cruisers, with *Sheffield* as Flag Ship.

The next week or so was taken up with various surface and air gunnery exercises at sea. We exercised with the other cruisers as well as the battleships. *Sheffield* was congratulated on her RDF (now called RADAR) work. These exercises were interrupted by the visit of Winston Churchill to Scapa Flow. We had expected him aboard, but instead, with so many ships to visit, we were visited by Sir Stafford Cripps. He spoke very well, stressing the importance of the Russian Convoys as well as the strategic importance of the fleet being at Scapa waiting for the opportunity to bring the German fleet to action. Later in the day we could see Churchill going round the fleet in the C-in-C's barge. Exercises continued for several days, followed by taking in more ammunition. Then, accompanied by *Jamaica*, *Sheffield* proceeded to the Clyde, where we carried out exercises with the aircraft carriers *Argus* and *Victorious*. On completion of these exercises we proceeded independently to Belfast Lough, anchoring some five miles from Belfast itself. The following day large quantities of bedding and other stores were taken on board. In all we embarked 600 US troops and 70 British ratings.

In the evening, whilst this was going on, I took the M.C. into Belfast to pick up two ratings who had been given permission to visit relatives. It poured with rain the whole time and visibility became so poor that for a while I had to steer by compass. On the return journey, a steep sea came in from the Lough making it very uncomfortable and at times threatening to swamp the boat. It took us an hour and a half to go in. The return journey took over two hours. According to the stoker, we used half a gallon of fuel on the way in to Belfast and two gallons on the return journey.

It was not until we were at sea again that it was revealed that all this was the prelude to Operation Torch, the landings in North Africa. We sailed from Belfast in the early hours of the 27th October, turned north and joined the fast convoy KMF I. By 1100 the 38-ship convoy was in cruising order of ten

12. Prelude to Operation 'Torch', the invasion of North Africa, Convoy KMF 1 en route. By courtesy of the ship's photographer.

columns, each of four ships. Our position was No 62, with the aircraft carrier *Biter* astern and the combined operations ship *Bulolo* flying the flag of Rear Admiral Burroy ahead. He was in overall command of the convoy. The Convoy Commodore flew his flag on the *Largs* in position 31. There were five Combined Operations ships in the convoy: the *Largs*, *Bulolo*, *Glengylee*, *Princess Beatrice* and *Queen Emma*. Close anti-submarine escort was provided by four corvettes, *Rother*, *Spray*, *Exe* and *Swale*; three sloops, *Ibis*, *Enchantress* and *Aberdeen*; two cutters, *Walney* and *Harland*.

October the 28th and 29th were uneventful. There was the usual Atlantic weather, overcast sky and heavy swell. 'As usual the *Sheffield* rolled like a cow.' To our surprise, the Americans stood up to the weather very well. Those who were ill were sick in the right places.

Oiling at Sea

One of *Sheffield's* duties with the convoy was to oil the escorts. This was carried out with varying success. The standard method adopted by the Navy big ships was that known as the Trough Method. This consisted of slinging an armoured oil hose between the two ships, with the oil hose being held in the bight by a preformed metal trough. In our case this was held by a hoist from

13. Operation 'Torch'. Oiling one of the escorts at sea by the 'trough' method.

the aircraft recovery crane. The two ships were held together by two wire ropes. As long as the sea was calm, the method worked well, but if there was any swell it became fraught with difficulty.

Between October 30th and 3rd November we had goes at oiling six ships of the convoy's A/S escort. The Corvettes *Swale, Rother* (2 attempts) and the *Spey* (2 attempts): the sloops *Enchantress* and *Ibis*: and the destroyer *Claire* (3 attempts). Two of the oiling attempts were broken off because of U Boat alarms. On the other occasions oiling had to be temporarily broken because of the gear parting. Although on the 1st November the swell had moderated, the day did not go well. It was the worst of them all. The programme went like this:

0915   *Rother* secured alongside.

0920   The breast and spring parted when the two ships simultaneously rolled in opposite directions. Oiling temporarily abandoned.

1235   Ex US Destroyer *Claire* secured alongside.

1242   Spring parted, *Claire* slipped the breast.

1345   *Claire* secured again alongside
1355   Commenced oiling
1415   Periscope reported sighted by *Biter*, *Claire* slipped and rejoined
        convoy
1530   *Claire* secured alongside.
1536   Started oiling.
1630   Spring parted, slipped the breast and only just recovered the oil
        pipe in time.

The main cause of the wire ropes breaking lay in their lack of give as the ships rolled. The next day a modification was tried. This consisted of the ship being oiled putting a breast across to us; we put the bight of the rope round the bollard and passed the end back. The ship being oiled then either took both ends to her capstan or secured one end and took the other to the capstan. In either case, she would haul in or veer the breast as the ships came together or parted, thus keeping an even strain on the rope. On the following day this was tried with the *Spey* and all went well for an hour, when the spring parted. She was alongside later in the day and oiling was completed. We also oiled the *Enchantress*, the *Ibis* and the *Rother*. During these oiling episodes one of the ships in the convoy, the *Orbita* was also oiling escorts. She used the towing method and never lost a rope. This was the standard method used by the Western Approaches Command for oiling escorts at sea from tankers. I never could understand why the Navy persisted in attempting to tie ships together at sea. I noticed that this method was still being used during the Falklands campaign.

On completion of the oiling of the *Rother*, the *Sheffield* left the convoy and proceeded towards Gibraltar at 22 knots. We entered the Straits of Gibraltar in the evening of the 4th November, but stayed in the Straits all the night. We entered Gibraltar at first light on the morning of the 5th, securing alongside the *Rodney* at the South Mole. For security reasons, all the soldiers on board had to dress in sailors uniform if they ventured onto the upper deck. Hopefully their brown shoes would not be noticed from the shore! After oiling, we sailed at 1930 accompanied by the *Soytla* (sic), *Caribdus*, *Argus* and four destroyers and steamed into the Mediterranean. Dawn on the 7th found us off Cape Palos on the south-eastern coast of Spain. We turned and steamed slowly westwards.

Operation Torch. We Support the Landings

At 0930 the Captain broadcast to the ship's company and outlined the operation. The proposed plan was to land a large army at 0100 on Sunday

8th November at Algiers, Oran and Casablanca. The objective was the occupation of the whole of the French Territory in North Africa and eventually attacking Rommel from the back.

The convoy that we had escorted in the Atlantic had split up, one half going to Algiers and the other to Casablanca. The *Sheffield's* part in the operation was to escort a slow convoy, that was just in sight, to Algiers and to give support to the troops during the landing, and if necessary to bombard any point of resistance as required by the army.

The one half of KHF1 (14 ships) and our slow convoy were so routed that they would arrive at Algiers at the same time. We did not actually join the convoy but steamed in the vicinity in support of the *Argus* and *Avenger* whilst they flew off aircraft. Each ship carried some 16 Hurricanes. Both carriers flew off four aircraft at a time. I reflected on the contrast to my earlier operations in the Med. and enjoyed the comfort of the security that you feel when you know that you've got air support at a moment's notice. Because the landings were supposed to be done by Americans only, all the aircraft were given American markings. During daylight hours each carrier maintained a patrol of four aircraft. The patrols were relieved at the end of an hour.

At 1320 the first aircraft casualty occurred. A fighter coming in to land on the *Argus* overshot the landing point, tried to abort the landing, but failed to get up sufficient speed and nosed into the water just ahead of the *Argus*. The pilot got free and was picked up by a destroyer. An hour later the same thing almost happened again. A Seafire came in too fast and the landing hook either snapped off or disengaged from the arrester wire. The aircraft, unable to stop, crashed into the tennis net, knocked it down and got the net entangled with the landing wheels, tipping the aircraft up. The pilot got out obviously shaken but otherwise unhurt. The plane itself suffered a broken screw and dented bow. Later on the engine was taken out and the aircraft hull ditched overboard.

Before dark the *Malcolm* and *Broke* came alongside to embark our passengers. The two destroyers were to force their way through the boom, land the troops, who were to board the merchant ships in the harbour to prevent them being scuttled, preserve the harbour installations and generally cause panic amongst the defenders. We closed up at action stations and remained closed up all the night.

At 0100 on the 8th the troops landed according to plan. It looked as though the French had been taken by surprise. There were no sounds or signs of gunfire and the town's lights shone peacefully over the bay. The first signs of resistance came about two hours later when the *Broke* and *Malcolm*

14. Operation 'Torch'. American troops aboard HMS Sheffield.
Supporting 'Woolworth' carriers in background.

nosed their way towards the harbour mouth. A searchlight began to sweep
the sea, swung slowly round and caught the *Broke*, swung away then slowly
swung back again on to the *Broke* and held her. In a few minutes the forts
opened fire and shell splashes could be seen jumping up around the ship.

On board the *Broke*, they first had to steer west across the mouth of the
bay, turn round and then steer a south-easterly course so as to strike the
boom at the correct angle. It was on this last course that they were seen. So
dazzled were the officers on the bridge by the searchlight that they could not
see any landmarks and had to sheer off. Three times they tried but each time
they were confronted by a blazing wall of light, stopping them from picking
out any details ashore. They had to lay off until dawn. Meanwhile the
Malcolm had been hit in the boilerroom, putting two boilers out of action,
killing eight men and wounding twenty others. She retired.

At dawn the *Broke* had another try. This time landmarks could be seen and
she crashed through the boom at 15 knots. The *Broke* went alongside and
disembarked her landing parties. Unfortunately the forts that should by now
have been put out of action by the Commandos were very much alive and

gave the *Broke* a warm time. She sought shelter behind a merchant ship. This relieved her from the heavier armaments, but she was soon subjected to fire from lighter weapons. By this time it was about noon. There had been no attempt to scuttle any ships, so it was decided to withdraw. The recall was sounded on the ship's siren and most of those who had landed returned aboard. Going out to sea would be ticklish because she would be exposed to all the guns of the forts. However, all went well. The helmsman did a first-class job. He had four men killed around him and was nearly suffocated by the fumes from the smoke floats lit on the bow. He stuck to his post and brought the ship safely out of the harbour.

In the meantime *Sheffield* had returned to Force 'O' some miles off Algiers, where both carriers were constantly flying off aircraft in support of the soldiers.

By 1900 the French at Algiers were still resisting but a truce was being negotiated. The airfield behind Algiers had been captured by British paratroops, flown straight from England.

At Oran there had also been resistance. The *Aurora* had met two French destroyers. One was now on fire and sinking. The other was damaged and standing by her. The *Aurora* was keeping a mother's eye on both.

The Forts at Algiers Surrender
At 1420 the *Sheffield* left Force 'O' and proceeded to Algiers at her best speed. We were going to bombard a 7.5"-gun fort by the name of Dupe Perre. These guns had a range of 30,000 yards.

When we arrived, we found the *Bermuda* already in action against another fort called Mattefou. Her shooting was excellent and she seemed to score a direct hit with every salvo. Unfortunately or fortunately, Dupe Perre surrendered just as we arrived on the scene. We closed in and lay off the fort some two miles distant, ready to open fire at a second's notice. It was found that Admiral Darlan himself was in the fort at the time. The capitulation of Dupe Perre ended French resistance in Algiers. The ships that had brought the troops to the beachhead began to retire and anchor in the Bay of Algiers.

At about 1630 the *Sheffield* turned to rejoin Force 'O'. At this point a single Caproni bomber came in to attack and was driven off by gunfire and believed to have been shot down. The sun had set, so taking advantage of the gathering darkness, four or five torpedo bombers attempted to attack the shipping. Four torpedoes were dropped in our vicinity, but no damage was done.

During the attack two shells exploded near the ship, one off the starboard quarter and the other up forward. The first did no material damage but one look-out was hit by shrapnel in the arm and a signalman in the neck. Luckily neither of them was seriously hurt. The other shell sent fragments over the foc'sle, puncturing the deck in several places on the port side. It also nicked the anchor cable and smashed one of the cable holders. With the attack over, we rejoined Force 'O'.

Early the next day, the 9th November, the armistice was signed in Algiers and our ships began to enter harbour to unload stores. We remained with Force 'O' throughout the forenoon. In the afternoon the *Sheffield* left the carriers to pick up a small convoy off Algiers. This convoy was destined to land troops further east down the coast. However, because of a choppy sea, the operation was postponed.

At 1630 five JU 88s attacked shipping off Algiers. It looked as though one AA ship was hit. Once the attack was over and one had time to look around, there was the ship on fire aft. Judging from the sudden shower of sparks upwards, it looked as though ammunition was blowing up.

The JU 88's attack was followed up by an attack by torpedo bombers. No damage was done. With this attack over, there was no sign of the AA ship. Either the fires had been put out or she had sunk. It was learnt later that the *Ibis* had been torpedoed.

It was during this attack that I came to realize how disorientating close sustained gun fire can be. My air action station was above and slightly aft of the aft starboard side twin 4" HA gun. Some of the attacking aircraft passed close to, or over, our starboard quarter. This resulted in that gun firing at a fairly high angle and almost against the after safety stop. The gun muzzles seemed very close to the oerlikon gun platform just below the after control tower. The oerlikon guns' crews did not seem to be affected. Possibly this was because they were wearing earphones, whilst the loaders could stand well sheltered inboard. For myself, I found the repeated gun blast most disconcerting and made worse when an early salvo blew my tin hat off. I found it very difficult, under these conditions, to concentrate on watching for incoming aircraft and directing the gun crews. My ears rang for days afterwards.

Sheffield rejoined the carriers at dawn and stayed with them until the afternoon. She then returned to Algiers to pick up our small convoy of three ships. These we were to take to Bougie and Djidjelli, some 120 miles east of Algiers.

There were two convoys, a slow and a fast one. Ours was the fast one and due to arrive at Bougie at 0200 on the 11th. The slow convoy, escorted by the monitor *Roberts* and bringing back-up supplies, was due to arrive during daylight hours when all the shooting should have been over.

Whilst we were away from Force 'O', it was heavily attacked. Special attention was given to the *Argus*, and she received a direct hit on the outboard edge of the port after end of the flight deck. Luckily this did not seriously impede flying operations. Two enemy planes were claimed destroyed. One was shot down by Force 'O' and the other was shot down in flames over the land by fighters.

During the night, whilst on passage with the convoy, we were in collision with one of the AS escorts, the sloop *Cabdus*. Her station had been on the port beam of the convoy, ours in the middle. For some reason we wished to get to the stern of the convoy, so we increased speed. When ahead of the convoy, we turned and passed down the port side in an opposite direction. In the pitch dark of the night the *Cabdus* was not seen until too late. We went hard a starboard, but she hit us a glancing blow in the band room and slid down the port side. In her passage she ripped off most of the bulkhead of the potato locker, as well as the whole of the bulkhead of the well below the catapult. Unfortunately, Stoker Spond was in the way and was killed. The *Cabdus* was holed for'ard above the waterline. Otherwise she was undamaged.

The convoy arrived at its appointed place at 0500. One transport was detached and proceeded to Djidjelli. At the same time a parachute force landed and occupied the airfield. The troops were not landed on their beaches until daylight. A signal had been received from the authorities to the effect that they had been ordered to hand over the port to us at 1100.

We lay off Bougie all forenoon, keeping an eye on the three forts there. Two of these mounted 3" guns and the other 5" guns. At 1100, ships from the slow convoy that had arrived at 0800 began to enter harbour. We left Bougie at noon and rejoined the *Argus*, which had been providing air cover. Stoker Spond was buried at sea with full military honours at 1530. At 1700 we were attacked by four torpedo bombers with no result to either side.

On the morning of the 12th, the BBC news revealed that Operation Torch had involved 500 merchant ships and 350 warships. Surely the biggest sea operation since the Spanish Armada. During that night the *Claire* had caught a U boat on the surface. The submarine crash-dived and *Claire* dropped depth charges. After these had exploded, there was another explosion. The submarine was claimed as sunk.

At dawn on the 13th, whilst off Cape Palos, we joined up with a convoy of three ships. The *Dempo, Almark* and *Samuel Chase* and four escort vessels, entering the Straits of Gibraltar during the night. The convoy continued on whilst we remained outside Gib until 0745, when we secured to buoys. Permission was granted to send air-mail letters and cables. The postman sent

off just over £36 worth of cables from the ship. At 1800 Rear Admiral
Harcourt hauled down his flag and re-hoisted it on the *Bermuda*. Thus ended
the *Sheffield*'s part in Operation Torch. In speculating on the effects of this
operation on the War, I commented at the time as follows:-

> Who can tell what effects it will have on the war? They can anyway only be
> good ones for the United Nations. The immediate effects can be gauged. The
> Germans have had to occupy, and will most probably strengthen, the defences
> of Southern France. Vast amounts of food and materials have now been
> diverted from Germany. Germany has had hastily to organize and transport by
> air a new army to Tunisia thus putting another great strain on her resources.
>
> For the Allies the Mediterranean is now, or will be in a few months, open to
> our shipping. We have a grand bombing base from which to bomb Italy and
> make the lot of those unhappy people even more miserable. We have acquired
> important bases from which to launch an invasion of Southern Europe. Apart
> from the tactical advantage, we have captured a nice lot of shipping in Algiers
> and Bougie.

Encounter with General De Gaulle

Because of my position as the Navigating Officer's Tanky, I was liable to be
sent ashore to collect our sailing orders. I think that it was on this occasion in
Gibraltar that I had my first encounter with General De Gaulle. I was
waiting in the Chief of Staff's Office when Admiral Somerville, Flag Officer
Force H, emerged from his inner office escorting General de Gaulle. I was
diagonally across the room from the General, who paused and for a moment
we made eye contact. As we did so, I could feel the small hairs at the back of
my neck rise and was swept by a feeling of intense dislike. The incident
probably lasted less than ten seconds but was burnt for ever onto my
memory. This was the first and only occasion that I have had an incident like
this. Reflecting on it, I recalled the completely different impression created
by General Sikorsky. He inspected a parade of Polish Troops on the quay
alongside the *Abdiel* in Alexandria. He was such a nice old gentleman and
genuinely concerned about the soldier who had fainted on parade.

Return to Scapa

On the 16th and 17th *Sheffield* and *Jamaica* cruised on the lookout for raiders
and supply ships sailing from French Ports. At dawn the *Jamaica* would part
company and take up station 16 miles away on the port side, returning at
dusk. On the 18th that part of the cruisers' duty was completed and we
headed home for Scapa arriving there on the 20th.

To the disgust of many of the crew, workmen came aboard on the 21st to make good the damage done during our collision with the *Cabdus*. It had been hoped that we would go to a dockyard for repairs and give leave. During the night of the 21st/22nd, in a wilful act of sabotage, some of the workmen's tools were thrown overboard. The Captain cleared lower deck and gave a very strong address on the subject. He explained that because of a number of ships being away and only a few ships at Scapa Flow that weren't broken down or working up, it was imperative that we should remain here in case the *Tirpitz* or some other ship tried to break through.

On the 26th November a message was received from Admiral Cunningham, who had had overall naval command of Torch. He had signalled:

> In my message to you before this operation started I called on you for all your efforts in a hazardous operation of supreme importance to our countries. The response has been all and more than I had hoped, and I thank Captains, Officers and Men alike for the courage, efficiency and resolution with which they played their part. My pride in the work of the Merchant Navy and the confidence I have learnt to place in them after two years of hard warfare in the Mediterranean has been proved yet again. This was my first contact with the United States ships and I emphasize that this message applies with equal force to them in this operation. I send Captains, Officers and Crews my thanks and wish them Godspeed.

It was also announced on that day that service pay in the Navy had been raised to bring it nearer that of the Army. Amongst other rises, Midshipman's pay was now 6/10d per diem.

On the 29th November Winston Churchill broadcast to all the English-speaking peoples of the World. I made two notes on this speech. Firstly he said that when he was leaving the Kremlin in the middle of August, he had said to Stalin that 'when we have decisively defeated Rommel in Egypt, I will send you a telegram: and he replied, 'When we make our counter-offensive here' and he drew an arrow on the map, 'I will send you one. Both messages have duly arrived'.

Referring to the landings in North Africa, Churchill said:

> 'For every transport or supply ship we have lost, a U Boat has been sunk or severely damaged. For every ton of Anglo-American shipping lost so far in this expedition, we have gained perhaps two tons in the shipping acquired or recovered in the French harbours of North and West Africa. Thus in this respect, as Napoleon recommended, war has been made to support war.'

In all this War this was by far the most cheering of speeches made by Mr Winston Churchill since the War began.

The Beveridge Report

On the 2nd of December I noted that Sir William Beveridge's report on improvements of social security was published. I commented in the following manner:

> The chief proposals put forward are that insurance companies in existence today should all be amalgamated together and work as agents to the Government. Everybody will contribute towards insurance paying 2/6 to 5/- a week according to age.
>
> Benefits range from birth to the grave of every single person. They include free medical and hospital treatment. Children's allowances after the first child. Increases in unemployment benefit, abolition of the means test and an industrial pension in place of workman's compensation. A grant for housewives, including a marriage and maternity grant. A widow's benefit and a separation or divorce allowance. Free domestic help in times of sickness. An increase in old age pensions and a funeral grant.
>
> To keep the plan in operation the Government will be required to contribute some 86 million pounds a year towards the scheme. Surely when the country spends thirteen millions a day on war, it can afford 86 millions a year spent on ensuring that nobody will suffer from want in peace time. For those that say the scheme is impracticable, much the same idea has been in operation for some years in New Zealand.
>
> If after the war this scheme is proved satisfactory, could it be applied world wide? That surely would be a correct and final step towards a peaceful world, a world without fear of want, without fear. Thus can one see the fulfilment of the Atlantic Charter.

Exercise at Scapa

For the next two weeks the ship was exercised hard. Gunnery shoots, damage control exercises and night encounter exercises. These were a prelude to more important things to come. The programme was interrupted by a severe gale in the early hours of the 8th December. The anchors started to drag in a gale force 7 (28-33 knots). Although a second anchor had been let go, this failed to stop the ship drifting into the harbour boom, with one buoy fouling the ship's rudder. As soon as it was light, divers went down to inspect and survey the damage. They found that the mooring wires of a buoy were foul of the rudder. Three tugs came to our assistance. One went to the bow to keep the ship steady. Another to the port quarter and tried to haul the stern to port, whilst the third stood by ready to give a hand if needed. Thanks to the tugs' combined efforts, *Sheffield* was pulled clear of the boom and back to her allotted position at 1415.

The account of the night encounter exercise may be of interest. The ships involved were the *Sheffield* and *Penelope* on the one side and the *Anson, King George V (KGV)* and screening destroyers on the other. The two battleships were representing the *Tirpitz* and the *Scharnhorst*. We proceeded to sea at 1545 and went to action stations at 1800. In the first run the *Sheffield* and *Penelope* were the target ships. The battleships opened fire at very long range with starshell. Their shells could be distinctly heard whooshing overhead and then exploding in the air. It served as a good introduction to the sort of noises one would meet with during a night action.

Sheffield and *Penelope* were unable to get close enough to use long-range starshell and were unable, in the time available, to shift to extreme fuse settings, so we were obviously badly shot up by the enemy. Round one to them. At the end of this run, we gathered up the destroyers and disappeared into the night.

In the second run we separated from the *Penelope*, came in fine on the battleships' bows and fired all our torpedoes from a good position. We illuminated the head of the battleships with starshell and fired at them with all twelve guns. Then we made smoke and dropped a smoke float in exactly the right place completely spoiling any chance of the enemy illuminating us. We then came through the smoke screen and illuminated the battleships, thus greatly helping the destroyers to press home their torpedo attack whilst we continued to fire broadsides at the battleships. Round two to us.

The third round was an RDF exercise. We shadowed the enemy force from their port quarter, keeping outside the critical ten-mile range to prevent them effectively opening fire on us. The whole time we were making enemy reports to *Penelope* and Scapa W/T. To *Penelope* so that she knew what was going on and to Scapa so that they could tell the world that this was an exercise. The shadowed force made an aggressive turn towards us, but the RDF tracking gave us sufficient warning to enable us to conform and turn away. Third round all square.

For the fourth round the battleships represented three Koln-Class cruisers. We picked them up rather late at nine miles. By careful tracking and clever tactics we managed to cross their bows and put them against the sun when dawn came. Out of the darker sky we delivered a number of 'suicide' attacks with both torpedoes and gunfire. We claimed that the enemy was damaged and reduced in speed and that one of the cruisers had been sunk. *Penelope* co-ordinated her attacks with *Sheffield*, adding confusion to the enemy force. We returned to the Flow late in the afternoon.

Exercises continued the following day, this time for the benefit of two destroyers who were working up. Oiling at sea exercises were carried out with the *Musketeer* and *Matchless*.

Support Force for a Russian Convoy

On the 13th December Rear Admiral Burnett hoisted his flag on the *Sheffield*. We sailed for Loch Ewe the next day, anchoring in the Loch late in the afternoon. We stayed at anchor all the next day. In the afternoon all the midshipmen were ordered ashore. The general idea was that we were all to take a long walk. However, the weather was foul with very heavy continuous rain, so we decided to spend the afternoon in the warm comfort of the only hotel. We spent a very pleasant afternoon reading and talking over an open coal fire. This was followed by an excellent tea of scones, bread and butter and some very good fancy cakes. Not the sort of tea one expected to get with the rationing. I concluded that the peaceful afternoon spent in congenial company and surroundings did us just as much good as a long walk would have done.

RA Burnett briefed the ship's company the following day. The operation was to cover an important convoy bound for Murmansk. On the afternoon of the 15th the convoy would sail from Loch Ewe. On the 16th *Sheffield*, *Jamaica*, *Matchless* and *Opportune* would sail and overtake the convoy on the 17th. We would then take up a position some 50 miles south of the convoy. All went according to plan, the convoy arriving safely at Kola Inlet on Christmas Day without the loss of a single ship.

It was on that voyage that I came to dislike the song, 'We're going to have a White Christmas'. This was played over the ship's loud speakers every single morning at reveille. I got very fed up with it.

We had arrived before Christmas Day, which was spent as far as possible in the traditional manner. I had the morning AA watch on the bridge and had the dubious pleasure of sounding off the air action stations alarm in response to a general Yellow Warning just as the crew were starting their Christmas dinner. Luckily the raid was over quickly and did no damage. The local Russian ENSA party entertained the ship's company with a spirited performance of Russian dancing and singing.

Whilst at Kola Inlet there would be air raids two to four times a day during daylight hours. As far as we could see from the ship, very few bombs were dropped and they did no damage. It was noticed that all the defending aircraft were Spitfires.

Shortly before we sailed on the 27th, I was sent ashore to collect our sailing papers. I had been issued with a special pass and was one of only two people allowed ashore from the ship. The other was a Supply P.O. sent ashore to obtain vegetables. We felt that the Russian guards on the quay were there more to stop anyone going ashore than to protect us from enemy action. This was what one might call a hostile alliance.

Battle of the Barents Sea

Sheffield, *Jamaica*, *Matchless* and *Opportune* sailed to take up a position south west of Bear Island so as to make contact with, and escort, another inward-bound convoy to Kola Inlet. Then we would turn round and take up position to cover the returning empty ships from our first convoy.

At 0100 on the 28th we went to action stations and remained at Second Degree of readiness until nearly daylight. Second Degree of readiness meant that, when off watch, one had to be in the immediate vicinity of one's action station. On these occasions I found a fairly comfortable sleeping place in one of the flats (small open spaces below deck between compartments) and discovered that the inside of a tin hat stuffed with gloves made quite a good pillow. The outside temperature dropped to about 21°F. The weather continued to get colder and rougher. The destroyers were finding it heavy going and were getting short of fuel. As a result, they were detached and proceeded to Seydisfjord for fuel. By this time we had turned round and were now sailing on an easterly course. The 30th provided lower temperatures and increasing seas. *Sheffield* once again demonstrated her ability to roll. The upper deck became covered with snow and ice started to accumulate from the spray. Some seas came inboard. One of the midshipmen, having just come off watch, reported seeing the Captain's steward coming over the hanger deck bearing the Captain' lunch. The midshipman, seeing a large wave towering over the deck, had just enough time to scramble up the ladder. The unfortunate steward had nowhere to go. He just hung on. When the wave had passed the steward was still with us, but no sign of the Captain's dinner.

On the last day of the year the hands went to action station messes for breakfast, as was usual. Just as the cooks were returning their gear and tidying up, the Captain broadcast that we had picked up an RDF contact. We immediately closed up to action stations. This was at 0858. The *Sheffield* with the *Jamaica* astern, investigated the echo for an hour. It was at first thought to be an enemy ship because of the speed, 28 knots, given by the plot. This was an error. At 0930 gunfire was sighted on the starboard beam, immediately followed by an enemy report from D17 (Captain V Sheerbrooke) reporting an enemy cruiser and three destroyers.

Captain Sheerbrooke in HMS *Onslow* divided his force and engaged the enemy destroyers with one division whilst he attacked the cruiser with the other. During the ensuing action the enemy was four times compelled to retire under smoke to avoid torpedo attack. Every time *Onslow* gave chase, driving the enemy ships out of range of the convoy and towards *Sheffield* and *Jamaica* who were coming in at high speed.

After being continuously in action for forty minutes, the *Onslow* was hit and forced to retire, both forward guns being out of action and Captain Sheerbrooke severely wounded in the face, losing the sight of one eye. Nevertheless he continued to direct the ships under his command until he was satisfied that his next-in-command in HMS *Obedient* had assumed control.

It was only then that he agreed to leave the bridge and go to his cabin for treatment. He insisted on receiving news of the action until the convoy was out of danger. For this supreme act of leadership and courage he was awarded the Victoria Cross.

In the meantime *Sheffield* and *Jamaica* were steaming to the sound of the guns at full speed. They continued to close until a large enemy cruiser, thought to be the 8 in Cruiser *Hipper*, but which was later known to be the pocket battleship *Lutzow*, was sighted. This ship was engaged at about 1123 using flashless cordite. This is almost essential in a night action. The flash from the standard cordite completely destroys night vision. The flashless cordite, however, seemed to produce much more smoke. The central gun in each turret was loaded with tracer shells. From the after control tower *Jamaica*'s tracer shells arcing up into the sky made a fine show. Although fire was opened at almost extreme range, hits were scored on the enemy ship with the first four salvos and the enemy retired under cover of smoke. We ourselves were fortunate not to be hit. Shells were landing very close and I felt extremely vulnerable with only a canvas screen as protection. Huge gouts of water reared up close to the port quarter as the shells plunged into the sea. I tried to comfort myself with the thought that, if the shells exploded, they would do so under water, thus preventing any splinters whizzing through my canvas screen. Later when I talked to the RDF operators, I found that they too had had some uncomfortable moments. As a result of our gunnery exercises off Scapa, they were well used to watching the echoes of our shells on the RDF screen heading out towards their target. To see blips of shells heading towards us was a new and disturbing experience.

At about this time, with the enemy disengaging, an enemy destroyer was sighted at close range on the port bow. The threat of torpedo attack forced *Sheffield* to shift target and alter course. The Captain asked the Admiral for permission to ram. Fortunately our first salvos from A and B turrets smashed into the destroyer's bridge, blew the forward funnel over the side and enveloped the destroyer in flames. *Sheffield* altered course to port and the destroyer passed down her starboard side at very close range. The main armament continued to fire at her under local control over open sights. They were joined by the 4" guns and the pompom. The destroyer, now known to have been the *Eckholdt*, was left burning furiously from stem to stern. Whilst this side action was going on, the *Jamaica* had also engaged the accompanying destroyer, the *Beitzen*. She however promptly turned away under smoke and escaped damage.[3]

At the very start of the action the concussion from the first salvo of *Jamaica*'s B turret smashed her RDF 273 set. As a result, she had to keep in close touch with *Sheffield*. This lack of RDF probably contributed to the cruisers losing contact with the main enemy when *Sheffield* was distracted by the destroyer. Contact was soon regained. At 1226 fire was opened on a forward bearing at long range at an enemy cruiser, either the *Nuremberg* or *Hipper*. The enemy ships returned a rapid and accurate fire.

The preceding account of the action is, with some slight editing, as I had described it in my log book. Admiral Schofield writing in 1977 described this latter part of the action as follows:-

> Meanwhile, having dealt with the *Eckholdt* group of destroyers, Burnett resumed the chase of the *Hipper* which was now 12½ miles to the south-west. She came into sight briefly at 12.15 hrs, but soon afterwards the threat of torpedo attack by the *Beitzen* and Z29 obliged him to turn towards them and the *Sheffield* was just about to open fire on them when the *Lutzow* appeared on the same bearing and at 12.29 both cruisers opened fire on the pocket battleship at a range of 14,500 yards. The *Lutzow* replied and the *Hipper*, from a position somewhat further ahead, joined in. The *Lutzow*'s shots fell short but those of the *Hipper* were dangerously accurate, so Burnett turned away to disengage and also to avoid any torpedoes which the destroyers might have fired. At 12.45 hrs, when he resumed his westerly course, the enemy ships had disappeared from view and although they were tracked by RADAR until 14.00 hrs, no opportunity occurred of renewing the engagement. Not wishing to be drawn too far away from the convoy – the position of which was still in doubt – Burnett abandoned the chase and swept towards the south in case the German cruiser *Nuremberg*, should be lurking in the vicinity.
>
> (Schofield, *The Arctic Convoys*, p. 92).

It was not until many years later that I learned of the extreme strategic importance of this action.

The U 354 had been shadowing the convoy since the 24th December. On the 30th he reported the convoy as being weakly protected. It was this signal that stimulated the sailing of the German force. The U 354 had observed the action, but could have had little appreciation of what had taken place. In spite of this the commander signalled at 11.45 hrs: 'According to our observations, the battle has reached its climax. I see nothing but red.' This message was

---

3. Vice Admiral B.B. Schofield; *The Arctic Convoys*, p. 91.

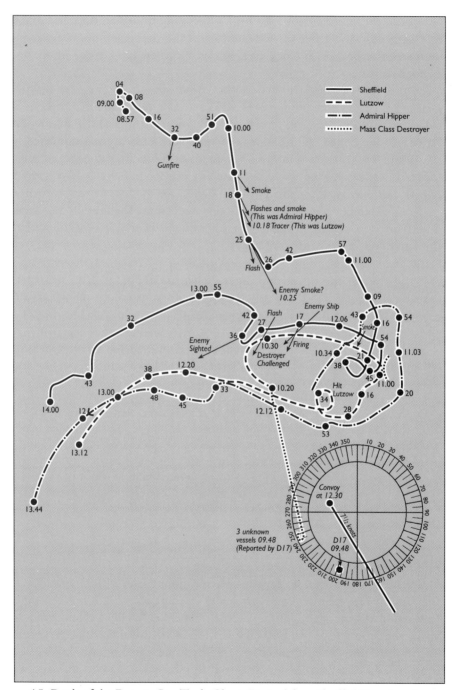

Sheffield

Lutzow

Admiral Hipper

Maas Class Destroyer

04
09.00
08
08.57
16
51
32
10.00
40
Gunfire

11
Smoke
18
Flashes and smoke
(This was Admiral Hipper)
10.18 Tracer (This was Lutzow)

25
42
57
26
11.00
Flash
09

Enemy Smoke?
10.25

13.00 55
Enemy Ship
32
42 *Flash* 17 12.06 43
54
27
16
36
54
Smoke
Enemy
10.30 *Firing*
10.34
Sighted
Destroyer
21
Challenged
38
45 11.00
43
12.20
11.03
38
10.20
16
13.00
48
33
Hit
20
45
Lutzow
14.00
12½
12.12
34
28
13.12
53

13.44

Convoy
at 12.30
7½ knots

3 unknown
vessels 09.48
(Reported by D17)
D17
09.48

15. *Battle of the Barents Sea. Track Chart. Derived from* Sheffield's *action plot.*

taken to mean that the operation had gone according to plan and the convoy had been destroyed or very badly mauled. The message was passed on to Hitler at his headquarters. On the return of the German ships, the report of the action to Hitler was unduly delayed. Hitler, angry at the delay and furious that the expectations arising from the U 534's signal had not been fulfilled, decreed that all the heavy ships should be decommissioned. Admiral Raeder was ordered to report to him. Raeder's resignation was accepted and Admiral Donitz, the very successful chief of the U boat arm, was appointed to succeed him.

The *Sheffield* and *Jamaica* continued to cover the convoy until midnight, Jan 1st-2nd, when they steamed for Seydisfjord. This was an uneventful passage except for a fine display of St. Elmo's fire on the RDF 284 and 285 aerials. I had only seen this once before. That had been on the *Canton*, where the points of fire had appeared on all the sharp points of the bridge. One could even run one's finger along a stanchion and momentarily pick up a point of fire on the tip of the finger. It was so strange to have this small blue/green flame glowing on the finger tip without the slightest sensation of anything – no heat, no tingling. it just glowed for a second or so and died away.

As the *Sheffield* with *Jamaica* and the 17th Destroyer Flotilla in company were entering Scapa Flow on the 6th January, the following signal was received from C. in C. Home Fleet 'Your defence of the convoy was most gallant. The boldness of your action was entirely responsible for the safe conduct of the ships under your escort, a fact of which you may be proud.'

The two cruisers entered Scapa Flow with their battle ensigns flying. These were about twice the size of the usual ensign and made a fine show when they were first hoisted at the start of the action. That evening our Admiral transferred his flag to the *Tyne*. The next day was occupied in re-ammunitioning ship and getting everything ready for the C. in C.'s visit the next day.

Admiral Tovey came aboard on the 8th and addressed the ship's company. He congratulated everybody on the part that they played in the action. He also told us of the valiant action by the destroyers and particularly of the gallant action of Captain Sheerbrooke.

Up till then we had had no idea of what had happened in the early phases of the battle. Admiral Tovey announced that he had given orders to the Captain to proceed to Greenock for repairs and said that he might take the opportunity to give leave to the ship's company.

We sailed for Greenock that afternoon, arriving there shortly after noon the next day. The Port Watch went on leave for three days at 1800.

On the 12th the ship went up river with the aid of tugs to the Dalmier Basin to carry out repairs. The damage was mainly confined to fan trunking and fan motors brought down from the deckheads during the action, all caused by concussion. The only damage directly caused by enemy action was a small splinter hole in the Admiral's day cabin. Whereas fan trunking and cable arrays coming down when the six-inch guns were fired on the *Canton* was not unreasonable, I found it strange that this should happen aboard a purpose-built warship. On the 14th most of the Port Watch returned and the Starboard Watch went on leave until the 16th. By the next day there were still some twenty men adrift from the Port Watch and we sailed without them, arriving back at Scapa Flow on the 19th.

It was also about this time that I really began to dislike dockyard workmen and trade unions. We were in the hands of the dockyard and the ship's hands had put a lot of effort into clearing up the hanger where we kept our Walrus. It was a wet day. The dockyard workmen were making a horrible mess tramping through the hanger, so, as Officer of the Watch, I had the hanger doors closed and signs put up directing the workman along a route that took them over the top of the hanger. The Commander sent for me. He was sympathetic as he explained that whilst he supported my action, he had had to open up the hanger to avoid a strike. The workmen had objected to having to walk over the top of the hanger in the rain.

About ten days after this episode, it was found that one of the ship's food stores had been broken into. The dockyard workmen had used an acetylene cutter to cut through the centre panel of the food store door. They had removed most of the stores and then welded the panel back in place again.

Russian Convoys again

On the 21st we weighed anchor and joined the *Anson* and the destroyers *Falkner, Ingelfield, Eclipse* and *Montrose*. We were proceeding on an operation to cover Convoy JW.52 bound for Murmansk. This comprised 16 ships escorted by 7 destroyers and 5 other small escort vessels. The convoy speed was to be 7.5 knots. The convoy was already at sea.

Force R, consisting of *Kent* (First Cruiser Squadron), *Glasgow* and *Bermuda*, had already sailed from Seydisfjord to cover the convoy to the southward during its passage from Long. 10°E to the Kola Inlet. Battlefleet cover was being provided by *Anson, Sheffield* and four destroyers. We were to proceed to 66° 12'N, 11° 50'W. There the destroyer screen would be relieved by *Queensborough, Raider, Echo* and the Polish destroyer *Orkan*. These would have re-fuelled at Seydisfjord. The force would then proceed to 72° 40'N and cover the convoy until it crossed longitude 32°E. The support force would

16. HMS Sheffield. *Arctic frost on the whaler.*
By courtesy of the ship's photographer.

then return to Akureyri for fuel. The Altenfjord would be under surveillance by a British submarine to watch out for *Lutzow* and *Hipper*. It was thought that the *Hipper* was operationally unfit.

The operation proceeded smoothly and almost without incident. Although the convoy was attacked on the 24th by four torpedo bombers, no damage was done and two of the bombers were shot down. During the remainder of the convoy's passage, it was shadowed both by aircraft and submarine, but no attacks developed.

Our main problem was the cold. The temperature dropped to 10°-12°F. This caused the funnel fumes to condense and form a thick fog downwind. Because of the cold, the guns had to be moved every twenty minutes or so to stop the hydraulic fluid seizing up. Although my cruising station at the torpedo control point was not draughty, I put on so many clothes to keep warm that it was a struggle to get through the emergency hatch covers on the way to and from my station on watch. The sheepskin jacket given to us

17. The author in winter gear.

on the *Abdiel* at Cape Town was an absolute boon and a cause of envy on the part of the other midshipmen. Feet were a problem. Thick sea boot stockings over one's socks in a rubber sea boot made the feet sweat. The lack of insulation in the boot allowed the sweat to freeze, or so it seemed. Leather shoes were no good; you couldn't put on thick enough socks to keep the feet warm. You just always seemed to have cold feet when on watch. Another problem was internal condensation below decks. Condensation formed on the ship's side and froze. Yet the central heating and warmth of the mess melted the inboard side of the ice, that would form up to about an inch thick. This melt water trickled down onto the deck, resulting in a constant film of dirty black water sloshing back and forth across the deck.

On the 30th of January we were at sea again with the *Anson*. This time our task was to cover a convoy returning from Russia. The cruiser force consisted of the *Bermuda*, *Kent* and *Glasgow*. These would operate some 50 miles south of the convoy. On February 1st air reconnaissance over Altenfjord had failed to find any of the German surface ships that were usually there, except for one destroyer. It was assumed that they were out in force searching for our convoy. At that time *Anson* and *Sheffield* were some 90 miles north-west of the convoy and steaming down on a south-westerly course at 20 knots. The next day *Anson* and *Sheffield* were about 100 miles ahead of the convoy and steaming on a similar course. There was still no news of the German ships. Several w/t transmissions were heard from U boats in the vicinity of the convoy whilst it was passing Bear Island. The next day, with no enemy activity, we were ordered to return to Iceland and proceed to Hvalfjord. Various gunnery and RDF exercises were carried out on the way.

During our brief stay at Hvalfjord, the liberty men were having trouble with the Canadian beer that was being served in the canteen there. The beer was about twice the strength of the existing wartime British beer and the men, being out of training for such strong stuff, were feeling the full effects of it.

However the boys and most of the officers landed on the north shore of the fjord. There there was no beer, but excellent opportunities for strenuous exercise in climbing the snow-covered hills that came right down to the fjord shore.

The view from the top was marvellous and well worth the effort of getting there. The whole fjord was mapped out at one's feet. The ships at anchor looked far too small to accommodate some eight hundred men. In the other direction, a valley was laid out flat before our eyes, with its frozen lake and a small road exploring its way past the lake and into the distant mountains.

The descent down the mountain-like hill was accomplished in a quarter of the time of the ascent. We found that the best way was to choose a long stretch of snow unbroken by any rocks and just to slide or roll down in a flurry of whirling snow and accompanied by shouts of encouragement from one's companions, until some deep snow drift barred further progress.

Battle Exercises in the Denmark Strait

We sailed from the fjord on the 8th and turned north-west. The Captain told us that we were going on an exercise and that *Anson* and *Sheffield* were representing a German force attempting to break out into the Atlantic. The *Anson* represented the *Tirpitz* and the *Sheffield*, the *Hipper*. We could expect to be attacked by aircraft and by the *Howe*, *Kent* and *Berwick*. The Captain also announced that this was to be his last voyage with *Sheffield* because he was about to take an appointment as Naval Aide de Camp to Field Marshal Gort VC, C. in C. Malta. He would be relieved by Captain C. T. Aldis.

The exercise started when at 11.00 on the 9th we turned south down the Denmark Strait. It was not long before we were found by aircraft. Throughout the afternoon we had one, and sometimes two, Hudson or Catalinas circling around out of range. We tried to evade them by steering towards snowstorms, but the storms persistently drew away from us, so we gave up the attempt and steered towards the clear weather.

In the evening we made contact with the 'enemy' and turned towards them to try and engage. They detected our move and conformed with our turn, so we resumed our original course. The enemy continued to shadow us until midnight when the exercise came to an end. We steamed towards Scapa Flow, where we were to have a number of AA shoots and night encounter exercises. However the weather turned foul and the exercises were cancelled.

This serves to illustrate how we were constantly exercised in all the various tactical situations which we might encounter. No doubt this made us a very efficient fighting force, as the recent action had demonstrated. The downside was that we spent a lot of time at action stations and had little time for off-watch rest and sleep.

Storm Force Winds off Iceland

The weather continued to be foul and during the night the wind increased to gale force and we dragged anchor. On the 12th the wind moderated and we were able to anchor in the Flow, where we had plenty of space in which to drag our anchor. On the 13th Captain Clark left the ship and it was not until the 15th that the weather moderated enough to allow us to get back to our proper berth. There we took on stores, aircraft fuel and two aircraft. We sailed for Seydisfjord that evening.

The weather continued to deteriorate, forcing us to heave to during the last dog watch of the 17th on a course of 265° and making about 5 knots. The wind and seas slowly moderated, allowing us to steer north and increase speed to 15 knots, which we did until 0400 on the 18th. By this time the wind was increasing and the seas had become very steep and severe, making us bump very hard in the seaway. We were once again forced to heave to.

By 0800 the wind had reached hurricane force and the waves were piling up in great hills some 50-60ft high. Visibility was down to about two miles and the air was soaked with flying spray. The wind tore off the tops of the waves and drove the spray horizontally over the sea.

On the whole, the ship was behaving very well. There was comparatively little rolling, the ship being kept with a slight starboard list by the press of the wind. She was not taking a dangerous amount of water over the foc'sle. She would stagger up one vertical side, hang poised at the top, then rush down the other side. The gun turrets were all trained to starboard on an after bearing so as to protect our flimsy wartime tampons and keep as much sea as possible out of the barrels.

18. HMS Sheffield. *Storm force winds off Iceland, 18th February, 1943.*

I was on watch at the time and had quietly crept to the back of the bridge to see what was going on. Thus at about 10.00 I watched one enormous wave tower over the ship fine on the port bow. Higher and higher it rose as the bow slipped down the trough to its base. The wave poised above the ship, a menacing mountain of water. Everyone held their breath. Slowly the top began to curl over, gathered speed. Crash! The whole foc'sle was buried under hundreds of tons of water. The wave swept on over the hanger deck and buried the quarter deck under fifteen feet of water.

The ship shuddered under the blow, and still shuddering, slowly came up for air. As soon as the spray had cleared, those on the bridge rushed forward. A gasp went up. The forward part of the top of A turret had vanished. Almost immediately a muffled explosion was felt from aft. This was from the depth charges that had been swept overboard and were now exploding 300 fathoms below.

The tops of the turrets were built in three sections. It was the port side section that had gone, exposing the left gun to the sea and sky. On arrival at harbour, it was found that the port side of the turret had been bent inwards. This would have been enough to wrench the rivets apart.

19. HMS Sheffield. *Photograph taken a few minutes after the port side section of the top of A Turret had been swept overboard.*

The depth charges had been set to safe, but when they were washed over the side, the diaphragms would have given way under the huge pressure, causing the charges to go off at 300 fathoms.

This huge devastating wave marked the height of the storm. By 20.00 the wind and seas had moderated enough to allow us to proceed to Seidisfjord at 18 knots.

We arrive at Seydisfjord at 0900 on the 19th, unfit for action. In addition to the damaged turret, the asdic compartment was making water fast through distorted rivets and the asdic dome was badly damaged by the pounding of the seas. The quarterdeck had been cleared of all carley rafts, depth charges and smoke floats, except for one very flattened survivor rolling in a drunken and disorderly manner from one side to the other. Abaft of Y turret, the starboard accommodation ladder was lying in pieces, having been torn from its lashings on the screen. The starboard whaler was completely wrecked, with only bits and pieces still hanging from the davits.

At Seydisfjord we met the *Cumberland* and *Belfast*. Both ships had been in the storm. *Cumberland* had got through unscathed but *Belfast* had had damage to her capstan. The next day *Norfolk* entered harbour. It was rumoured that she had had the stanchions supporting her capstan bent.

On the 23rd *Sheffield* left Seydisfjord bound for Glasgow for repairs. One felt sorry for Captain Aldis, to have his command so severely damaged on his first voyage with her. On our passage home we again had to heave to for a few hours because of the severity of the weather. On arrival at the Clyde, the ship was delayed going up river because of the weather, but this did not stop the first leave party from leaving the ship for three weeks' leave. In due course *Sheffield* was towed up river and put into No 5 drydock. Whilst in drydock, A turret was lifted out, the asdic dome replaced and the damage sustained in the collision in November made good.

At this point I left the ship for three weeks' leave. However, after ten days at home, I received a wire appointing me to the *Newcastle*, to take effect from April 2nd. As I received the wire on the 1st, I did not have much time to get to Glasgow, collect my gear and then proceed to Scapa Flow. Furthermore, by the time I received the wire, the last train that day for Glasgow had already left. However, in spite of wartime train delays, I joined the *Newcastle* on the 3rd. On the 5th, the day before she was due to sail for Greenock to give leave prior to going out east, I was drafted to the *KGV* (*King George V*). So once again I packed my gear, caught the drifter and reported on board the *King George V.*

CHAPTER 5

HMS *King George V*

THE OTHER RNR MIDSHIPMAN on the *Sheffield*, Lowein, had the same posting as I. First to the *Newcastle* and then to the *KGV*. By this time we were both fairly senior midshipmen and only a few days of seniority separated us. There had always been a bit of rivalry between us. Because he preferred the protocol of the quarterdeck while I enjoyed messing about in boats, we had had little contact with each other as far as work was concerned. We were both into gunnery. His action station was in the main Transmission station,[1] while mine was in the after (back up) control tower.

Seniority in the Gunroom
Lowein had apparently scanned the Navy List just before we transferred to the *KGV*. On the way over in the boat, he told me that he reckoned that we would be the two senior midshipmen on board. Because he was senior to me, he expected to be the Senior Midshipman and did not want any trouble from me. My reply was that if he did not interfere with whatever I was doing, there would be no problem. I mention this here to illustrate the then very hierarchical nature of the Navy. Whoever was senior was in command. Seniority was based on the day one was commissioned or promoted. Lowein had been appointed as a midshipman three days before me. If we had been appointed on the same day, then I would have been senior, because G comes before L.

So it turned out. We were the two most senior midshipmen in the Gunroom. I found out that the position of Navigator's Tanky was vacant. I saw the navigating officer and the job was mine. Word of my previous gunnery experience had gone ahead of me. I was quickly put through a run on the gun control simulator that they had on board. As a result, my action station became Rate Officer in the main gun control tower. I kept this post throughout my time on the ship. It was very satisfying to be a member of the main armament control team in the Flag Ship of the Home Fleet. This does not mean that it had been my intention to specialize in gunnery. My sights

---

1. All gun control commands are passed through the Transmission Station (TS). It was situated well below decks and within the armour-protected section of the ship. Mechanical computers there calculated the amount of elevation and lay-off of the guns.

were on the position of Hydrographer to the Navy. I had also let it be known that my preference lay in running boats rather than being the Midshipman of the Watch. In this too I had my way.

Air Defence Exercises
A week after joining the ship, Admiral Tovy, C.-in-C. Home Fleet, transferred his flag to the *Duke of York*. When leaving the ship, he was given a formal rousing cheer by the ship's company and escorted to the *Duke of York* by the ship's boats. These were manned entirely by officers. That evening we left Scapa Flow for Rosyth for a short refit and to give home leave. On the approach to the Firth of Forth the following day, several Swordfish and Beaufighters carried out a torpedo bombing exercise. Their co-ordinated attacks from different directions and heights were most impressive and caused our air defence organization considerable embarrassment. We usually carried out these exercises when leaving or approaching the coast. The attacks by the squadrons that were regularly harrying German ships and shipping off the Norwegian coast were particularly effective. The exercises were of obvious benefit to both sides. My own feeling was that we, on the *KGV*, probably benefited most. Our look-out drills and RDF detection improved considerably. It was not long before we were rarely caught out by secondary and tertiary attacks coming in from different directions and heights.

Royal Navy and Merchant Navy Seamanship Compared
To go under the Forth Bridge. we had to wait for low water and send down our topmast. I was much impressed by the speed and efficiency of that exercise. This was unusual for me, because at this time I had become very critical of the naval way of doing things and tended to compare them unfavourably with the methods of the Merchant Navy. To my mind, a major problem for the Navy was that they had too many hands available, so that they got in each other's way. Often the chain of command was too long and there were differing views within that chain of the way the job should be done. This criticism applied mainly to seamanship activities. When it came to damage control and gunnery, things generally went very well. Here a long tradition of fighting ships and well-rehearsed drills paid off.

Firing Broadsides and Gunnery Exercises
High winds delayed our entry into drydock until the 19th. The lucky 14-day leave party had two extra days' leave, not having to report on board until the 29th. We sailed from Rosyth for Scapa Flow on the 30th April and carried

out a 5.25 gunnery shoot when approaching Scapa, followed by a 14"
bombardment of Stack Skerry. Our Walrus was spotting for us.

There is something extremely satisfying in firing large-calibre guns; it is
almost sensuous. A moment before the firing of the guns, the firing gong
sounds. 'Ding ding' it goes in the Control Tower, on the bridge, the TS and in
each turret. This warns everybody that the gun layer is about to press the
trigger. As the gunlayer moves his sighting telescope up and down in
response to the ship's motion, so the huge guns below respond. Then as his
cross wires come onto the target he squeezes the trigger. The guns boom and
the whole ship responds to the concussion. The muzzles dip to the loading
position. Then in the Control Tower a klaxon gives its harsh cry a split
second before the shells are due to land. This allows the gunnery officer to
recognize his own fall of shot from the shells of any other ship that may be
engaging the same target. If all has gone well, huge splashes rise up dead in
line with the target. Some will be short of the target, some beyond. A
straddle has been achieved. Given a reasonable fighting range and well-drilled
turret crews, by the time one salvo splashes down, there will be two others in
the air on their way.

During these exercises, to conserve ammunition, we would normally fire
only one gun at a time until we had obtained the correct line of fire and
range. Then we would go into salvos, probably with only one gun firing
from each turret. Under battle conditions one would establish the line and
range with salvoes and then immediately go into broadsides. Then every gun
from every turret that could bear would be fired. Broadsides with the ten 14"
guns of the *KGV* were a vastly impressive sensation. I had thought the
broadsides of the six-inch guns of the *Sheffield* were impressive enough until
I felt the power and the thunder of really big guns.

On completion of these exercises we anchored in the Flow, only to go to
sea again near midnight. The immediate objective was to carry out night
encounter exercise with the *Berwick*, that had sailed two hours earlier. This
involved the 14" Control parties and the 5.25" starshell parties and searchlight crews. Three runs were carried out. In the first two, *KGV* was firing
ship while in the third the *Berwick* had a go. Our starshell and searchlight
illumination were very good on the first run, making the inclination of the
Berwick easy to assess. There was however a disagreement between the TS and
myself about the *Berwick's* speed, the TS claiming 32 knots against my
estimate of 20 knots. On the second run the starshell illumination was again
very good, but somehow the glare from the searchlights was a hindrance.
During the third run, with the *Berwick* as the attacking ship, we confused her
gun control by turning our searchlights on her.

We Join Force H

On completion, *Berwick* returned to Scapa Flow and we started our voyage to Gibraltar, arriving there on the 6th May. Reports of many submarines near our track resulted in us closing up to a second degree of readiness for 24 hours and in altering our track westwards. To avoid arriving late at Gibraltar, we had increased speed from 18 to 20 knots and, for the last few hours before entering Gib., to 25 knots.

There was a disturbance to the usual routine one night during the middle watch. *Tuscan*, a screening destroyer stationed on the port side, switched on her fighting lights. We immediately went hard-a-starboard to keep clear. However there were no depth charges and the fighting lights went out. The *Tuscan* vanished and we could not regain contact by WT. She reappeared on station about 30 minutes later.

When we left Rosyth, there were still some dockyard workmen on board. They had a pleasant cruise to Gibraltar, where we disembarked them when we had moored to the south mole. On the following day (7th) Rear Admiral Bissett hoisted his flag on board as Rear Admiral Second In Command of Force H. Force H's task was twofold. First, it was to act as a hunting unit in the Atlantic in case any German capital ship broke out into the Atlantic. Second, it was to keep open the supply lines to the First Army and if possible to bring the Italian fleet to action.

At this time the Tunisian Campaign was drawing to a close. Cape Bonne Peninsula had become a trap for the Axis troops. The First and Eighth Armies were slowly driving a wedge up the peninsula with the objective of splitting the Axis forces in two.

As usual we were kept busy with practice shoots of various kinds. On the night of the 14th May a night-tracking exercise showed up electrical failings in the 14" control system. That night star shell control was a shambles. After this had been sorted out, both the forward and aft control towers suffered misfires. However, later this was compensated by a very successful exercise in holding a target that was nearly end on and weaving from side to side to avoid punishment. We were very quickly in line with our shot and culminated in getting two successive salvos dead in line while the target was steaming dead away from us. That is, all our shells fell within the width of the beam of the target cruiser.

We then stayed in harbour for the next two weeks. During this time the fleet was reinforced by the *Howe* and the *Formidable*. A day or so after the arrival of the *Formidable*, she went outside to carry out dummy air attacks for a film being made about the Fleet Air Arm. Some senior midshipmen went out with her.

A Tour of Fortress Gibraltar

It was during this lull in operations that a party of us visited the Fortress of Gibraltar. This was confined to visiting the new tunnels being excavated in the rock. A senior officer met us at the Governor's House. Some of us thought that it was the Governor himself. We had been told that the Governor was going to conduct us round. To us lowly midshipmen that was not altogether an unreasonable supposition, considering that the leader of our party was the Commander. Our first visit was to the gallery, where six- and twelve-pounder guns were placed to fire through narrow loopholes covering the landward approaches to the Rock and the airfield. Off this gallery was one of the many W/T stations, a very well lit place but hot. The array of transformers and W/T equipment was most impressive. From there we went by car through the town and up towards the summit of the Rock, the overloaded cars growling up the gradient. We stopped opposite a large entrance into the rockface and entered an impressive cavern, where a workshop was being fitted out. Leaving this, we went along a gallery and came out on to a north-facing ledge. This gave a sweeping view across neutral ground littered with concrete pill boxes, and on into Spain. Entering the rock fastness again, we followed a seemingly endless gallery running dead straight on a slight downgrade. We walked past a bakery where the bread for 4,000 troops was mixed by hand and baked in electric ovens. We called in at a workshop, a power station under construction and another in action.

Returning to our cars, we went round to the south side of the Rock and into the store houses. There there were thousands of cases of every imaginable tinned food, tyres, and all the minor paraphernalia of war that keeps the machine going. The tour ended in an instrument repair workshop. From there we called at the hospital. Since it was obvious that we had come to the Med. for action, it was disappointing to find that the hospital was still under construction. It would include an operating theatre, dispensary, laboratory, gas cleansing centre and several huge wards. I feared that by the time it was completed, it would be too late for us. This was the last place we visited on our tour. When we got back to the cars, it was found that the cads' car, which is the car that always took the rearguard and carried the midshipmen and Warrant Officers, had broken down. We all piled into the next available one and went carefully back to the Governor's house with the mudguards almost down on to the tyres.

We entered a large room where several senior officers, including the Governor and General De Gaulle, were having a stand-up tea. Recalling my previous encounter with De Gaulle, I was careful not to look at him directly. Strangely, my previous feelings of instant dislike were not repeated. Perhaps it was prejudice that made me write in my journal: 'It was immediately apparent why De Gaulle is not very popular. He had a haughty air but did condescend to be introduced to our Commander. He left soon after.' To my surprise, the midshipmen's supervisor, who read our journals, did not make any adverse comment on this observation.

Working up for Operation Husky

On 15th June we sailed for Gib., carrying out day and night gunnery exercises en route. Some ten days later *Howe* (*KGV* Class Battleship) joined the fleet. From then until July 9th the two ships worked together, sometimes at Gib., sometime at Mers el Kabir, the Naval port of Oran (MEK) or Algiers. We went through a whole series of gunnery and damage-control exercises. For exercising torpedo and dive bombing attacks we were joined by the *Formidable*. On June 20th Rear Admiral Bissett transferred his flag to the *Formidable* and so we became the junior capital ship of the fleet.

Full calibre 14" gunnery exercises were carried out on June 22nd with the *Howe*. This was an interesting throw-off shoot, with the ships starting the exercise at 28,000 yards apart (14 nautical miles) and steaming at high speed on slightly converging courses. Fire was opened at 26,000 yards and the exercise continued until the range had come down to 12,000 yards (six miles). Because of poor visibility, we had to rely more than was usual on RDF for establishing the enemy's course and speed. This was followed by a 'fun' shoot at a splash target towed at high speed, and at some risk, by a destroyer. As this was an anti-E Boat exercise, all the small calibre guns were engaged. Afterwards the oerlikons showed what they could do to a low-level sleeve target.

That was a good day. Sometimes things did not go so well. Once, during a night-encounter exercise with the *Formidable* as the enemy, all started well. The starshells burst almost in the right place and the RDF worked out bearings and spreads. On the point of opening fire, it was found that the training transmission on the control tower had gone. We switched to the after control tower. The same thing had happened there. B turret control was the last alternative to go to. Heavens above! B turret couldn't find the target even though the *Formidable* was silhouetted by the starshells. In disgust we called it a day and sent the technicians scurrying round to find out what had gone wrong.

Ship's Boats and Mooring Problems

When at either Algiers or MEK, we were invariably moored stern to in basins with the bows facing out to sea. This was for obvious reasons. Usually the *KGV* and *Howe* occupied adjacent basins. Getting into these basins was a tricky affair. After entering harbour, the ship was turned through 180 degrees within a very restricted space. Then she reversed into the basin, paying out kedge anchors forward and getting stern lines ashore aft. This latter task presented certain difficulties. We used a launch to land a mooring party. The launch was then used to take feeder ropes from the shore party to the ship. These were used to haul out the mooring ropes to the shore. Controlling the launch astern of the ship within the ship's wash was very difficult, especially when the screws on the ship were going ahead. After watching the first operation, I had suggested to the Commander that the operation could be handled better by using the alternative launch (sometimes called the pinnace). This was fitted with a Kitchen rudder. It comprised two half-spheres of bronze-like material placed either side of the pinnace's propeller and attached to the boat like a rudder. By means of a wheel below the helm, the spheres were moved to the 'full ahead' position when they lay parallel to the propeller shaft, or to the 'full astern' position. In this position, the after-end of the spheres came together abaft the propeller, so that the wash from the propeller was directed forward, thus driving the boat astern. Forward and astern speeds were controlled, with the engine continuing to be run at full revs, by the degree of opening between the two spheres. Moving the helm to port or starboard directed the force from the propeller to the opposite side, thus giving a powerful steering action. This gave great directional control when going astern. In the conventional arrangement, the effect of the rudder when going astern with only a single screw was far less effective than when going ahead. It was this directional control that was the key to using the pinnace when mooring. By going astern to carry out all the necessary manoeuvres, it was possible to counteract the effect of the ship's wash and retain control of the pinnace. The next time we moored to in a basin, the Commander gave me a chance to prove my point. Using the pinnace in this way became standard practice when mooring at either Oran or MEK.

The Quality of Senior Officers

The approachability of the Commander illustrates the high quality of the senior officers of the *KGV*. The Commanding Officer, Captain Hawsley, was a very junior Captain to command such a ship as the *KGV*. He was obviously destined for much higher rank. Even then one sensed that at a future date one would say with some pride, 'I served under Captain Hawsley.' As a midshipman on a ship of that size, I had little direct contact with the senior officers. Of those that I did, the Commander, the First Gunnery Officer and the Navigating Officer, I found all these approachable, fair and firm. In no way could you overstep the mark, but if you had a valid point, they would listen. Since then attitudes have changed. In the 1940's the Navy was very hierarchical and protocol was important. You were told just as much as you needed to know. If ordered to jump, you jumped, and if necessary asked questions afterwards. One small story may also illustrate the point that I am trying to make. It concerns gambling, which regulations forbade on board ship. The scene was the bridge of the *KGV* on a sunny afternoon in the eastern Med. We were at cruising stations in a relaxed atmosphere. There were the usual officers on watch on the bridge. The Captain was there too. The gun's crews on watch were relaxing in the sunshine and a group of them were on the top of B turret. They couldn't be seen; only heard. An officer made a move to look over the bridge to watch them. 'I wouldn't do that if I were you,' interrupted the Captain. 'You might see them gambling.' One of the arts of discipline is to know when not to exercise it.

Harbour Patrols

While in the Med., I continued to enjoy working with the ship's boats. My pride and joy was the picket boat. This had twin diesel engines with all controls centred on a bridge amidships between cabins fore and aft. On the sternpiece were two 25lb depth charges. The picket boat was regularly used for patrol when Operation Alert was in progress. This was put into effect when calm conditions prevailed. They were considered suitable for attacks by miniature submarines, such as the one in November 1941, when the *Queen Mary*, *Valiant* and other ships were torpedoed in Alexandria harbour by this type of vessel. The human torpedo-ers and limpet-ers could only operate when there was a minimum sea running. Throughout the night, the harbour defence booms were kept closed and MLs or motor gunboats continuously patrolled outside the harbour, while within the boom defence, a launch or motor boat patrolled around the entrance with rifle, Bren gun and demolition charges. These were small charges of up to 5lbs each attached to Pickfords fuse and a float. If the alarm was sounded, they were cast overboard every ten to fifteen minutes. On the picket boat we would usually have a Bren gun and one .303 rifle, also a 4" searchlight and a R/T set.

At weekly intervals, roughly speaking, when at MEK, I would be required to take someone to Oran. This would give us about a half-hour high-speed run in the picket boat. Or rather it should have done. There was some design fault either in the propellers or in their configuration, perhaps a combination of the two. What would happen was that after five or ten minutes of full speed, the boat would suddenly slow down. At first I thought it might be that the drive plates on the prop. shafts slipped because they had become hot.

However the engineers could find no trace of that. After that I concluded that the propellers must create some kind of vortex, so that there was virtually nothing for the props. to bite on. The outcome was always the same. An initial high-speed dash, with the boat suddenly coming off the step and the rest of the passage being done 3/4 full revs. Even so she was a grand boat to handle. Coming alongside could sometimes be difficult. With only two hands, one had simultaneously to control the wheel, two throttles and two gear levers.

The cutter with the Kitchen gear was only used for carrying either many people or heavy gear. Its most frequent use was to take hands to bathe off the breakwater and on Alert patrol.

The relationship between the midshipman in charge of the boat and the coxswain of the boat's crew, usually a leading seaman, could be difficult. The difficulty arose occasionally when manning boats during Alert operations. Because the boats were out working all night, several crews had to be provided. Sometimes this resulted in the midshipman and the coxswain not being familiar with each other. This certainly happened one night in my case. We were using the pinnace with the Kitchen rudder. I knew that the coxswain was familiar with the gear, but he did not know that I too was well used to it. This was not unreasonable because few of the midshipmen had ever handled such gear before. In the very early hours of the morning we were returning to the ship at the end of our watch. Dawn had barely broken. The approach to the gangway was not easy. One had to pass and duck below the mooring ropes and avoid the trot of boats moored astern. I had the boat running in on half revs with the gear set to give about fifty per cent ahead speed. The intention was to go into full reverse at the critical point and use the powerful steerage effect to swing the bow clear of the trot of small boats. Then go into ahead mode for coming alongside. Suddenly the coxswain decided to take charge and ordered full revs. The boat leapt ahead and the helm snagged a mooring rope. All control of the boat was lost. She rammed the nearest boat in the trot up its stern. In the semi-dark we examined the boats and made a note of the damage done. This I reported to the Commander the next morning. Several days later I was sent for. The Commander said that he had had requisitions for the repair of much more damage than that which I had reported. How did I account for that? I explained that I had reported all the damage that I could see in the semi-dark. This apparently satisfied him as I heard no more on the subject. I also noticed that afterwards the coxswains did not try to interfere with whatever I was doing.

It was obvious that we were being trained hard for a major operation.

However, it was not all exercises. There was the occasional air raid warning and once or twice we had a target to fire at. There was great competition between us and the *Howe* about who would open fire first. *KGV* won more often than not. *Howe* had an unfortunate incident when they had a flashback in a 5.25 turret. It set alight the thin film of oil that always seemed to cover the inside surface of these turrets. Luckily no one was killed but several of the guns' crews had very nasty burns.

Operation Husky

For us, all that we had been waiting for started on the 5th July 1943. With *Howe* we sailed from Gibraltar for Oran, steaming at 25 knots. During the day we joined company with the *Nelson*, *Rodney* and *Indomitable*, keeping eight miles astern of them. Early the next morning we waited at anchor outside Oran until the *Nelson* and *Rodney* had finished oiling their destroyers inside the protective baffle. They left at 14.30 and *Howe* entered harbour followed by the *KGV*. Conditions were not made easy by a strong northerly wind. We both had to use tugs and they had difficulty in keeping control of the two ships. The uneven cooling of the turbine drive to the port inner screw kept that engine out of action while manoeuvring, adding to our problems. We remained at one hour's notice for steam during the next two days. Even so, we were able to give swimming leave to the breakwater. During the dog watches on the 9th we moved out of the harbour and anchored in the bay. When the engines had been rung off, lower deck was cleared and the Captain briefed us on the forthcoming operation.

Our main task was to intercept and sink the Littorio-Class battleships, should they attempt to intervene in our invasion of the southern beaches of Sicily. This was due to take place at 0245 on the 10th, preceded by an airborne landing at 2200 on the 9th. We would spend most of our time either at Algiers at one hour's notice, or between Algiers and Cape Bon. There was a chance that we might carry out a bombardment of coastal defences in support of our troops. Shortly after dark that night we went to sea to cover the passage of the last invasion convoy leaving for Sicily. The 8th Army under Montgomery and the American 7th Army formed the invading forces. The two armies were under the command of General Eisenhower. Admiral of the Fleet Sir Andrew Cunningham was in command of all the naval forces. Some 2,500 ships and craft took part in the operation.

We steamed eastwards until 20.00, by which time we had reached 9°E. For a time *Dido* and *Sirius* joined us to provide additional AA fire power. We then patrolled westwards until 1100 on the 11th when we turned east and steamed at full power. Our dirty bottom made us slower than the *Howe*, so we had to cheat a bit on the zig-zag pattern in order to keep up. We were moving into position to bombard Trapani and the island of Levanzo on the western extremity of Sicily. The ship went to action stations at midnight.

'As we approached Trapani, we could see the flash of bombs bursting in the town and the pin-point flashes of flak in the sky. A bomber caught by the searchlight beams and surrounded by bursting shells twisted and turned until it escaped.

The weirdest thing was what appeared to be a huge red V suspended in the sky. As we got nearer we could see that it was formed from fires burning on the hillside with the V pointing to the town below. It was strange that none of the points of light flickered, as one would expect from a fire.

All was quiet as we approached Levanzo, our first target. It seemed improbable that we had not been seen. Were they just waiting for us to come within range? So the tension built up. At 0145 *Howe* opened fire with starshell and 5.25. The star shells burst short of the island. Howe's first salvo burst on the beach. We opened fire the moment the star shell burst. Almost simultaneously two twin mountings on the island, one on each end, opened fire, but we were well out of range. The fire from *Howe*, ourselves and escorting destroyers was intense, smothering the island with shell bursts.

In two and a half minutes our 5.25s had expended their ration of ammunition. Ten minutes later *Howe* opened fire on the town of Trapani with 14". We immediately followed suit. At the same time our 5.25 and the destroyers bombarded the harbour installations. *Howe* and *KGV* each fired 40 rounds of 14" shells into an area of the town 1,000 yards long by 500 yards deep. The explosions of the 14" shells were awe-inspiring, sending up huge bright red flashes. We were both firing in two- and three-gun salvoes. The fall of shot was difficult to observe because of dazzle from Howe's 14" salvoes and from our 5.25s. None of us were using flashless charges. Warned by our own 14" firing gong, we could close our eyes the moment before the main armament fired. However, in the 14" control tower we had no pre-warning when our 5.25s or Howe's 14" guns were about to fire.

As we turned away at the end of this brief bombardment, we dropped overboard several devices designed to keep the enemy alert and guessing after we had gone. These consisted of Snowfire rockets mounted on floats, smoke floats and depth charges. All were fitted with delay-action fuses timed to come into action some 30 minutes after we had left the scene.

The enemy's reaction was better than anything we had hoped for. When one rocket went off, searchlights swept round and guns opened fire. When another soared into the air, they shifted target for that one. Pandemonium broke out when the first of the depth charges exploded. Guns blazed away in all directions and the searchlights swept frantically back and forth looking for a target. The drifting smoke from the smoke floats added to their confusion.

We heard later that in response to this bombardment and phantom invasion, the Germans diverted a division of troops to the north-west coast of Sicily, thus relieving the pressure on the hard-pressed American troops in the south. The naval attack was a great tactical success.

Explosions in the Harbour and Loss of HMS *Arrow*

We were back at our moorings at Algiers by 1520 the next day (13th), then at sea again the following day in response to reports that the Italian battleships had put to sea. This proved false, so we returned to Algiers, arriving there at 1830 on the 15th.

At 1530 on the 16th there was a large explosion at the southern end of the harbour. A stock of ammunition on the wharf had blown up. This was close to the bow of a 2,000 tonner engaged in loading army salvage. This consisted chiefly of empty 25-pounder cartridges and spent rifle cartridges. Just round the corner from this ship lay another, an 8,000 tonner, discharging a cargo of petrol and aviation spirit in tins and aircraft fuel tanks. Dumps of discharged fuel containers were located in several places 100 yards from the ship and about the same distance apart from each other.

When the ammunition blew up, the 2,000 tonner was blown off the wharf and everything on her foc's'le blown on to the bridge. She was severely holed in the bow and quickly sank, her bows resting on the mud and the stern floating at an angle of 45° to the wharf.

The explosion, besides killing all those in the vicinity, set the 8,000 tonner alight as well as the petrol dumps and petrol containers alongside the ship.

Immediately after the explosion, the 2nd Gunnery Officer took the skimmer to find out what help was required. Meanwhile the launch was ordered to pick up survivors. When the Gunnery Officer returned, the pinnace was hoisted out. At the gangway we picked up a 20-strong fire-fighting party with Lieut. Monk in command. Firefighting equipment included a portable pump unit, numerous lengths of hoses, branch pipes and firefighting (fearnought) suits.

As we approached the burning ship, she was a terrible sight. Flames and smoke pouring out of all four holds. Intermittently there would be a muffled explosion from within the ship, followed by a great ball of red hot burning gases shooting up into the air. A variation would be a burning petrol tin leaping out of the hold with a loud whoosh and landing sizzling in the water.

I took the boat up to the bow of the ship. We were told that we were not required to fight the fire on board; that was hopeless. So I landed the firefighting party between the sunken ship and the 8,000 tonner.

We had arrived before the casualty clearance party had finished their job. Inadvertently, I secured the boat at a point where two corpses were lying, one without a head. Nearby an American nurse was out there searching the debris.

The fire-fighting party ran one hose to the sunken ship to deal with a small fire on the poop. The other hose they ran to a dump of aircraft fuel tanks to help with the cooling down process. From then on time ceased to exist. A British tug came along and took inboard the blazing ship's head ropes and started to tow her away from the wharf. When they reached the harbour entrance, the head ropes had either burnt through or parted under the strain. The destroyer G96 went up bow to bow and towed the ship out stern first. She took her across the bay and beached her there.

Soon after the ship had been towed away, we shifted the boat to that side of the wharf. This allowed our hoses to reach a petrol dump that had suddenly blazed into life. Our task now was to keep the petrol tin dumps cool.

The army was there with foam producers. These successfully smothered the fires but they had to be constantly cooled down. Otherwise, as the foam slid off the dumps, the tins would burst into flames again. In the middle of all this, the oil and petrol that had flowed into the bottom of the crater created by the explosion burst into flames. We got one our hoses on to it and were slowly bringing it under control with spray. Soon the army came along with foam and quickly finished the job.

By 2100 all the fires were out and the petrol dumps sufficiently cooled down. We returned to the ship.

Eight days later I went over to have a look at the wreck of the 8,000 tonner. The bridge had collapsed into No 2 hold. The gallows on the mast were just twisted bits of metal. Smoke still poured from the holds, heavy soot-laden smoke with an occasional flicker of flame. After all this time the ship's side was still almost red hot. Waves hissed as they hit the hull.

An extraordinary thing was that in the region of No 2 hold the ship's sides had caved in towards the centre of the ship. It was as though the 'tween decks had melted, given way and pulled the ships' sides down with them.

By this time it began to look as though the Italians had had enough of the War. Mussolini had resigned and the government had been taken over by Marshal Badaglio. The immediate future of the Fascist Party was in doubt.

We sailed with the *Howe* late in the afternoon on the 26th July, heading east at 23 knots. At noon the following day we joined company with the *Indomitable* and two destroyers. She had been torpedoed and patched up at the Malta dockyard several weeks before, and was now on her way home. We escorted her as far as Algiers, where we again took up our place at the southern mole.

During the early afternoon of the 4th August there was another violent explosion in the harbour. A British merchant ship with a cargo of smoke floats, ammunition and other stores caught fire in No 1 hold. The destroyer *Arrow* went alongside to help with fire-fighting. She reported that the fire had been brought under control and that all the explosives had already been unloaded. Some five minutes later the merchant ship blew up forward, destroying the whole of the ship's foc'sle. The *Arrow* was very severely damaged up forward and was set on fire. The merchant ship's main mast fell across *Arrow*'s X gun.

After the explosion, all power boats in the water were ordered to pick up survivors. I missed the pinnace but joined her later outside the harbour from the skimmer.

When we arrived on the scene, the merchant ship's stern was high in the air with the screw clear of the water. What remained of her bows rested on the bottom. The bridge superstructure was just above water and burning hard. There were a few other small fires elsewhere on the ship.

The *Arrow* was in a bad way. Her bow, as far aft as A gun, was torn open and twisted over to one side. The bridge superstructure was on fire. Another fire was burning in the port alleyway beneath the bridge. Small fires burnt amidships on the upper deck. The main mast of the freighter had fallen across the barrel of X gun. The crosstrees had smashed through the roof of the cabin on an army cabin-cruiser, pinning it alongside. A completely naked leg and thigh were tangled in the boat's rigging.

A rating was sitting beside X gun. He said his leg was broken. I climbed up to him over the remains of Y gun and other wreckage. Parker, the other midshipman with me, tried to get aboard from further forward but his way was blocked by a fire in the Captain's cabin. He retraced his steps and came aboard the way I had done. As I was climbing up, a man from the merchantman shouted across that there was another man with a broken arm. I told him that we would pick up him and the other man when we could. Shortly afterwards an American launch tried to get them off. They came under a shower of burning oerlikon ammunition from the merchant ship. Tracer shells fell into the boat and they shoved off. *Howe*'s launch then went between the two ships and took off the men.

While we were getting the man down to our boat, a fire broke out forward of the after superstructure. At the same time a very hot fire burst into life in the after hold of the merchant ship. Oerlikon ammunition jumped around like fire-crackers. I noticed that some of *Arrow*'s depth charges had got very hot. The explosive was starting to leak out through the weld at the edge of the depth charges. I persuaded myself that the explosive was more likely to catch fire than explode.

We could hear shouts for help. They seemed to come from below deck up forward. We couldn't find out where the men were trapped. The rating said that he had been the only one on the after end of the ship. As there were no signs of there being anyone immediately below deck, we cast off. We passed slowly up the *Arrow*'s port side. Seeing nobody alive, we doubled back and crossed the stern. A French motor launch waved us towards the bridge of the merchant ship, but another pinnace got there first and took off two or three men. There seemed nothing else we could do, so we returned to the ship.

The pinnace was then loaded with fire-fighting equipment and an acetylene cutter. Meanwhile a launch with a mixed British and American crew had come alongside the *Arrow* with acetylene burners, trying to cut out some men who were trapped in a lower messdeck. The men died before a hole could be cut through the hull to them. When that launch had left, a submarine tried to sink the merchant ship by gunfire by holing the stern at the water line. If the merchant ship still had explosives aboard, this would have been the safest way to put out the fires.

When we arrived in the pinnace, the submarine had already started shelling the ship. Captain Hawsley ordered us back to the ship. Once the merchant ship was sunk, the launch was loaded with fire-fighting gear and a fire-fighting party of 40 led by Lieut. Monk. We followed an hour later in the pinnace with food and water. By then it was about five and a half hours after the initial explosion.

When we returned to the *Arrow*, she was down by the head. The RADAR cabin abaft the bridge was on fire. There were fires in the port alleyway, under the bridge and in the whaler.

The *Howe*'s fire party arrived shortly afterwards. It was found that their small barrel of water was foul. We took it to a boom defence vessel nearby to refill it with fresh water. On the way we picked up various items of flotsam. While we were alongside the boom defence vessel, the officer on deck told us that they had got a boat in tow with two dead on board. This was the boat that I had previously seen alongside the *Arrow*. It was thought that one of the dead was a Captain RNR, the Divisional Chief Transport Officer. I returned to the launch for orders, went back to the boom defence vessel and towed the boat to the *KGV*.

The launch returned about half an hour later at 2230. They had managed to get near the mess decks, but as the ship was sinking, they had had to abandon her.

The next day volunteers recovered the dead from the *Arrow*. They were buried at sea from an ML during the dog watches.

Later, at about 2230, an American destroyer rammed one of our MLs. The launch went to assist. They bound a wire round the boat each side of the damaged section, thus pulling the sides together and helping the bulkheads to hold. At 2300 the order came to 'Carry Out Operation Alert'. The pinnace was loaded with charges etc. Meanwhile the launch was recalled and also made ready. The picket boat was already being hoisted out when the order was cancelled. So ended a strenuous evening.

We remained at Algiers for the rest of August, and had a comparatively free time with few exercises. The main event was a fairly comprehensive damage control exercise followed by listing the ship 5° so that we could get at the more accessible marine growths on the ship's bottom.

An Exercise with the Marines
One morning two other midshipmen and I went ashore with the Marine Landing Party. At first we travelled in three lorries a certain distance along the coast towards Sidi Farouch. We then marched the next five miles. While we were on the march, the ship's Walrus carried out dummy strafing attacks dropping thunder flashes and taking photographs. When attacked, we had to scatter the right way and the wrong way as directed by Lt. Edmunds, the Marine Officer in charge. Subsequently we were shown the photographs taken from the Walrus, so that the marines could see for themselves the benefits of scattering and taking cover the right way. It was only then that we realized the reasons for including us in the party. We had had to wear normal white shirts and shorts. Of course we showed up strongly in the photographs and it served to emphasize the benefits of camouflaged clothing.

We reached the beach at Sidi Farouch at about 1100 and stayed there bathing and lying in the sun for the next three hours until the lorries arrived to take us back to the ship. So apart from the march in the hot sun, we had a good relaxing day.

The rest of the month was a boring and frustrating time, with no sea time. Rumours were around that the Germans had developed a guided bomb that had severely damaged several cruisers supporting the armies in Sicily from the sea. There was also a general buzz to the effect that all the *KGV*-Class battleships were destined for the Far East. Our Lordships had no intention of unnecessarily risking these ships before they went east

Things livened up early on the 7th September, when we put to sea and
headed for Malta at 24 knots.

Surrender of the Italian Fleet

During the morning we were briefed on the coming operation. The general
plan was to land two army corps of British and American troops at Salerno,
some 50 miles south of Naples. The landings would be early in the morning
of the 9th. Because Salerno was beyond the range of fighter support from
Sicily, five aircraft carriers were to provide air cover. These would be the
Unicorn, Hunter, Stalker, Attacker and *Battler.* They would be supported by the
cruisers *Sycilla, Euryalus* and *Caribdus.* The *Nelson, Rodney, Warspite, Valiant,*
and other cruisers would cover the landing. *Howe* and *KGV* would stay at
Augusta to deal with any of the Covior battleships that might come out from
Taranto to attempt to oppose the landings.

Our immediate task was to rendezvous with the AA cruisers and carriers,
Force V. This would be off Malta on the morning of the 8th. The force
would then steam towards Corfu. After dark it would turn back, pass through
the Straits of Messina under cover of darkness, and be off Salerno in time for
the landing. We would go to Augusta and wait events.

We arrived off Malta after a moderately quiet trip. En route there had
been some tense moments when, unexpectedly, we steamed bang through
the middle of a convoy of laden landing craft. Collisions were avoided. It
must have been quite scary on the landing craft. At Malta it was learned that
the operation had been speeded up. This meant that the carriers and cruisers
would now go straight to Salerno.

At 1730 the BBC broadcast that Italy had unconditionally surrendered
and that she had been granted a military armistice. The Italian people had
been ordered by radio and leaflet to do all in their power to hinder the
Germans. Italian troops were to wage war on the Germans. Italian warships
and merchant ships were to leave for ports in the hands of the United
Nations. If they did not have enough fuel to do so, they were to sail for a
neutral port. They were only to scuttle their ships if all else failed. *Howe* and
KGV sailed to Taranto with orders to see that the Italian ships kept the
armistice terms.

At dawn on the 9th we were joined by the *Aurora, Dido, Sirius, Penelope,*
Boise and *Abdiel.* All had troops on board. The plan was to enter Taranto at
1600 and then send boats to the cruisers and land the troops.

We arrived off Taranto at 1500 and steamed up and down waiting for two
pilots and for minesweepers to prepare a swept channel. Eventually *Pathfinder*
went in and brought back one pilot. She reported that all was quiet in the

20. Cruiser force en route to occupy Taranto, 9th September, 1943.
Abdiel *(her last voyage),* Boise *(USN),* Dido *and* Sirius.

harbour and that no Germans had been seen there for some days. Because it was now getting late, we were ordered to remain outside whilst *Howe* and the cruisers entered harbour. We would rendezvous off Taranto at 0800 the next morning.

At dusk two large ships were sighted astern. They flashed the Italian recognition signal GA. They were Covior-class battleships. We closed up to first degree of readiness of main armament and continued on course, tracking the ships by 273 RADAR. The RADAR detected five ships in all. At about 2200 we turned and passed them on opposite courses, letting them go ahead. During the night we were ordered to Malta.

We arrived at Malta at 1900 on the 10th. There we saw three Italian battleships, one cruiser and one destroyer. This was the force that we had been tracking during the night. The next morning two Littorio-class battleships escorted by *Valiant* arrived off Malta. Admiral Cunningham had the huge satisfaction of signalling to the Admiralty:

'Be pleased to inform their Lordships that the Italian Battle fleet now lies at anchor under the guns of the fortress of Malta.'

On the 16th we weighed anchor and with *Howe* escorted the Italian Fleet to Alexandria. The combined fleet consisted of *Howe*, flying the flag of Rear Admiral Bisset, the *KGV*, the 8th Destroyer flotilla, two Littorio-class

21. *The Italian Fleet steams out of Taranto to surrender. Left to right:* Eugenio de
Savoia; Duce Daosta; Baimondo Montieuron, Vittorio Veneta, Italia.

battleships, four cruisers and four destroyers. Once clear of the swept
channel, we steamed towards Benghazi at 20 knots. When fifteen miles off
the North African coast, we followed the coast line to Alexandria. I
personally derived great satisfaction from this voyage. I had joined the
Eastern Mediterranean Fleet almost two and a half years earlier and had been
somewhat surprised and relieved to have survived that event. Here we were
back in Alexandria, with the surrendered Italian battle fleet following us into
harbour. This however was tinged with great sadness over the loss of the
Abdiel. She had been landing troops at Taranto when, swinging at anchor, she
struck a mine and sank in a few minutes with heavy loss of life, especially
among the heavily equipped troops.

The ship's photographer had taken a picture of *Abdiel* on her way into
Taranto. I kept a copy of this in my pocket books for years afterwards.

A visit to the Alamein Battlefield

During our stay at Alex a group of us toured the El Alamein battlefield. The
party comprised 14 officers, seven from the *Howe* and seven, including
myself, from the *KGV.* I wrote an account of this visit for my log book.

At 0800 a party of officers landed from *KGV.* We were to meet with a similar
number of officers from the *Howe* and go by car to tour the El Alamein
battlefield. However, as often happens on occasions like this, the meeting place

was changed at the last minute and the signal saying so had not left the CCO (Communication Control Office) in time.

We learnt from some soldiers standing at the entrance to the old C. in C.'s Offices that we should have gone to No 18 gate. We scrounged a lorry, and with all our food, bathing costumes, and last but not least, the precious block of ice that the Senior Engineer Officer had brought with him, we bounced along the hard and very twisting dock road.

When we arrived at No 18 gate, the South African sentry there said that he had been told that 'If he saw a party of Naval Officers looking very lost he was to tell them to wait there.' The driver, turning his lorry towards the Custom House, collided with a passing lorry. No one was hurt and little damage done except to one fender. We climbed out and prepared for a long wait in the shade of the Customs House.

After ten to fifteen minutes, the *Howe* party turned up with two cars, two brakes and a small lorry. Another lorry with a party of army sergeants joined us later.

We put our food, etc. into the lorry, although it was already half full with petrol cans.

The cavalcade left the dockyard only half an hour late, which was considered very good going. Outside Alex we drove for half an hour before stopping to allow the food lorry to catch up. When it arrived, I found that our food was in danger of being contaminated by leaking petrol. We transferred all our supplies to our car. Incidentally, I consistently followed this policy in later years whenever travelling in bush or in convoy with other vehicles. Always have your basic supplies travel with you.

When we approached the 90 KM mark, we began to see the first signs of a battlefield, in the form of concrete pill boxes and silted up slit trenches on either side of the road. We passed the occasional burnt-out lorry and roads turning off to the south marked 'Springbok Rd' and 'Anzac Rd' and a sign-post pointing to El Alamein.

At the 100 Km mark we turned off the main road on to a dirt track. There we stopped and gathered around our guide, a Captain in the Intelligence Corps. With the aid of a map, he explained the tactics and general plan of the battle.

He told how after two unsuccessful attempts to dislodge Rommel, the 8th Army, leaving only a small holding force, was withdrawn to be trained in the new tactics that were to be used in the coming battle.

Previously, in desert warfare, the tanks had always gone into action first, followed by the infantry and supported by an artillery barrage.

The new plan was to send in the infantry first, cross the minefields and then fan out sideways to get at the enemy from behind. Then when the gap had been cleared of mines, the tanks would advance and consolidate the position, attacking any enemy armour that presented itself. While the infantry were

22. 'Be pleased to inform their Lordships that the Italian Battle Fleet now lies at anchor under the guns of Fortress Malta.' Admiral Cunningham. Left to right, Vittorio, Venito, Italia.

going through the minefields, the artillery were to put down a very heavy barrage to keep the enemy's head down. The attacks in the north and the south were to be the same, with the heaviest attack in the north.

What actually happened was roughly this:-

Under cover of the barrage, the infantry made a gap eight yards wide and poured through. This was then widened to 20 yards for the motor transport, and finally to 48 yards for the armour. After the armour had passed through the first minefield, they ran on to a mini-marsh in which mines had been laid indiscriminately. The tanks, in the confusion of battle, mistook this for a proper minefield and tried to clear it. In the meantime they dug themselves in.

The next night the tanks advanced again but ran into a nest of anti-tank guns that should have been cleared by the infantry. Lacking tank support, they had been unable to do so. The result was that we lost 98 tanks out of a force of 133.

The following night the two opposing armours went into battle, and the Australians crossed the German lines. They turned north aiming to reach the sea. Although they cut the road, they were unable to reach the coast. Most of the enemy then escaped along the sea shore. Meanwhile our tanks had cut the supply road to the enemy's forces in the south. The position had became impossible and Rommel pulled out.

We followed the road along which the Australians had advanced. Because of the large number of uncleared mines, barbed wire enclosed the road. At the time the mines were only cleared where a road was required. We crept along the road, bouncing from rut to rut. Dotted about the landscape were burnt-out tanks and lorries, shell and grenade fragments and bits of discarded equipment and clothing.

We stopped for lunch at Victory Orchard, an ex-German brigade headquarters. The dug-out, obviously well constructed, had, after a year's disuse, silted up. Dogs had got at the graves of two Italian soldiers. Spilt boxes of mortars, small calibre shells, mostly unfused, empty machine gun belts and pieces of shrapnel were lying about all over the place. In the middle of this scene of desolation and hasty retreat were ten olive trees with small birds flying around.

We had our lunch here. After one of the brakes had had its punctured tyre replaced, we drove around a small area of the battlefield. Burnt-out wrecks still lay around, even though the salvageable stuff had been recovered. We stopped to have a look at a burnt-out German Mark IV tank, the largest type they had then. The tank had first been stopped by A/T fire, then demolished either by our engineers or the Germans.

Some thirty years later, with a group of irrigation engineers in the vicinity of El Alamein, we had stopped to check our position. A front tyre of our Landrover had stopped within an inch of an anti-tyre spike used in the war to disable lorries. Even now the debris of war still litters the desert.

Later in the afternoon of our tour we passed a graveyard of German aircraft containing the remains of some fifty planes. We rejoined the main road about 20 KM further along from where we left it. From there we went to a tank salvage depot where there were about 300 British, German and Italian tanks and self-propelled guns. Our guide said that there was the best part of a complete Italian armoured division at the depot. We spent a very interesting half hour looking at the various types of tanks and self-propelled guns.

Leaving the graveyard, we retraced our steps to stop at a spot where the road passed close to the sea. There we bathed and had our tea. After tea we went back to Alex as fast as we could because it was getting late. We just managed to catch the 1930 liberty boat back to the ship.

The ship's bottom was getting quite foul. This had already been demonstrated when we could not keep up with the *Howe*. The Commander decided to do something about it in earnest. Accordingly, on the 30th September the ship was heeled 10.5° to starboard. This list gave added realism to the various damage control exercises that we were put though. Such exercises included the removal of an unexploded bomb from the wardroom bathroom, hoisting out the kedge anchor and preparing the launch to receive it. At the same time, some of the 5.25" guns' crews rigged out harbour davits. I had not seen these before. They are quite cunning devices. The heel of the davit lies horizontally on deck and it is kept in place by two brass pins. The davits jut out at right angles to the ship. They are just long enough to keep a boat clear of the armour belt when the boat is being hoisted or lowered. The davits are used for whalers or motor boats. Although the boats could be hoisted by winch, there were so many hands available that it was just as easy to run them up.

At 0800 on the 1st of October *Howe* and ourselves slipped moorings and started on our way back to Gibraltar. At first visibility was under 1,000 yards. The destroyer screen of *Echo*, *Eclipse*, *Fury* and *Falconer* was ordered to keep within visibility distance. Soon the heat of the sun lifted the mist and the destroyers went to their usual screening positions. When off Malta during the night of the 2/3rd October, the screen was replaced by the *Queensborough*, *Quinton*, *Quail* and *Raider*. They took us as far as Algiers, where we spent four days before going on to Gibraltar.

By this time we had learnt a thing or two concerning the snags of getting a large ship berthed at Gib. At the southern entrance there is often a slight set to the eastwards. This is a trap for the novice. There is no visible sign of it until the bow comes opposite the entrance and starts to swing to starboard. Because of the slow speed of the ship, the rudder has little effect. This time we entered harbour by the northern entrance, bound for berth 52 on the detached mole. When we turned round, we departed from the usual procedure by turning to port. So as to come up again past the southern entrance, we were ready to counter the slight eastward set. When we came opposite our berth, we were closer than usual. This saved time in getting the lines across and made it easier for the tugs to push us in.

A Flight in a Barracuda

At 05.30 on 11th October, all the executive midshipmen went aboard the *Illustrious* with the purpose of flying and learning at first-hand how a carrier operates aircraft at sea. It was still dark when we clambered over two destroyers lying along her starboard side and found *Illustrious'* Officer of the Watch. He recommended that we find our way to the wardroom, which we did at the first attempt. A few Air Arm Subs. and some even more tired and bored-looking stewards completely ignored us. We retired to a corner and looked over the latest magazines from the UK.

Six midshipmen from the *Howe* joined us half an hour later. Shortly afterwards we were told that only twelve midshipmen would be able to fly. The first flight, a practice torpedo attack, would be at 0730; the second at about 1430, would be a dive-bombing exercise.

We arranged with the *Howe* that four *KGV* mids would go up to two of theirs. We drew lots to decide who would go up. I found myself to be one of the chosen eight and decided to take the first flight. As it was now getting near to seven o'clock, the others and myself, who were going up on the first flight, went in to have breakfast. A very good and large breakfast it was too. However, I must admit that I did not feel like eating very much.

Seven-thirty found us in the air operations room, where the crews were being briefed and given last-minute instructions as to the method of attack.

Mae Wests, helmets and parachute harness were laid out for us. After a couple of shots, we all managed to get the gear on the right way. I was allocated to plane 'B'.

Out on the flight deck I joined the observer of B for Baker. As we walked off together towards the parked aircraft, he asked me if I had been up before. When I told him that I had, in a Blenheim, he seemed quite relieved, saying, 'Oh that's good, you know all about it then, what to do and not to do. The last passenger I had pulled the rip cord of his parachute to get it up from under the seat and filled the cabin with billowing parachute.'

We were flying in Barracudas. A Barracuda is a single-engined plane with the rudder plane three quarters the way up the tail fin. They can carry one 18" torpedo or four five-hundred pound bombs or depth charges. The crew of three consists of the pilot, observer and rear gunner.

I was shown into the rear gunner's seat. My intercom was connected and I was shown how to get out of the plane in a hurry. To do this you pulled hard on a red coloured wire. All being well, the centre panel of the hood would come out. The rigger then closed the hatch. I tested the intercom with the pilot and took stock of my position.

I was sitting facing the tail in quite a comfortable seat. Even the back of the seat was well upholstered. In front of me and level with my chest was a twin .303 mounting, and ranged on each side, eight spare drums of ammunition. The barrels were inside the plane. When being operated, part of the fuselage slid back and the guns came up. On my left was a W/T set, receiving and transmission. It could also be used for DF purposes. All around my head was the perspex cabin top. Down by my feet on either side was another perspex panel giving a view below. My view forward was blocked by the wings.

By this time the engine had been started, and was now gently turning over, warming up. Soon, over the intercom the pilot's voice said 'Here we go.' The engine roared and we started taxiing into position. Soon we gathered speed. When just past the island, I felt the plane lift off; we were airborne. We circled round climbing, and caught up with A for Apple, the leader, and took station on his starboard beam. The pilot continued to fly round the ship until the remaining six 'planes joined up. When in formation, we headed east.

Looking up, I could see two aircraft together on each quarter, rising and dipping as the air currents took them. Down below the blue Mediterranean glittered with scattered white horses.

I found another cushion on the deck and put it on the one already on the seat. My head was now just clear of the roof and I could get a much better view all round.

We flew east for half an hour, turned north for a few minutes and then flew back west. In another thirty minutes we were over the fleet at about 10,000 feet. The ships looked very small, but the wake showed up remarkably well. It occurred to me that an aircraft probably saw the wake of a fast ship before the ship herself.

After flying over the fleet, we went on west and turned round over the Straits. The formation opened up considerably, sideways and upwards. The up currents were more marked now, no doubt caused by the high hill below.

Without warning, A for Apple disappeared in a steep dive to port. We followed. The plane tilted alarmingly and the wind shrieked past the aircraft. I was watching out to port and saw the air brakes come up. The result was surprising. One could feel the plane slowing down. Soon we flattened out and began our run in, 200 feet above the sea and doing about 180 knots. The moment our smoke bomb dropped, we did a steep turn to starboard and began to zig zag furiously as we made good our escape. After circling round, we came in on another attack but this time without such a steep dive and without dropping a smoke bomb.

The 'ALT' (Aircraft low level torpedo) attack was now over and we flew round the ship waiting for the signal to start the next exercise. This was to be an anti-submarine bombing exercise. It was then that we found that we had dropped two bombs instead of one.

We did three bombing attacks, all very similar to each other. A shallow dive, then a quick get away. On the first run we again dropped two bombs and concluded that there was a mechanical fault.

When the practice was over, we circled for some time waiting for permission to land. We did one run in but were waved away. The next time we came in to land. I was very nervous about this landing business, having watched many planes crack up on landing during Operation Torch. However, all was well. We came in from the port quarter with air brakes down and the engine throttled back, with occasional bursts of revs. to give more speed. Over the flight deck the engine was throttled back and we pancaked down. The arrester wires pulled us up short. When stopped, the arrester wire was unhooked and we taxied to the parking area. I got out feeling pleased with myself and very thankful for such a smooth landing. We had been in the air for two hours.

Afterwards in the briefing room, the flight commander commented on the morning's work. The torpedo attack, he said, was quite good but required more practice and better timing, especially for those who attacked from the starboard side. The bombing of the splash target was described as 'bloody'. Most of the bombs fell either too far over or far too short. The timing was rotten. Evidently there should have been only fifteen seconds between individual attacks. If the aircraft attack too close together, one aircraft can be hit by the bullets aimed at the first. If the aircraft are too far apart, the gunner has plenty of time to shift target after the first plane has attacked.

After lunch we went on deck to watch the Barracudas taking off for the dive bombing attack on the splash target. One plane veered when taking off but just managed to get off the deck, narrowly missing a ventilation shaft in the port forward corner of the flight deck.

After the bombers had taken off, another Barracuda took off to go on anti-submarine patrol. Once up, he found that his hydraulics were faulty. He could not raise his wheels and his airbrakes were difficult to move. He made an emergency landing. This was beautifully done. He came down without the slightest bump. The moment he stopped at the parking position, the starboard undercarriage slowly and gracefully subsided, followed by the port one. The air-screw chewed itself up on the deck. Otherwise the plane was undamaged and no one was hurt.

We were then shown the marvels of the Flight Direction Office. It was a wonderful place, putting our control system to shame. It was like comparing a 14" TS (Transmission Station) to a Vickers clock.

The Flight Direction Officer (FDO) with his two assistants sits facing a large transparent plot. The plotters, in communication with the RADAR offices, plot the aircraft as the reports come in. The plotters have to learn to write backhanded to make the numbers readable from the other side.

The communications are very good indeed, allowing the FDO to speak to as many or as few positions at a time as he chooses merely by pushing a few buttons. He can speak to the fighters whether they be Fleet Air Arm or RAF planes. After leaving this wonder, we repaired to the wardroom, where we were hospitably treated until about 1800, when our boat came for us after the ship had secured.

At 1000 on the 13th October we put to sea in the company of the *Howe*, *Formidable*, and *Illustrious*, flying the flag of the Rear Admiral and with a destroyer screen comprising the *Savage* (Capt. D) *Obedient, Forrester, Hobson*

(US Navy), *Venus*, *Inglefield*, *Chaps* (US Navy) and *Stord* (US Navy). We were bound for the UK.

We now come to a small hiatus in this account because of the lack of written records. Soon after we arrived back in the UK, I was given six months accelerated promotion to Sub-Lieutenant and promptly stopped writing anything in the Journal. Journal writing was compulsory for Midshipmen and because of that I hated having to do it. This also meant that I was now old enough to sit the Board of Trade examination for 2nd Mate. I was given leave to attend a cramming/revision course at Newcastle.

Rejected for the Merchant Navy

The first day was occupied with revisions and implications of the Rule of the Road. I was dismayed to find that all the courses were given as points of the magnetic compass. Apart from the occasional check of the gyro compass against the magnetic compass, I had not used a magnetic compass since training on the *Conway*. I was very slow in these exercises because I had mentally to convert the bearings and courses from compass points to numeric bearings and back again. What really appalled me was the thought that most merchant ships at that time, apparently, did not have gyro compasses.

Unfortunately during the second day I failed the BOT colour blindness test. I saw all the colours OK until they turned on the smallest red test light. I didn't see any light and guessed white. I was sent for further tests in London, but still failed. On the other hand, the Navy was quite happy with my colour vision. It was eventually diagnosed that I suffered from colour blindness only when I was tired. Certainly the initial tests had been carried out after we had spent several days at a high degree of alertness and with little sleep. So the Merchant Navy would not have me but the RN would. I set my sights on becoming the Hydrographer of the Navy.

A Very Important Passenger

In either late December 1943 or early January 1944 we again sailed for the Mediterranean. What we did when we first got there I do not remember, except that before we finally sailed back to the UK, we spent some time at Algiers. During the last few days rumours flew around that we were going back to the UK on a special mission. The ship's office was completely cleared out and all sorts of mysterious cases were brought on board, including, so it was rumoured, numerous cases of brandy and whisky. All was soon revealed. We arrived at Gibraltar on the 12th or 13th of January 1944. On the 15th Winston Churchill came aboard to take passage to the UK. Travelling with him were Beaverbrook, Lord Morton, his physician, and several other very senior people.

Churchill's War Map Room had taken over the ship's office and some of the mystery cases did indeed contain brandy.

After consulting with the Wardroom, the Gunroom sent the Prime Minister an invitation to dine. The reply came back that the PM regretted he would not be able to dine with us, but that he would be pleased to call on the Gunroom after dinner on the 17th.

We all waited for him nervously and expectantly, and all dressed up in our best uniforms. In he came. All smiles, double chins, cigar and bulging tummy. He relaxed and fully occupied our best chair and soon put us all at ease. He talked of how the War was going on; of the importance of attacking the soft under-belly of Europe. After twenty minutes or so, he invited a few of us to his Map Room. The few, of course, meant the most senior and that meant the Sub-Lieutenants.

Maps of all the theatres of war covered the walls of the ship's office. Churchill, like a great jolly garden gnome, perched on what seemed in relation to his proportions, a tiny stool. Swivelling on the stool, he could see all the maps and gave us a quick resumé of what was going on. Finally he left his perch and approached the map showing the northern part of the Adriatic. Pointing to an arrow located on the north-east shore he indicated an on-going operation to land supplies and ammunition for Tito's Guerilla Group. Tito, he said, is our man and we will support him all the way. He was the only guerilla leader in Yugoslavia who was really fighting the Nazis. That ended a most memorable evening.

I have often wondered since what it was about that evening that made such an impression. After all, one already had a tremendous faith and liking for the man, partly because one's superiors so obviously admired him. Remember the famous signal sent out by the Admiralty when Chamberlain made Churchill the First Lord of the Admiralty again. 'Splice the Main Brace, Churchill is back'. There were also, of course, Churchill's speeches. So what was it that confirmed all those feelings when one met him briefly in the flesh? He put us at ease. After all, to be confronted by an Admiral was frightening enough. To have the Prime Minister as one's guest was something far more. He was friendly; he did not talk down to us. It was just sheer personality.

We approached the English Channel in low visibility. Our cruiser escort (I forget which one) loomed ahead out of the early morning mist. As luck would have it, I was on watch on the bridge at the time. On a reciprocal course, the cruiser emerged through the mist and immediately flashed the recognition signal, followed by her pennant number. There was a rush to look up her Captain in the Navy list. The cruiser Captain was senior to Hawsley. Almost simultaneously, a message was flashed across by aldis. 'In view of your distinguished guest, I have pleasure in placing myself under your orders.' And so it was. The cruiser was ordered to take station ahead and so we steamed into the Channel and to Plymouth.

For a ship the size of the *KGV*, Plymouth is a tricky harbour to enter. The Navigating Officer had spent a long time in preparing his entrance plan. I was impressed how, without constant reference to the chart, he guided the Captain through the approach courses. He was frequently taking bearings of key positions and referring to his note book. This accompanied by a running commentary in the form 'So many minutes to altering course to Y. 45 seconds to alter course'. Later followed by a run-down to the time left before letting go the anchor.

What to do with a Surplus Sub.

After Churchill and his party had disembarked, our departure was not quite so successful. While manoeuvring in the harbour, the wind caught us and drifted us slightly off line, resulting in us ever so briefly touching bottom. No damage was done.

We went back to Scapa Flow via the west coast. I was on watch again the next morning when we were between Cape Wrath and the Pentland Firth. The Captain suggested to the Officer of the Watch that I should take over, and he guided me through manoeuvring the ship past some smaller and slower vessels. At one point he gently admonished and corrected me for giving too large a helm order when too close to one of the vessels. He pointed out that I had not allowed sufficient room for the ship to swing about the centre of her turning circle. I would probably have swung the ship's stern amidships into the overtaken ship's side. He had already taken my Sub-Lieutenant's training in hand.

Before leaving Scapa to pick up Churchill, I had been asked by the Captain what type of posting I wanted, there being now a surplus of Subs. on board. I told him that my first choice would be to rejoin the Fast Minelayer Squadron. Failing that, I would choose something that would involve me in the coming Second Front. Back again at Scapa, the Captain sent for me and told me that the Admiralty had said that there were no vacancies in the Minelayer Squadron. He had therefore recommended that I be posted to a minesweeper. They would be closely involved with preparations for the invasion. He also thought that I was better suited to a small ship. I left him agreeing with the last sentiment, but not too sure about the minesweeping part. Minesweepers were often caught by the mines they were meant to dispose of. Being small, they sank very quickly.

During the short time that I had left on the *KGV*, the ship was engaged in a series of gunnery exercises. These involved relying much more on RADAR for the 14" guns. We were also still trying to identify the best fighting range under different conditions. The RADAR control exercises culminated in a combined shoot at Stack Skerry with the *Howe* and *Anson*. All ranges and direction would be arrived at entirely by RADAR. The range-finder lenses and the control tower layer's and trainer's ports were closed. Each ship was firing shells which, when they exploded, produced coloured smoke, a different colour for each ship.

We steamed off the Skerry in battle formation and opened fire together. Ours was the only first salvo to obtain a direct hit.

On this note, in late February or early March 1944, I was sent on leave pending a new posting.

CHAPTER 6

HMS *Tintagel Castle*

First Impressions

I DON'T THINK THAT MY LEAVE lasted more than a couple of weeks. I was appointed to some obscure shore establishment and told to report to the SNO at Troon on the 17th February 1944 for the *Tintagel Castle*. The shore establishment was of no concern. One had to be on somebody's books. I speculated about the *Tintagel Castle*. What sort of ship was she? Perhaps she was ex-Union Castle Line and was a troop transporter of some sort. She didn't sound like a minesweeper.

At Troon I was to go to the yard of the Ailsa Craig Ship Building Co:. There in a tiny office, surrounded by very worn-looking files, signal logs and other administrative junk, I met the first of my future fellow officers. I forget who it was. It was probably Lieut. Courtold, our harassed No 1. Almost immediately I met Sub-Lieut. Despard. We formed an immediate friendship and were close companions for the whole of the commission. He was the Anti-Submarine (AS) Officer and, of course, a specialist in the Asdic equipment. He had recently come from serving on a very ancient destroyer that had been on convoy escort duties between Gibraltar and Freetown. He took me outside to see our future home.

Why does a ship in the hands of the dockyard always look so squalid? Rusty plates partially covered by red paint protruded through the Navy grey. The superstructure was draped with air pipes and welders electric leads. Flashes of welders' torches distracted the eye and our ears were dulled by the tireless clang of struck metal.

There she lay in all her squalor. Then the eye and the brain began to separate out her form. The long rake and wide flared bow spoke of a dry ship. This was confirmed by the gentle downward curve of the hull line to her cutaway quarter deck. The line of the superstructure from the single forward-mounted 4-in gun to the low bridge structure gave her a firm squat appearance, accentuated by the funnel that barely rode above the bridge. Between the bridge and the funnel, the tripod mast surmounted by the RADAR dome provided an air of firmness. The lack of depth charge throwers on the quarter deck puzzled me. In spite of all the worst that the dockyard could do to her appearance, it was love at first sight.

114

23. HMS Tintagel Castle.
By courtesy of the Castle Class Corvette (Frigate) Association.

Despard and I were soon aboard, exploring the ship. He explained the absence of the depth charge throwers as he extolled the virtues of the Squid. This was the strange canvas covered object on the raised platform abaft of the 4-inch gun and immediately for'ard of the bridge. It was a three-barrelled mortar that threw its 200lbs bombs ahead of the ship. Much of his enthusiastic description of the asdic sets that controlled the squid went over my head. No doubt about it; this was the ultimate in anti-submarine weapons.

I was impressed. I had had little to do with anti-submarine warfare and had not had much faith in the way Fleet Destroyers went about this task. I had heard of the effectiveness of the 'Hedgehog' fitted to the smaller, Flower-Class Corvettes. This threw a large number of smallish charges ahead of the ship. The system had the great advantage that the attacking ship was able to keep in contact with the submarine right up to the point when the charges actually exploded. The high speed attack by destroyers resulted in contact being lost as the ship passed over the submarine and before the depth charges were dropped. The blanket use of depth charge throwers and several depth charge rails for dropping them overboard was a desperate attempt to compensate for this 'guess-and-by-God' type of attack. The major innovation of the Squid was its connection to asdic equipment that accurately measured the depth of the submarine. This enabled the fuses on the mortar bombs to be set automatically the moment the bombs were fired. Because the attacking speed was so slow, the bombs exploded ahead of the ship and there was no risk to the hull. The slow approach speed to the submarine meant that the submarine's range, course and speed could be accurately assessed, maximising the chance of exploding the bombs in the immediate vicinity of the U boat.

The rake and flare of the bow indicated a dry ship. She was squat, with little top hamper and therefore unlikely to roll badly. Access to the working parts of the ship at sea would be good. Below decks everything had been done to make the crew comfortable. The messdecks were lined throughout with crews' lockers, neatly fitted into the lining between the ribs. There should not be a lot of condensation such as we had had on the *Sheffield*. The wardroom and cabins looked fine too. The bridge was clear of clutter. Abaft the compass platform there was the asdic hut and an automatic plot as well as a RADAR Plan Position Indicator (PPI). For'ard of the platform and under cover was a table for a ready-use chart on the port side and radio TSB equipment on the starboard side, all under cover and well protected from the weather. The positioning of the voice pipes was good.

For close convoy work, the single screw driven by a steam reciprocating engine seemed sensible. This, together with the fitting of a large rudder, gave excellent manoeuvrability. Yes, this was going to be a nice ship to work.

Accommodation for the officers was provided at a boarding house in the town. After fixing ourselves up, Despard and I went out for a drink. He always seemed to know where the best pubs were. On the way back from the pub, I developed hiccups and was still hiccuping when introduced to Lieut. R. Atkinson RNR DSC and Bar, our CO. I was glad that he was RNR and I was at ease with him.

It was probably the next day that the more formal interviews took place. My previous experience of working with the navigating officer more or less secured me the job of pilot. Similarly my connection with gunnery control on the *Sheffield* and *KGV* made me the logical choice for gunnery officer. It was generally concluded that serious use of the Woolworth single-barrel 4" in action was unlikely. If a submarine surfaced and had to be dealt with by gunfire, then I would be on hand from the plot abaft the compass platform. The gun could be controlled by megaphone from the bridge. So it was decided.

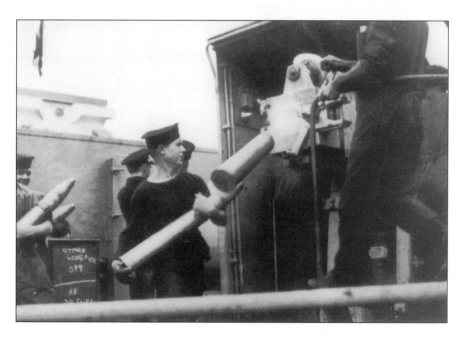

24 & 25. Gunnery exercises.

Pre-Commissioning Courses

I was a bit surprised at the speed of what happened next. Atkinson had obviously had everything worked out before hand. I was to go immediately to Greenwich for a short course on gyro compasses, then to Portsmouth for a gunnery course on the 4" gun. On completion, I would join the Captain at the A/S Tactical School at Liverpool for a course with him on anti-submarine tactics.

We had not learnt much about gyro compasses on the *Conway*, so this course was invaluable. The main thrust of the course was about maintaining the gyro compass and correcting errors. In practice it proved most useful. At Portsmouth, for the first time ever, I entered barracks. As far as I was concerned, it was an efficient and not too Spartan hotel. The gunnery course itself was a 'synch' and I passed out top of the class without really trying.

At Liverpool the A/S tactical course was really interesting and intense. It comprised a mixture of lectures and exercises in the simulator room. The COs and their navigators worked as a team. Each pair represented the ships of a convoy escort. Usually all was darkness. In the background various fiendish Wrens operated the side effects as well as the plot of the exercise. Some of them made the 'Bridge' roll, whilst others operated a fan to give the wind effect. Every now and again they would throw a bucket of water into the air stream so that the bridge party got soaked. In the meantime the signals were pouring in. Asdic repeater sounding, flashes of light representing ships being torpedoed. I soon realized that there was much more to keeping an action plot than I had realized. It was all hectic, fun and interesting. After three days or so, all this was shattered by an imperious signal from Portsmouth demanding my presence there to participate in a gunnery course for our gun crew elect. I pleaded with the Captain that this should be ignored. The tactical course was of far greater importance than working with the gun's crew. 'No,' he said. 'The signal cannot be ignored.' I would have to go back to Portsmouth. So I returned to Southport, where I had been staying with my two great-aunts. I packed my bag and returned to Portsmouth.

At Portsmouth I was ordered to report to the CO's Secretary. When I did so, I was surprised to be marched into the CO's Office as though I was a defaulter, complete with caps off.

Why had I left the barracks without orders?

I was acting under the orders of my CO, who had told me report to the A/S Tactical School on completion of the gunnery course.

Why was I doing the tactical course?

Because I'm the ship's navigating officer.

This really seemed to upset them. To them it was quite impossible for a navigating officer to be a gunnery officer at the same time. To suggest such a thing in the home of Naval Gunnery was close to sacrilege. I did not improve things by suggesting that because my action station was in the plot at the after end of the bridge, I could easily control the gun by megaphone from the bridge. My attitude of denigrating gunnery to a subsidiary role was not to their liking. However, they realized that I had been acting under instructions and in good faith. I was dismissed with the warning not to leave barracks again without permission.

The next few days were, to my mind, a waste of time. The leading hand in charge of the gun crew knew his job, and, with the Petty Officer Gunnery Instructor, soon had the gun's crew well drilled. It was a relief to get back to Troon.

Soon afterwards we commissioned the ship and started acceptance trials in the Clyde. At this time we were joined by an RNVR Midshipman, Nick Kimberly. He became the Gunnery Officer, thus solving the problem of my dual role. *Tintagel Castle* officially joined His Majesty's Fleet once she was accepted on the 7th April 1944 on completion of acceptance trials. These were carried out in the Clyde off Troon and went off smoothly. There was, however, one alarming incident. As we started the count-down for the first test firing of the squid, a small low flying monoplane was on course to cross our bows a short distance ahead. As the mortar fired, the dummy Squid bombs rose up towards the aeroplane. At one point it seemed certain that we were going to be the first to bring down an aeroplane with an anti-submarine mortar bomb. They drifted up towards the aeroplane and skimmed beneath its belly in a calculated parabola.

The School for Corvettes

Our first shake-down cruise took us to Rosyth, where we ammunitioned ship. There we were joined by one of the instructors from the school for corvettes at Tobermory. He took passage with us back to Tobermory, where we were to start our working-up routine. This Lieutenant did me a great service as we passed westward along the north coast of Scotland at night. He realized that I was having a problem in identifying our position and showed me how one could take bearings and ranges of prominent points off the PPI, draw appropriate position lines on tracing paper, and then move the tracing paper over the chart until one achieved a good fit. This was a technique that I had never seen before but frequently used afterwards. The RADAR operators were quick to understand what I was after and gave me accurate bearings and distances of the points that interested me. This could be done straight off the PPI display in the plotting room abaft the compass platform, but not with the same degree of accuracy.

The training at Tobermory was intense. The school was under the command of the Commodore Western Isles, Admiral 'Puggy' Stephenson. There can be little doubt that the vigour of the training that he put the corvettes through played a very significant role in the eventual defeat of the U. Boats. There was no time to relax. The training officers, whilst being firm, were helpful. Only two incidents remain firmly in mind.

We had been practising with another Castle Class corvette, towing and being towed. It was at the end of the exercise. We had just completed our turn of being towed and were preparing to take in the towing wire. To make certain that the towing pennant did not foul the screw or rudder whilst it was being taken in over the bow, we rang down to the engine room for slow astern. We were not too surprised at a slow reaction. After all, the engine had been stopped for a long while. To our consternation, the ship started slowly to move ahead. 'Stop engines.' Then again 'Slow Astern.' The ship once again moved slowly ahead. 'Stop Engines.'

The Captain, turning to the training officer, asked him to go down with him to the engine room. I was instructed to give them a few minutes to get below, then ring down 'slow astern'. This I did. Once again the ship moved slowly ahead. This time I left things as they were. The towing hawser had been hauled inboard and all was clear ahead. The ship slowly moved forward. In the meantime I was still keeping an eye on what was going on aft. In due course a small procession of people appeared on the quarter deck, moved aft and together peered over the taffrail. Heads turned to each other and nodded. In a moment the group broke up and the Captain and training Lieutenant moved towards the bridge. I ordered 'Stop Engines'. The Captain, having noticed the position of the engine telegraph as he came through the wheelhouse, ordered 'slow astern, Pilot', as he came onto the bridge. The ship slowly went astern. Sighs of relief and satisfaction all round. 'Full ahead 80 revs, carry on Pilot,' ordered the Captain and we proceeded on our way. He then described what had happened down in the engine room.

'When the order came down "slow astern", they opened up the steam valve and the engine started turning. I said to the Chief, "we have a right-hand screw; the engine is going ahead."

'No Sir,' he replied, 'look' and pointed to the indicator on the reversing engine. 'It's at astern. The engine is going astern.'

'At this point,' the Captain said, 'I was getting a bit confused myself, so we all went up on deck to see which way the ship actually was going. Sure enough we were going ahead.'

What had happened was that the Chief, knowing that we were going to be towed and that the engine would be stopped for a long time, had shut off the steam to the reversing engine. This would prevent steam condensing in the engine itself. Unfortunately this was forgotten when the order came down to go astern. The reversing engine control was moved to the astern position and the main engine steam valve opened. Of course the reversing engine had not moved the valve, so the engine went ahead.

All this created a tremendous fuss. The chief was getting near retirement age so I don't think any actual charges were made. He was quietly sent ashore. In due course he was replaced by a large jolly rotund Sub-Lieut (E) by the name of Wallace.

On another occasion whilst at the Corvette School, we had been exercising off the west coast of the Island of Mull with a submarine. In these exercises it was the custom to communicate with the sub by means of hand grenades. Dropping a different number of hand grenades over the side at a time meant different things, the most usual being, say, three hand grenades. Three bangs, for example, would mean, 'I have lost you. Please surface.' At the end of the exercise, it was too late to make it worth while returning to Tobermory, so we anchored for the night inside the entrance to a small loch. The chart showed a small river flowing towards the loch, finishing in a pool at the loch head. Despard was sure that there would be salmon in the pool for the catching. The lack of fishing rods did not matter. We had a whole boxful of hand grenades. So, with the Captain's permission, the three of us, Despard, Kimberly (the Mid) and myself launched the ship's 14ft dinghy and rowed to the head of the loch. This was less than half a mile away. There was no one to be seen as we tossed in the first of the grenades. Nothing floated to the surface. We plastered the pool with grenades and didn't even catch a frog. By this time it was getting late and to our dismay, the tide had turned. It was a very long hard pull back to the ship, made doubly so by the lack of the makings of a good supper. Punishment, we assumed, for daring to attempt to poach salmon with grenades.

Whilst at the school, we were able to fit in a double run along the measured mile in the Sound of Mull. Flat out at 185 revs we managed 16.5 knots, but the average over the two runs was a little less than that.

The final day of exercises and drills took place in the harbour. These were all basically damage control exercises. The Commodore's staff did their best to drive us to a chaotic standstill. We had an un-exploded bomb in the wardroom, a raging fire in the paint locker, and various other hair-raising activities elsewhere in the engine room, messdecks and so on. Just to stir things up a bit, some satanic-minded instructor would throw thunder-flashes into a group of struggling sailors. It is said that in the midst of the general chaos, 'Puggy' Stephenson, walking on the upper deck, met a young RADAR operator who was apparently not doing anything. The Admiral threw his cap onto the deck, calling out. 'This is an incendiary bomb'. With great equanimity and precision the RADAR operator, with a bland 'Yes Sir,' flicked the cap with his toe under the bottom wire of the guard rail into the harbour and proceeded on his way. Not to be outdone, the Admiral roared 'Man Overboard', promoting the immediate lowering and manning of the whaler.

We Start Work. The B3 Group.
We had spent three hard weeks at Tobermory, so it was with some relief that we sailed from there on the 7th May to Greenock and thence to Londonderry. There we joined the B3 Escort Group (HMS *Towy*; Cmdr H. King) with the *Antigua*, *Knaresborough Castle*, *Leeds Castle* and *Anguilla*. We left Londonderry on the 14th May, arriving at Gibraltar on the 25th. My main memory of this voyage was of discovering that actually doing the navigation was not as easy as earlier training had suggested. After a few days Atkinson realised that I was struggling. He was most helpful in putting me right and for a few days we took noon sights together. We assumed the traditional Merchant Navy practice of my reporting to him every day with the noon position, together with the formal report that the chronometers had been wound.

Our return voyage to the UK went off to a very slow start. Our orders required that we should gather up the first half of the convoy, already assembled at Gib. We steamed at four knots, taking the convoy eastwards into the Med. to join up with the other half of the convoy steaming west from Malta. Matters became more complicated when it was found that the other half of the convoy was two hours ahead of its expected position.

With successive slow motion turns, our half of the convoy was turned around. In the meantime a number of the ships were getting agitated. They expressed in explicit signals that they had no desire to steam eastwards into the Med, when their destination was the UK.

For one used to the comparative high speed manoeuvres of the Fleet, this was an eye-opener to what close convoy escorting entailed. The Skipper, however, took advantage of the slow restful conditions by taking detailed observations of our fuel consumption at slow speeds.

These manoeuvres resulted in the two convoys forming a very broad front. Further adjustments of speed and positioning had to be carried out so as to squeeze the combined convoys through the narrow throat of the Straits of Gibraltar. By this time it was getting dark. Next morning the convoy was

26. Noon sights. The author at work.

found to be widely scattered and it took most of that day to get all the ships together.

With a new crew to make into a working whole, the skipper organised various exercises. The most onerous of these was to prepare for towing. This entailed hauling by hand a section of the anchor cable to the quarter deck, and of course getting it back again once the exercise was over. We practised streaming paravanes. We practised steering engine breakdowns. We practised and we practised. In the meantime we got into a regular routine of steaming from the Clyde to Gib and back. Generally all was pretty quiet. Most of the U-Boats were operating against the North Atlantic convoys, leaving our part of the ocean quiet. Even so, one could not help being nervous when, homeward bound, we had to stop to repair a defect in the engine room. To start with, the boiler safety valve blew. With the funnel at almost the same level as the bridge, the racket was horrendous and seemed to go on for far longer than was reasonable. Then came the complete contrast. The only sound now was the regular pinging of the asdic loudspeaker on the bridge. Soon the convoy had gone out of sight and we looked anxiously astern for the sub that might be trailing the convoy from a distance. Everybody was enjoined to keep as quiet as possible. The ship rolled in the low swell and the boats creaked in time in their davits. At last, a little before sunset, the repairs were completed. The ship came to life as we rang down near maximum revs and hastened after the convoy.

Between April and the end of August 1944 we did three round trips to Gib. and back. On the final voyage *Tintagel Castle* flew the flag of the Senior Officer, who brought two of his specialist staff with him, the Navigating Officer and A/S specialist. I enjoyed working with the Group Navigator, a Lieutenant Commander. He used a bubble sextant as used in aircraft, the first time that I had seen one. He also used what, to my mind, were short-cut navigating tables. I think that I assumed that in a fast travelling aircraft great positional accuracy was not necessary. Therefore the navigation tables would only provide an approximation of one's position. However we never disagreed as to our position, so the tables were reliable enough. He also took only half the time that I did to work out the position. The great advantage of the bubble sextant was that one did not have to be able to see the horizon in order to take a star or sun sight. Later, when working in the North Atlantic, I regretted not having tried to get hold of one.

These three voyages were pretty routine affairs, most alarms being caused by whales. On one occasion, when homeward bound shortly after D Day, we became a little disconcerted when the Admiralty advised us that a group of German destroyers had left a North Western French port and were steaming in our direction. If they had attacked the convoy, there would have been little that we could have done to stop them. The best that we could hope for would have been to have placed the close escort between the destroyers and the convoy and make as much smoke as possible. With luck most of the ships would have dispersed by the time the destroyers had penetrated the smoke screen and help had arrived. It seemed more likely that the destroyers were heading for the invasion fleet lying off the landing grounds. After a mildly anxious few hours, the destroyers were reported to have turned north and we did not hear of them again.

It was either with this convoy or the next northern bound one that we tangled with sections of the Mulberry Harbour being towed to the south-west approaches to the Channel. Visibility was not good and we had had no warning that the two convoys were on opposite tracks. Apart from some strong language over the r/t, we passed each other without incident. I think that it must have been on the same occasion that we met a Command/Communication ship proceeding south at high speed. Our plot of her suggested that she was due to hit the Scilly Islands within the next forty minutes. We signalled to her to that effect, receiving the bland reply, 'Thanks. We know.'

We join B1 Escort Group

At the end of August 1944, we transferred to Londonderry and joined the B1 Escort Group under the command of Cmdr. Eaden DSC RN. He flew his 'flag' in *Chelmer*. The Group consisted of two frigates, *Chelmer* and *Inman*, four Flower-Class Corvettes, *Lotus*, *Poppy*, *Dianella* and *Starwort* and the Castle Class Corvette, *Tintagel Castle*. These seven ships formed the core of the Group and remained together until the end of the War in Europe. From time to time Canadian Corvettes were attached, usually only for one outward or homeward bound voyage. Among these were the Canadian Navy corvettes *Cap de la Madeline* (twice), the *Calgary*, *Lindsay* and *Port Arthur* (each, one occasion only). If *Chelmer* was not available, then *Tintagel Castle* carried the Group Commander. This occurred during the period 9th December 1943 to 16th February 1944 for Convoys ON 271, HX 328, ON 279 and HX 336.

Although the ships worked very well together as an Escort Group, there was little social contact between the wardrooms of the different corvettes. I do not recall one wardroom entertaining another. This was in marked contrast to the socializing and friendly competition between destroyers of a flotilla in the Eastern Med. Possibly it was because of the different tradition between the mainly RN manned destroyers and largely RNR/RNVR manned escort vessels.

In the B1 Group, esprit de corps was helped by each ship painting the Group's logo on her funnel. This was a representation of a bulldog with a large bone in its mouth. Accredited U-Boat sinkings were represented by a small painting of a sub below the bulldog's front paws. Rivalry between ships was generated by a series of 'Bone' exercises carried out at sea. Before sailing, each ship received an envelope of sealed numbered envelopes containing 'Bone' exercise instructions. When all was quiet and when so disposed, the Group Commander would send a general signal, 'Carry out Bone exercise!' This might instruct all ships to stream paravanes, or carry out some emergency procedure such as going over to hand steering, or perhaps for all general service officers (other than COs) to take a sun sight. Results on completion of the exercise had to be signalled as quickly as possible. Laggards would receive a rude signal from the Group Commander. Most of the Group's Convoy Reports contained references to carrying out Bone Exercises. However, there was one exercise that was never officially referred to. This was carried out when we were steaming to St John's after handing over the convoy to the Canadian Escort Group south of Newfoundland.

If the conditions were right, the exercise would start by the Group being disposed in line abreast formation. The Escort SO's ship would be in the middle and searching ahead with her asdic. At the same time the SO would be flying the code signal reading:- 'Drop one Depth Charge.'

Once he had made suitable contact, the executive signal flag would be dipped and each ship would drop one depth charge set at a fairly shallow setting. This would immediately be followed by the SO flying the signal 'Pick up survivors.'

At the executive signal, each ship would turn in her tracks, stop where her charge had exploded and send off the whaler. The enthusiastic whaler's crew, armed with poled nets, waste paper baskets and the like would swoop upon the stunned fish rising to the surface, scooping as many as possible inboard. They had to be quick because the cod soon recovered consciousness and swam down out of sight. All being well, the boat would catch enough fish to give everyone fresh fish for two days.

Whilst the whaler was away, lower deck would be cleared and the falls made ready for hoisting her inboard. Once alongside, she would be run up the davits and secured. Immediately the whaler was clear of the water, the ship's engine would be started and course resumed. Again speed of completing the operation and numbers of fish landed earned brownie points. Of all the Bone Exercises, this was the only one that was popular. The others were considered a chore and an irritating interruption to a peaceful routine, especially if you happened to be off watch at the time.

Neutrals at Sea

It was, I think, in the autumn when, with a west-bound convoy, we received warnings from the Admiralty of a possible encounter with the combined Spanish and Portuguese fishing fleets, homeward bound from the Grand Banks fishing grounds. The weather was quite calm, with a long swell rolling out of the south-west. The south-western horizon was tinged with red as the evening drew to its close. The first call came from the RADAR hut was followed almost immediately by a hail from the crow's nest. Slowly more and more masts and sails came into view until a whole arc of the south western horizon was dotted with sails and masts. In their midst there was the small outline of a naval patrol boat. Gradually the hulls of the nearest of the fishing fleet emerged over the horizon, soon to subside again as the two convoys drew apart. No sign or signal passed between the two fleets. In fifteen or twenty minutes the Banks fishing fleet had sunk once more below the horizon. The meeting left a strange impression. Here were all these boats sailing home at the end of their traditional expedition to the Grand Banks, just as they had been used to doing for years. This in the middle of a major war and in one of its major battlefields. But it was not quite a normal peacetime activity. They too had had to adjust to the changed conditions. They had had to co-operate in order to combine and co-ordinate the sailing of the two national fleets. They had had to modify their peaceful occupation to take account of a war in which they were not involved.

Escort Work

Some inkling of the conditions that we might expect was given by a general signal from the C. in C. Western Approaches. This enjoined all COs to bear in mind the need to minimize weather damage during the forthcoming winter. Last winter many ships had been 'off duty' whilst weather damage was repaired. This had placed great strain on escort resources. However, now, with improvements of air cover, convoys would be routed further south during the winter. This was a reversal of the previous year's policy, when convoys had been deliberately routed northwards so as to take advantage of the difficulties U-Boats had in finding and attacking convoys during stormy weather.

By the time that we joined the North Atlantic convoy system, the Battle of the Atlantic had virtually already been won. The development of the system whereby Escort Support Groups reinforced the close escort defences as a convoy passed through a danger area had made the U-Boat pack attack much more difficult to sustain. Some of these Groups were disposed with the purpose of hunting down and destroying and dispersing any concentrations of U-Boats.

The U-Boats' tactics also changed. They began to operate closer inshore, often taking refuge close to a wreck to avoid detection. It was very difficult for an escort to distinguish between a U-Boat and a wreck. Eventually almost all the known wrecks were marked with an acoustic responder.

At the start of a voyage, each ship was given her sailing orders and escort position in relation to the convoy. In all escort operation events the reference point, known as Z, was the halfway point along the first line of ships of the convoy. If the convoy comprised ten columns, each of six ships, position Z would lie between the lead ship in column 5 and the lead ship in column 6. One of these ships would normally be flying the Commodore's Flag. The escorts were disposed one and a half miles to two miles from the convoy, those in the van of the convoy usually two to two-and-a-half miles ahead and those on the convoy flanks one-and-a-half to two miles from the outside columns. Each column would be half a mile apart. Within the columns the ships would be 800 yards apart (4 cables). A convoy of sixty ships disposed in ten columns each of six ships would, with the escorts, cover an area of some 52 square miles. The various escort reference positions are shown in Plate 27.

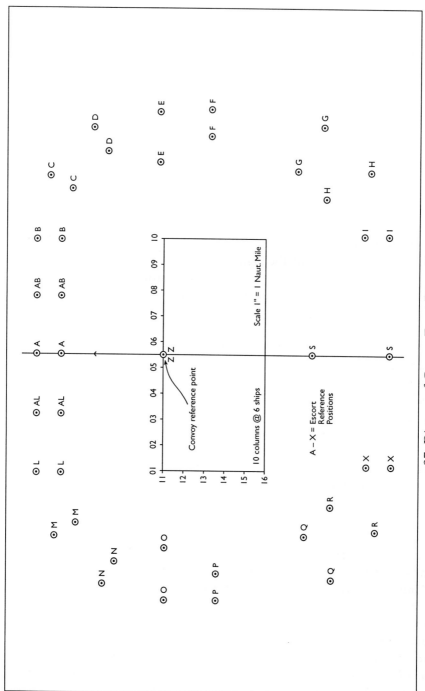

27. *Diagram of Convoy Escort Disposition.*

128

Under normal cruising conditions, the escorts would occupy the more distant positions. In the event of an attack or the suspected close proximity of U-Boats, the escorts would be drawn into the closer positions. The Escort Group Commander usually occupied position A. The other escorts would normally occupy positions M or N, O or P and B or C and E or F and S. *Tintagel Castle* was frequently allocated position S. With her Squid, proved as a more accurate weapon than either the hedgehog or depth charges, this put her in a good position to go to the assistance of any escort that had made a contact. Under reasonable conditions, she would be able to join an attacking escort in under half an hour.

In station S we usually weaved from one side of the convoy to the other. In this way we could quickly identify any ship that was going too slow and thus causing the ones astern of her to tail back. The RADAR operators soon learned to warn the bridge whenever they noticed a ship beginning to lag. This was invaluable during the night watches. Without loss of time, we could steam up the column to the ship that the operators had identified on the Radar Plan Position Indicator (PPI) as the one causing those astern of her to tail back. Once opposite the ship's bridge, a call across by loud hailer usually sorted out the problem. This, of course, meant that watch-keeping was far more interesting than just keeping station and pinging through the designated arc with the asdic.

Another aspect, foreseen by our skipper, was that opportunities were provided for rendering assistance to any ship damaged or broken down, with the added bonus of possible salvage awards.

On one of our very early calls at St John's, the skipper arranged for the dockyard to make a strong towing spring. It was stowed below the quarter-deck in the tiller flat, ready for instant use. The spring consisted of a long and very thick doubled manila rope with massive eyelets at each end. One end would be attached to the damaged ship's tow rope, the other to a section of our anchor cable that had been laboriously manhandled aft to the quarter-deck. The other end of the anchor cable section would be attached to our wire rope towing pennant. This would be eased in or out depending on sea conditions and so on.

Convoy escorts probably put in more sea time than any other group of naval ships. In the period 30th May 1944 to 30th May 1945 *Tintagel Castle* spent 206 days at sea on convoy escort work (Table II.1). This was quite typical for the convoy escorts. Those in the Support Groups were equally hard pressed. A round trip took about 33 days, with a turn around time at St John's NF of 6-7 days, whilst the turn-around time in the UK was about 10 days. The UK turn-around period gave little time for granting leave or for training. Those remaining on board had to carry out any necessary maintenance work and store ship. Once the liberty men were back on board, there would be several days of training sessions either on land or at sea – often both. Only at St John's NF was there much time for relaxation, there being few if any training facilities there. Visits to Gibraltar usually involved some sort of training session, usually target practice of some sort or another.

The base staff at Londonderry were very supportive. Nearly always a gang of maintenance staff, many of them Wrens, would come aboard and service the guns, the squid and all the electrical, radio and radar equipment. A first-class chart correction service was also provided. It was a tremendous relief to come back off leave to find that all the charts had been brought up to date.

Transferring Personnel at Sea

Particularly when we were carrying the Group Senior Officer, it would sometimes be necessary to transfer a specialist or spare part to another escort ship. This was done using the whaler. The Group, and possibly the Western Approaches Command as a whole, had developed a neat and speedy drill for doing this. The two ships involved would steam to a position some four miles ahead of the convoy. When in position, the receiving ship would take up station about a cable astern of the transferring ship's starboard quarter. Both ships would reduce speed to 2 or 3 knots. The whaler would be lowered and slipped whilst still attached to the ship by a long pennant made fast well forward. The coxswain would put his tiller over so as to veer out from the ship until the whaler was almost directly ahead of the receiving ship's port side. In this position, the whaler would slip the tow rope. It was then easy for the whaler to be brought up alongside the receiving ship.

When the whaler had been slipped, the transferring ship would steam round to take up position astern of the receiving ship. In the meantime the receiving ship would have secured the whaler with a long pennant, also made fast well forward in the ship, and tow the whaler whilst it was alongside. Once the transfer had been completed, the whaler would veer out from the receiving ship, slip, and the transferring ship would steam up to bring the whaler alongside. The whole operation could be completed in a very short time with minimum effort on behalf of the oarsmen of the whaler's crew. No ship ever actually stopped, thereby reducing their vulnerability to torpedo attack. The main manpower effort was in hoisting the whaler up to the davits. This required all hands not actually on watch. Although it was possible to take the falls to the for'ard capstan, it was always considered safer to hoist the boat by hand. One had better control.

Oiling at Sea

The earlier version of corvettes, the Flower Class, did not have such a long range as the Castle Class. In the early days of the battle of the Atlantic, the Flowers would have to turn back when they reached 26° parallel if they could not re-fuel from a ship in the convoy. By the time the Castle Class corvettes came along, most convoys included a tanker from which the escorts could re-fuel. In the B. One Group, the Flowers, re-fuelled at sea on each voyage. Although the *Tintagel Castle* had the endurance to cross the Atlantic without re-fuelling, we were often required to do so for exercise. This was no doubt considered good for our souls. It also reduced any envy that might have developed amongst the Flowers.

The first time that we fuelled at sea, I recalled the experiences when in the *Sheffield* with some dread. Then, the idea of firmly securing two ships together at sea had always seemed to me to be against all the tenets of good seamanship. To my relief, I found that the Western Approaches Command had developed a very seamanlike method of fuelling at sea.

In essence, the fuelling ship, usually a tanker, streamed a fuelling hose. This was picked up by the vessel to be fuelled, coupled to the fuel intake point of the foc'sle and some of the tension on the oil hose was taken up by a wire hawser. At the same time, the tanker streamed a splash target – often just a small barrel. This was secured to lie a suitable distance astern of the tanker. All that the fuelled ship had to do was to steam on a parallel course to the tanker, maybe a hundred feet on its port side and at exactly the tanker's speed. Because the helmsman had a good view of the tanker, keeping a parallel course was not a problem, even if there was a bit of a sea running. There was enough slack in the system to take up a bit of cork-screwing. The major problem for the Officer of the Watch was to get the speed right. The ship was usually positioned so that the splash target, as seen from the compass platform, was in line with a stanchion on the starboard side of the bridge. Small adjustments of engine revs kept it in that position. This required first class co-operation with the engine room and not a little expertise on their part to make engine speed adjustments in steps of just two revs per minute. On the bridge it was vital that speed adjustments were made in only very small steps. If the changes were too big, one quickly got into a yo-yo situation, with the ship surging ahead or astern. This was very difficult to get out of. The other vital side of the coin was for the tanker to vary neither course nor engine revs. The system worked well. Corvettes were oiled at sea even when conditions were getting severe. To cope with the worst conditions, tankers were equipped with an extra 300 feet of oiling hose. This allowed for greater movement between the two ships. With this system, we could safely oil at sea under conditions that would have been impossible with the rigid system used by *Sheffield* during Operation Torch.

Sea Routines

At sea the ship's company worked normal watches. The crew were split into three watches which worked four hours on, eight hours off. Routine ship's cleaning and maintenance work was carried out by the watches off watch. Dog watches were worked in the evening. The hours between 1600 and 2000 were split into two dog watches, each of two hours. The result was that nobody always kept the same four-hour watches during the day or night. However in the wardroom it was mutually agreed that we would keep fixed watches. This made it more convenient for carrying out various off-watch duties. As the Navigating Officer, I kept the 8-12 watch. This was convenient for taking star sights at dawn and dusk and for the noon sun sight. As there were always two officers on watch at a time, it meant that I could take sun or star sights whilst on watch and work out the results afterwards. This was made easier for me by the skipper allowing me to use the chartroom, where there was a bunk, as a sea cabin. In most corvettes the captain would sleep in the chartroom whilst at sea. Atkinson only did so if there was a panic on or if we were carrying the Group Senior Officer. In that case I had to sleep in my cabin at sea. From somewhere we managed to get hold of a washstand that was secured in one corner of the chartroom. The bridge messenger was organized to bring hot water at the appropriate time in the morning. It was a very civilized arrangement.

If I had taken star sights during the evening watch, it was no bother to work out the results when I came off watch. I would plot the new position and turn in immediately. In the morning I would be woken up by the bridge messenger in time for star sights and only had to go up one ladder to the bridge to take them.

Four of the officers were keen bridge players and play would start on the first night of every voyage after supper. The game would continue every night at sea until we were back in Londonderry again. Not being a bridge player, I did not partake and had little understanding of the scoring. It seemed that each night each of the four players accumulated points. The one with the most points at the end of the round trip won. Tension would mount, especially when homeward bound. It was not unusual for the players to wander up to the bridge one by one at the end of the evening's play. Most evenings I would get at least two versions of the day's play. On one occasion scores were almost even. It was decided to have an extra session in the afternoon on the day that we were due to return to Londonderry. At that time we had to take on a pilot at the entrance to Lough Foyle.

'Entering the Lough in five minutes.' I reported down to the captain.

'OK, carry on, Pilot,' came back the reply, and so the dialogue continued.

' Pilot coming aboard, Sir.' Then some time later: 'Ten minutes to going alongside, Sir.' Only then did the bridge game come to an end, and the Captain came up to the bridge to perform the last rites of the voyage; to bring us alongside and ring off engines.

Later, after we had gone up and down the Lough a sufficient number of times, the CO was considered to have had sufficient experience to dispense with a pilot. When that happened, the skipper could claim pilotage money, which he shared with me – chiefly because it was I who usually took the ship up and down the Lough.

Pilot

Without a doubt this was the happiest time that I had during the War. Being the Navigating Officer, I was doing the job that I really wanted and enjoyed. Apart from the sheer interest in finding out where we were all the time, it was something that kept one wholly occupied. Part of the fascination was that it combined purely technical and mechanical tasks with intuition and skill. For example, taking a sextant sight was basically a mechanical task. One looked through the telescope and brought the star or sun down to the horizon and read off the angle. The skill and intuition came in deciding where exactly the horizon was. For star sights taken at dawn and dusk, the horizon was not always all that clear. Even when taking a sun sight, the horizon was not always all that well defined – especially during a gale.

The star globe was a wonderful tool. It was a globe sunk into a box. All the main constellations were painted on the globe. By setting one's dead reckoning position and the time, one could read off the bearing and altitude of any star of interest. So when it came to taking star sights, one set the altitude on the sextant and lined it up on the appropriate bearing. And there in the viewpiece was your star. With the sextant set up at the correct angle to the horizon, a star could be found long before it could be seen with the naked eye. In this way it was possible to take star sights when it was light enough to get a clear horizon line.

There was also the challenge of getting an accurate dead reckoning position when the weather prevented taking either sun or star sights. The ship was fitted with an automatic plot. It was driven by a repeater from the gyro compass and from an impeller protruding from the bottom of the hull to give distance. This plot was quite accurate over short distances. Its main function was to provide a tactical plot when in action. The plot made no allowances for wind drift or the set of any current. The ship was equipped with a conventional log. This we streamed and the Quartermaster and I spent a lot of time adjusting the length of the cord to obtain accurate readings. Daily runs were compared to those registered by the automatic plot and to distances run between sun and star sights. Strict comparison was difficult because of operational needs to adopt a zigzag course. After about a week of trials, I was satisfied that we were getting readings with not more than a ten per cent error. When U-Boats began to use acoustic torpedoes, we had to stop streaming the log because it would become foul of the noisy rattlers that we streamed to counter the acoustic torpedoes. The rattlers created an overwhelming noise such that the torpedoes would strike them rather than the ship. The noise of the ship's propeller would be completely drowned by the racket set up by the rattlers. The downside was that they made the asdic operators' job a lot more difficult and virtually precluded detecting a submarine astern of the ship.

During heavy weather I would spend some time trying to gauge the combined effect of the sea and wind on our course made good. The angle that the log line made with the centre line of the ship could, I thought, be taken as an indicator of any sagging down to leeward. I don't think that I ever came to any firm conclusions on this problem.

Frequent long spells of overcast sky or fog meant that we often had to rely for several days in succession on dead reckoning, with perhaps an occasional snatched sun sight. One of the more successful of these was when approaching the south-west of Ireland. After several days in fog, the message came down from the bridge that there was a window in the sky. I rushed up and managed to get a quick sight but with a very ropy horizon. It so happened that an hour or so later I was able to detect, with the echo sounder, the moment we crossed the Continental Shelf. This gave me two position lines and put about a five-mile correction to my dead reckoning position. This was confirmed several hours later when we got a bearing of the Scilly Isles. I was reminded of the occasion when we fixed the *Canton*'s position by simultaneous sights of the Sun, Venus and Pico Alto; the latter was the highest point of the Azores. This coincided with the rare occasion when our brightest planet, Venus, was visible during daylight.

I was much happier as a deep sea navigator. Coastal pilotage was always a time of tension. I took my responsibilities very seriously and stayed on the bridge for as long as possible when in coastal waters. I recall two particularly anxious moments.

Once we had brought a convoy to the Western Approaches, it then often broke up into smaller sections, depending on the ships' final destination. Each detachment would be placed under the care of one corvette, which, once she had delivered her mini-convoy, would then proceed to Londonderry independently. At that time UK-bound convoys were routed to the South West Approaches. We were usually detached to take ships either to Liverpool or to the Bristol Channel. This meant a final passage through the North Channel to Londonderry. Standing Orders said that we had to pass to the north of Rathlin Island. However, if one entered the narrow channel between Rathlin Island and the north Irish Coast at a time when the tidal flow in that channel was westwards, one could save some two hours' sailing time. We used to time our passage up the Irish Sea and into the Northern Channel so as to arrive at the eastern end of the Rathlin Island channel when the north-western tidal set was running. We would then slip between Rathlin Island and the mainland and so berth in Londonderry that much earlier. On this particular occasion, the voyage-long bridge game had reached a critical stage, so a final afternoon session was in progress. I had quite happily taken over the afternoon watch. The weather was rough with a strong north-westerly wind. We entered the Rathlin Island channel on schedule and all was well. That is until we began to clear the western end of the Island. It was not long before I realized that a particularly blocky and sharp-edged island, Shep Island, an outlier of the Giant's Causeway, was maintaining a constant bearing. Several small alterations of course to starboard did not improve the situation. I then realized that the gale had made the eastern tidal run start early. This, backed by the strong wind, was setting us rapidly on to a lee shore. We finished up steering a course some ninety degrees to starboard of what it should have been and cleared Shep Island by the narrowest of margins. Luckily for me, the wardroom was on the starboard side, so the skipper did not see how close we were to a premature arrival ashore. Although I suspect that he knew something had happened because he made some remark later on about the change in the ships' movement.

The approach to St John's Harbour was by a long swept channel running at right angles to the coast. The channel was quite wide, so not too difficult to find. One could usually see the flashing red light that marked its western end. Because of my difficulties with seeing dim red lights, I used to get the signalman to find the red light for me.

Just to the north of St John's there lies a bay which showed up on the RADAR PPI as almost the exact shape and outline of the harbour. More than one corvette had got into trouble in mistaking that bay for St John's. I remembered this well on the day that we approached St John's in thick fog.

We crept up to the harbour mouth but even with the PPI, could not clearly make out the entrance. We could hear the swell breaking on the cliffs. We could hear the blare of the lighthouse's foghorn. None of us on the bridge could agree on the direction from which the sound came. It was an extraordinary and eerie situation. We could barely see beyond the foc'sle. The swell washed up, recoiling from the cliffs. The sirens of equally bemused consorts echoed around us and above all was the overwhelming blast of the lighthouse's foghorn. The sound swirled around us like invisible wisps of fog. To seaward and to the north the PPI showed the stationary blips of the rest of the Group. Eventually the harbour sent out a launch to guide us in.

During the winter of 1944/45, the Atlantic Convoys were routed southwards, partially to avoid the severe winter storm damage caused to both escorted ships and their escorts during the previous winter. It was also during this time that we were issued with LORAN navigation equipment. This was an electronic navigational radio system. A system of master radio beacons sent out a series of pulses. Each pulse triggered a slave station to send out a pulse. The onboard system measured the time between receipt of the master signal and that of the slave signal. With a suitable set of charts, one could, with this data, obtain position lines. It was quite useful. However with our southerly routes, the angles between the position lines were too acute to give a firm position. After we had had the system for several weeks, we received charts and other necessary data to enable us to use a similar system set up by the Germans. This was based on radio beacons set up in Spain, Portugal and the Azores. As far as we were concerned, the German system, whilst of interest, gave weak signals and the position lines where we were operating tended to be of too acute an angle to be really useful. This was in the days before transistors. The sets were cumbersome and liable to breakdown. I recall being most impressed by the way our senior RADAR operator maintained the LORAN set and usually managed to keep the temperamental thing going. In peacetime he had been a fashionable hairdresser. I admired his remarkable adaptability. At about the same time the DECCA system had been installed around the UK coastline. This had far greater accuracy than the LORAN and I envied the ships that were fitted with it. It was, of course, a tremendous advantage for coastal work in fog. I believe that its main use was in mine sweeping.

At the end of each voyage there was always a large backlog of chart correcting that had to be done. This was no real problem except when it was one's turn to go on leave. Leave and A/S courses between convoys gave little time to get the charts up to date. The position was completely changed when a chart correcting service was set up in Londonderry. This would have been late in 1944 or early 1945. All the work was done by Wrens and they made an excellent job of it.

After the Group was broken up, I had my first experience of pilotage up the English Channel and along the east coast of the UK; a very nerve-wracking experience, especially as it started with a night passage. I was confused by the multiple flashing of the channel buoys. I would start counting the seconds between flashes and then a more distant buoy would flash, throwing everything into confusion. The chart would not show a buoy with that particular sequence. Of course at the same time I had to pretend to the Officer of the Watch that I knew what I was doing and had everything under control. After a closer study of the chart, I realised that adjacent buoys had different flashing groups and that provided one concentrated on one buoy at a time, the system worked. The next day I nearly got us tangled with a channel buoy. To keep a neat and accurate track on the chart, I liked to alter course as close to the buoy as possible. On this occasion I had realized that we were running against a strong tide. I had decided to alter course well up tide of the buoy. I steamed past the buoy and altered course to port. I had misjudged the strength of the tide and found to my horror that we were being set down on to the buoy. Only a burst of speed and a full helm order saved us. The Skipper, down in his cabin, had seen it all. We had hardly cleared the buoy when a few caustic remarks floated up the voice pipe about near misses and cleaning barnacles off the hull. No, I did not enjoy pilotage in strong tidal waters.

Seamen's Rum

On the whole the *Tintagel Castle*, like all the Castle Class Corvettes, was an excellent sea boat and dry forward. The sharp and pronounced flare of the bow ensured that we took very little water for'ard even in the worst of the weather. However at the back end it was a different story. The severely cut away quarter deck invited the sea to come inboard whenever we rolled to windward in anything of a seaway. This would not have mattered very much because there was little cause to go on to the quarter-deck. The two racks of depth charges we had at the stern were there more for decoration than for use (except for when we wanted to fish). In very heavy weather we took in the log line. The only access to the rum store was via a hatchway on the quarter-deck. On this particular voyage, when outward bound, it had not been possible to collect the daily ration of spirits. The day the weather moderated enough to allow us to get safely to the spirit room hatchway, I happened to be the Duty Officer. It was my job to accompany the Regulating Petty Officer (RTO) to draw the day's rations of rum. The

moment we opened the store room door, it was obvious that there had been
storm damage. The place was heady with the sweet sickly smell of rum.
There was even rum sloshing across the deck. Several jars in their wicker
baskets had broken adrift from the racks and smashed on the deck. Before
drawing the day's ration, we had to record all the damage and clear up the
mess. When all was done and the rum ration issued, I went up on to the
bridge for a breath of fresh air. I had hardly stepped onto the compass
platform before the skipper turned on me demanding to know why I had
been drinking rum. He was furious and I'm sure on the point of putting me
under open arrest. It had never occurred to me that my breath stank of rum.
I explained hurriedly about the broken jars and the rum fumes in the store,
denying vigorously that I had drunk anything. The RPO was summoned. It
wasn't until he had confirmed what had happened that the skipper relented.
This reminded me of a story told by the mother of my friend Dennis.
Dennis and his father had been working one hot day with a two-handed
cross cut saw, cutting a cider barrel in half. This they were going to make into
two troughs for the pigs. It was hot work. Once they had got halfway
through the barrel, the cider fumes began to waft out. She said that it was a
miracle that they ever completed the job. They were as drunk as two coots
by the time the two halves of the barrel fell apart.

Small Ship Command

The relationship between the Commanding Officer, his officers and crew,
particularly in a small ship, has a profound effect on how well the ship
operates. I had great respect for Atkinson as a CO. He kept a very tight and
well-trained ship. It was easy to see how he had obtained such a fine
reputation as a U-Boat killer. This reputation paid off as far as the whole ship
was concerned. As the 'deputy' Escort Group SO's ship, we gained certain
privileges. We were allocated special duties in connection with the assembly
and dispersion of the convoys. This enabled us, on occasions, to act
independently. Atkinson's reputation was also probably a deciding factor in
giving us the position as 'tail end Charlie' in escort position around the
convoy. This certainly made watch keeping much more interesting and there
was always the chance of picking up some salvage. However, the way
Atkinson set about things could sometimes be irritating.

There was a period when he was probably justified in thinking that watch
keeping had been getting a bit slack. There was the instance, nearing
midnight, when his voice called up from the quartermaster's voice pipe:
'Watch your course.'

We were way off course and none of us on the bridge had noticed it. The skipper had deliberately told the quartermaster to steer the wrong course. There were no recriminations, but we got the message. On another night when all was quiet and everything in order, the quartermaster reported that the ship was not responding to the wheel. My God! What do we do?

'Right. Go to emergency steering from the tiller flat.'

'And I hope to God that the quartermaster remembers the routine better than I do', I thought to myself. So we went to emergency steering and everything worked out fairly quickly. It was only later that I found out that the messenger sent to waken the Engineering Officer had been intercepted and that the whole episode had been put in motion by the skipper. No doubt it was a good training exercise, but it still rankled.

Away Sea Boat's Crew!

The CO's decision cannot be questioned. Not at the time anyway. One incident giving rise to this occurred on a November day with an outward bound convoy. The day was overcast with a strong wind and broken, disturbed seas. A merchant ship had reported sighting a periscope and *TC* was sent to investigate. Sure enough, there over on the starboard side was a spar bobbing up and down. The Skipper ordered the sea boat away. Dykes, the sea boat Officer, viewed the affair with much doubt and apprehension. It was difficult to launch the whaler under those conditions and in the high seas rowing in unison would not be easy.

During the launching process, the *TC* had been turned to give the whaler a lee. This put the spar on the port side, but in the limited visibility this was not noticed by the whaler, which gamely set out to starboard away from the *TC*. By the time this was realized, the spar was well astern and to get to it under oars in that seaway would be a long and exhausting effort. The skipper approached the whaler with the intention of passing a tow line and towing the whaler to the spar. We turned a full circle and closed the whaler. Let Dykes continue in his own words:-

'A Seaman crouched astride the forecastle bullring to hand us a line' – "To hand" indeed was very much a feasibility. Being approached bow on presented us with a towering raking bow one moment and the next, the ship so low in the water that we could have stepped from the whaler on to the forecastle.'

From my position on the compass platform it seemed almost impossible that we could avoid running the whaler down and I started to rehearse in my mind what we would have to do to rescue the whaler crew from the sea. Dykes continued:-

'The process of going from high to low presented us in the whaler with the

28. Sea boat's crew of HMS Tintagel Castle *searching for an object sighted from the bridge; North Atlantic, November, 1944.*
By courtesy of the Castle Class Corvette (Frigate) Association.

possibility of the rakish bow presenting itself to the side of the whaler as if it was a saw – the consequences of which I could plainly see – either being sawn in half down to the keelson or gradually being turned over port side first. With a large degree of strength and certainly urgency, we endeavoured to maintain a small distance of a foot or so from the plunging bow, by pushing ourselves away until we secured the tow line.

In spite of the numerous expletives and other seamanlike words of the whaler crew, by now very wet and chokker, the tow was passed to us and secured to the tabernacle. The tow began. I cannot recall whether we were towed astern of the *TC* in her wake, or alongside starboard side a matter of an oar's length from the ship's side. Although the *TC* could not have gone any slower without loosing steerage way, we, in the whaler, felt we were proceeding at a very fast rate. Certainly too good for comfort and with a degree of danger because of the large seas and strong wind.'

Once close to the object, the whaler slipped the tow and painfully pulled the remaining short distance by oars. With difficulty the 12 foot 4" x 3" plank was hauled aboard. One end had a metal collar with a swan neck secured to the wood, hence the reason why the plank stood on end in the water, looking, from a distance, like a periscope.

It was a difficult pull back to the ship and even more difficult to secure the falls in that type of seaway. In Dykes' words:-

'We eventually came alongside and engaged the falls fore and aft. *TC* proceeded to get under way slowly and our troubles began once more. Unfortunately *TC* did not roll in the same direction as the swell. *TC* would roll to starboard, the sea would roll towards the ship. The whaler would find itself on the crest of the sea, the falls and disengaging gear snatched with a loud bang as if it was all being pulled from the keel of the boat. As the roll to port continued, we were inclined to be pulled from the sea and swung towards the ship's side. Then the ship would right itself and start to roll back to starboard and dump us in the sea.'

The slacking and snatching of the falls in those moments presented the bowman with a difficulty which nearly cost him his fingers – but we made it. The Ship's Company "cleared lower deck" to hoist us clear of the water. The whaler was secured on the davits and the crew returned to their messes. The crew were given an additional tot of rum . . .'

What passed between a pretty fed-up Dykes and the skipper they kept to themselves.

U 878 Sunk

On the 7th April 1945 the B1 Escort Group [HMS *Chelmer* (SO)] sailed from Londonderry to escort Convoy ON 295 across the Atlantic. The *Tintagel Castle* and *Poppy* had been detached to escort the Submarine *Sidon* and to collect the ships joining the convoy from Milford Haven. We joined the main section of the convoy in the early hours of the 9th April. By this time we had also been joined by the 23rd Escort Group to provide additional A/S cover. It was a pretty busy time over the next two days, with the sea in our immediate vicinity seemingly crowded with ships and escort vessels. These included the Channel Section of our convoy escorted by the *Vanquisher*, *Sunflower* and *Alisma*. There had been the usual false alarms from non-sub contacts as we proceeded south through the Irish Sea and South Western Approaches. At one point the convoy was diverted to avoid a smoke contact reported by a shore-based aircraft. An aircraft was flown off from our MAC ship (*Gadila*) but nothing was sighted. Later *Poppy* had an asdic contact classified as probable. The convoy was diverted away to port to make more room. *Chelmer* joined *Poppy* in an attack. Subsequently the contact vanished and it was declared to have been a non-sub. With the convoy now clear, all the escorts resumed their stations. At this time the U-Boats were tending to attack in coastal waters. There they could take refuge on the bottom or close to wrecks. In either case they were difficult to find and each contact had to be carefully investigated. All this kept everyone very busy, especially the signalmen, who had to keep track of and log a constant stream of TSB (Voice radio) and light signals.

On the evening of the 10th April *Tintagel Castle* was in her usual position astern of the convoy in position 'S' when we gained a shallow contact and made two Squid attacks. No movement of the target could be detected so it was assumed that the contact had been a wreck. An hour after the first contact, the *Inman* was ordered to join the *TC* in case the contact was a sub. However twenty minutes later *TC*, who had been getting a number of echoes, had decided that the contact was definitely non-sub. We started to rejoin the convoy that was now some ten miles ahead. Shortly before midnight, whilst we were re-joining the convoy, *Vanquisher* reported sighting a U-Boat and opened fire. *Chelmer* lit up the area ahead of *Vanquisher* and the U-Boat was reported to have dived. Both the *Alisma* and *Inman* were ordered to go and support *Vanquisher. Vanquisher* and *Alisma* soon gained contact. By this time we were within two miles of them and were ordered to join in and immediately went to Action Stations.

Vanquisher, in contact with the sub, assumed the duties of the directing ship, and passed ranges and bearings. Within seven minutes we had an asdic echo at a range of 600 yards. This was quickly classified as non-sub. *Vanquisher*, who was still in contact, continued to send ranges and bearings and in about fifteen minutes we obtained a firm asdic contact at a range of 1,300 yards. Life in the asdic hut, which also contained the plot, was getting quietly hectic. The young ordinary seaman that I had with me did an excellent job in feeding me the messages and ranges and bearings as they came in, and soon a plot began to develop. We reduced speed to 6 knots and the target was plotted to be moving slowly right. A very deliberate attack was started and all instruments checked. Within ten minutes of making contact, the plot established the sub as moving at three knots on a course of 100° at a range of 400 yards. The depth of the sub was soon established as being steady at 600 ft. Half a minute later the Squid was fired and the pattern detonated 28 seconds later. Almost immediately a muffled explosion was heard. Shortly afterwards this was followed by another explosion, strong enough to shake the ship. *Vanquisher* confirmed having heard the explosion and of not having fired any depth charges. It was evident that the submarine had suffered a serious internal explosion. Contact with the sub was soon resumed and we opened up the range in preparation for another attack. The sub appeared to be stopped and blowing noises could be heard. Ten minutes after the first attack, the Squid was again fired with the target at about 600 yards and 300 ft deep. Three minutes later the target was stopped at a range of 400 yards and two small underwater explosions were heard. The contact now deteriorated and slowly disappeared amongst faint whistling noises. An hour after the first attack another small explosion was heard and another attack started. This was soon abandoned because of the poor quality of the asdic contact. A search for debris was organised by *Vanquisher*. Nothing was found and *TC* was ordered to return to the convoy after two and a half hours. The whole operation had taken a little over four hours. Most of it had been occupied in making certain that the U-Boat did not re-surface and in searching for evidence of its destruction. The actual attack was carried out from 2317 hours to 2338 hours, when the squid was fired in the second attack – a total of 21 minutes. *Tintagel Castle* remained in the vicinity until 0225 and rejoined the convoy some ten hours later. It was subsequently confirmed that this action resulted in the sinking of U-878.

This illustrates one of the tactical problems facing escort group senior officers. How to balance the need for maintaining a close escort around the convoy with the zeal of his commanding officers, not only in attacking firm asdic contacts, but also in their natural desire to obtain proof of the success of their attack. In this case the *TC* was away from her station on the escort screen for nearly 18.5 hours.

Icebergs and Fog

Although by mid-May 1945 the War in Europe had officially ended, there was uncertainty as to how the U-Boat commanders still at sea would respond to their orders to surrender For this reason, Convoy ON 303 UK – Halifax of 74 ships sailed on the 16th May escorted by the B1 Group. In spite of dense fog, the Milford Haven and the Channel sections of the convoy were joined without incident. Fog continued to be the theme of the voyage.

As the convoy neared the Grand Banks, it had already been steaming through thick fog for several days and the Admiralty diverted it southwards to avoid ice. In the early evening of the 27th May *Chelmer* (SO) obtained a RADAR contact three miles ahead fine on the starboard bow. There were several confused echoes. She went ahead to investigate and with visibility down to 50 yards, she found herself in close contact with a very large iceberg. Its full length could not be seen, but the RADAR picture suggested that it was nearly three quarters of a mile long. Growlers and another iceberg were detected to the north.

It was apparent to the SO that collisions would occur. If the convoy

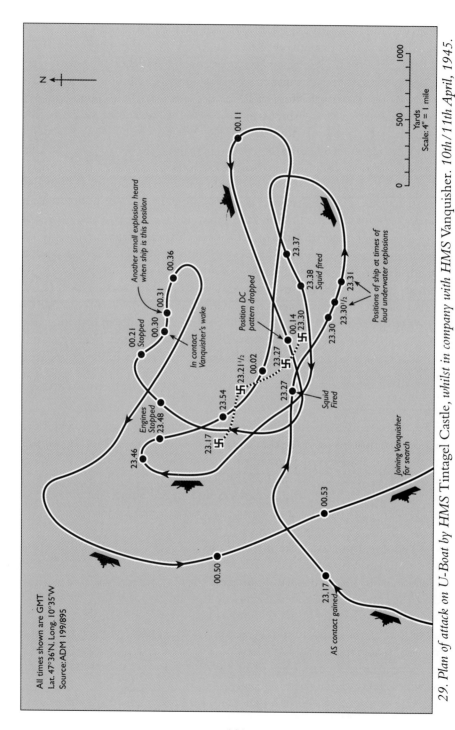

All times shown are GMT
Lat. 47°36'N. Long. 10°35'W
Source: ADM 199/895

N

Another small explosion heard
when ship is this position

00.36

00.31

00.30

00.21
Stopped

In contact
Vanquisher's wake

00.02
23.21½

23.54

Engines
Stopped
23.48

23.17

23.46

00.50

Position DC
pattern dropped

00.14
23.30
23.27

23.27

Squid
Fired

23.37

23.38
Squid fired

23.31

23.30½

23.30

Positions of ship at times of
loud underwater explosions

Joining Vanquisher
for search

00.53

AS contact gained
23.17

Yards
Scale: 4" = 1 mile

0   500   1000

29. Plan of attack on U-Boat by HMS Tintagel Castle, whilst in company with HMS Vanquisher. 10th/11th April, 1945.

144

continued on its present course, it would steam into the ice at 9.5 knots. The alternative was for the convoy to take violent evasive action, which in itself implied a very high risk of collisions occurring. The SO chose this latter course and asked the Commodore to make a 'double item' turn (i.e. 90° together). Because of the fog, this order could only be transmitted to the ships by radio. Not all the ships had more than one radio operator. Since we had been in thick fog for four days, it was probable that only a few of the operators would be on duty to take the message. The turn was executed twenty minutes after the first RADAR report. Inevitably there were a number of collisions. Almost immediately the Commodore asked the Vice Commodore to assume charge of the convoy because the Commodore's ship had been badly damaged. The Vice Commodore immediately declined, reporting that he too had been in collision. Command was passed to the Master of the *Empire Stuart*, who ordered all ships to stop whilst he figured out what to do. Eventually all ships were ordered to steer due south at a very slow speed and to rendezvous the next day at a position that was reported to be clear of fog. Three tugs were ordered to be sailed from Newfoundland and proceed to the scene.

In the meantime *Tintagel Castle* was ordered to find the Commodore's ship, take him off and convey him to the *Chelmer*. *Inman* was left in charge of the Convoy, whilst *Chelmer*, *Poppy* and *Lotus* together with the *TC*, were ordered to close the ships and render what assistance was required. *TC* soon found the *Villager* and, with the whaler, transferred the Commodore and his staff to the *TC*. This took over two hours. First taking across the personal luggage of the Commodore's staff and then make two further journeys to transfer the staff and the Commodore himself.

We then proceeded in search of stragglers to pass on the message to steam south so as to clear the fog. When one such had been picked up on the RADAR, we would close at speed and pass on the instructions.

During the second half of the middle watch a general kerfuffle in the wheelhouse and bridge woke me up and I went up to the bridge. It seemed that a ship had been picked up earlier some twenty miles away and we were now closing it at full speed. Visibility was still very poor with fog and heavy rain. The Captain was on the bridge and as the range was reduced, so was our speed. Suddenly the two lookouts stationed in the bows gave a yell and ran aft. At the same time a light appeared out of the fog fine on the port bow and almost immediately another over to starboard. A ship was right across our bows and very close. The engine was put full astern and action stations sounded so as automatically to clear the lower decks and close all watertight doors. The ship shook with the vibrations of the engine and the screw going full astern against our still considerable forward speed. As we approached the ship, it loomed out of the fog above us. A lone voice from amidships called out to us to go astern. They had already been in one collision and definitely did not want another. We stopped just a few feet clear of the unknown ship. We never did discover which one she was.

After this close encounter we continued south and I remained on the bridge. It was not long before we picked up another substantial echo on the RADAR. This time, still in fog and heavy rain, we approached more cautiously. On the PPI the echo looked very large. It might have been several objects so close together that they responded to the RADAR as one. Taking bearings of the two extreme ends, I concluded that the target was several miles long. Coming out on to the Bridge to report to the Captain, I could feel the chill wind blowing off the ice on to us. It reminded me of how it felt like entering Seydisfjord in Iceland in the middle of the winter. Ice-cold fingers reaching out for one from an invisible darkened shore. We continued to approach and soon could hear the waves lapping the base of the iceberg. Now I had never actually seen an iceberg, but I had heard how most of it floated submerged. If this thing was several miles long, how much of it protruded out sidewise? I nervously suggested to the Skipper that perhaps as we couldn't see the iceberg maybe it would be prudent not to get too close to such a huge one. Great was my relief when he ordered a course to take us away.

Incidentally, it transpired that the ERA on watch who so rapidly put us 'full astern' happened to have been the one who had failed to do so at Tobermory. His prompt action on this occasion earned him the forgiveness of the Skipper.

The next day we emerged from the fog into bright sunshine and during the morning and afternoon all the ships bar three or four were found and the convoy reformed. Eventually the convoy was handed over to the Canadian escorts and B1 Group proceeded to St John's.

In all, twenty ships had been damaged but only one of them had struck the ice. No lives were lost neither were any personal injuries reported. Although ships had been holed and compartments waterlogged, there had been no SOSs and none were expected. All the ships made it safely to port.

Homeward Bound

Convoy ON 303 was the last fast Halifax convoy to be escorted across the Atlantic in WWII. Shortly after B1 Group assembled at St John's, a signal came from C. in C. Western Approaches disbanding the Group. *Tintagel Castle* was ordered to proceed independently back to the UK.

The return passage was thus carried out with a certain light-heartedness. We were acting on our own with no other ships in company. The passage back to the UK was taken on a Great Circle course, the one and only time that the writer ever plotted such a course.

To add to the holiday atmosphere, the whole passage was in fine weather. One day in particular stands out. The swell was slight and coming up astern on the starboard quarter. The light wind was from a similar direction and very slightly faster than the speed at which we were steaming. Throughout the whole watch, a tern-like seagull circled the ship and did so with the greatest economy of flapping. He started his circuit abreast the funnel on the port side, and in a steep glide overtook the ship, skimming round the bow close to the sea, and turning into the wind. At this point his ground speed almost dropped to zero. As the ship passed, he soared upwards from the waves, until, a few feet above the funnel, he turned parallel to the ship and once again started his rapid downward glide. This was repeated time after effortless time. Later memories of this passage inspired the following lines:-

The Great Circle

In mid-Atlantic an Arctic tern hangs poised above the funnel,
The seaman's dove perhaps.
Subtle changes in the updraft, she loses lift and with wings stilled
Dives down the looward side, skims beneath the prow,
Turns, soars upward and hangs and hangs as before,
Till another swell disturbs the air, and so again and again.
        The great circle course
        The shortest route
        Act independently
        Homeward bound
The gale is over, the last convoy done.
'Disperse your Group' My lordships said,
'Put a tampon in the gun
Keep the squid alert and let the asdic ping'.
'Blow your tanks' it says, 'a black flag will keep you safe.'
        The shortest Route
        Act independently
        Homeward bound
        The Great Circle course
Summer on the bridge, shirts off in the sun
The look-out is relaxed, just good seamanship now,
Last week survival was the game.
The tern circles all the watch through

> Act independently
> Homeward bound
> The Great Circle course
> The shortest route
> Where once was talk of station keeping and codes of attack
> We speculate on rescue ships for homing GIs.
> On tedious weather stations whilst waiting for demob.
> Re-training for a life of peace
> Homeward Bound
> The Great Circle course
> The shortest route
> Act independently

A few days out from the UK, a U-Boat surfaced flying the black flag of surrender. It was escorted in to Londonderry. The U-Boat was ordered to take up a position on the port bow and warned that any deviation from this would result in dire consequences.

At Londonderry we had a glimpse of several of the new types of U-Boats that were just coming into service. These had a fast underwater speed and because of the propulsion fuel used, a very long submerged endurance. These subs were believed to have submerged speeds of around 25 knots, compared to our maximum of 15 knots. In training exercises on the tactical table, they proved extremely difficult to counter. The only saving grace was that at speed they were very noisy. So with two ships taking bearings, we would know where they were, even if we couldn't catch them. It was a relief to know that we would now not have to do battle with them.

A visit to Norway

With the end of convoy work, the *Tintagel Castle* escorted a group of passenger liners across the North Sea to Oslo, conveying the King of Norway's entourage back home. The King and immediate family and staff had already proceeded ahead.

On arrival at Norway, the ship spent several delightful days in Oslo. The ship rang with the sound of children invited aboard by the crew and the NAAFI canteen was soon denuded of chocolates and other goodies generously given by the lower deck. The officers had little part in this. To me it seemed as though the crew believed that the children were not allowed on board. At that time, whenever I ventured below decks, there always seemed to be a scuffle of children rapidly disappearing from view, which one pretended not to notice.

The grateful shore authorities provided a bottle of wine, recovered from stock looted by the German Occupation forces from France, to each of the ship's company.

One afternoon a party of us were taken to see the sights of Oslo. This culminated in a visit to high point overlooking the city and fjord. I think that this is where the ski jump is now located. It was a steep road back down to the city, and I noticed that our car driver was doing a lot of the descent driving on his gears. When we reached the bottom, I remarked on this. 'Oh, that,' he replied nonchalantly, 'I had to drive on the gears. The car's brakes are done for.' This was certainly a case of ignorance being bliss.

After about a week in Oslo, we took a Norwegian Pilot on board and sailed for Tromso. Near there we were to meet a freighter that was bringing back French POW's from Russia. It had no suitable charts and our task was to escort the ship to Boulogne.

On this operation we escorted a Norwegian freighter and the *SS Stratheden*, that was carrying the Grenadier Guards. They were to land at Tromso and take over the town from the German Army. The freighter carried their equipment. The two ships were to carry the German troops and their equipment on the return journey southwards.

This was a fascinating voyage through the Norwegian fjords. The scenery was terrific. Of particular note was the peak of an island lying off one fjord. The peak had a huge horizontal hole through it. Further north we struggled through a huge tide rip where one could actually see the slight difference in water levels. Throughout the passage, German-manned supply boats were freely plying up and down the fjords, each boat flying the large black flag of surrender. Tromso at that time seemed to be a small fishing port, but was already cashing in on the market for German war trophies.

The freighter was met as arranged. An old, sad-looking vessel, badly in need of a re-paint. She followed us at a slow speed back down the fjords, across the North Sea, down the East coast and into the channel. We left her off Boulogne in an early morning haze. *TC* then reported to Sheerness, where we stayed for a while amid rumours concerning our future. These varied from being sent out into the mid-Atlantic to act as a combined weather station and radio guide for Flying Fortresses that were repatriating American Soldiers from Europe, or some similar fate but based at Freetown.

A Radio Beacon in the North Sea
We finished up being based at Rosyth. There we were conveniently placed for us to go some fifty miles off the coast from Aberdeen to anchor close to a lightship. This was moored at the western end of the swept channel from Norway. There we acted as a homing radio beacon, gently rolling in

boredom. Sub-Lieut. Despard and I relieved this by devising various models of fishing gear designed for spinning for mackerel from the ship's dinghy, which had in the meantime acquired an outboard motor. We never caught anything or had sight of a fish of any description. The ship's cook was most patient with us as we occupied the galley from time to time melting down and re-shaping the lead weights we had made. It was whilst at anchor in the North Sea that we heard of the use of the two atom bombs.

VJ day was celebrated whilst we were alongside in the Naval Base at Rosyth. Recently, in the *Journal of the Castle Class Association*, there have been various accounts of what happened on that day. In essence we celebrated the defeat of Japan with our own firework display. In exhausting our supply of Verey Lights, we nearly set fire to the night-watchman's hut by the dock gates. As a grand finale, an illuminating rocket was fired. Some accounts said it was a 4" star shell. This was sufficiently spectacular for all hands to come to their senses and retreat below decks as though we had had no part in it. Making a guess at the range at which the flare burst, I estimated that we had given Admiralty House a well-deserved illumination. As far as I know, nothing more was heard of this until accounts began to appear in the Castle Class Association's Ship's Log.

In due course we returned to Sheerness, where the ship was paid off.

CHAPTER 7

HMS *Allington Castle*

I WAS THRILLED WHEN IN early January 1946 I received my appointment as Executive Officer to the *Allington Castle*. It took a while to sink in. Then all became clear. I was to be No 1; not quite as good as being the CO, but the next best thing. I danced a jig with my mother around the drawing room.

I found the *Allington Castle* at Sheerness with orders to proceed to Dover the next day. She was allocated to the Fishery Protection Service. Her patch was to extend from the South Western Approaches to the north of Iceland.

We arrived in Dover in foul weather; cold and driving rain. We were ordered to a mooring buoy. It was then that I realised that we had a fairly raw crew – at least one inexperienced in securing to a mooring buoy.

Most of the crew were Hostilities Only and, like me, waiting for their Demob papers. This attitude of 'how soon can I get out', pervaded the ship. The skipper was a young Lieutenant RN. He was a keen rugby player. This interest played a significant part in our cruising programme. Although we operated within the command areas of C. in C. Nore and C. in C. Western Approaches, we actually reported directly to the Senior Officer, Fishery Protection (S.O.F.P.), who had an office in the Admiralty. Thus the Skipper, Lieut: P Aylwin RN, had a pretty free say in where and when we went,

Fishery Protection Duties

At first we cruised the SW. Approaches and the Irish Sea, making our home port at Fleetwood. This was the centre for the west coast fishing industry. It has a nasty sand-bank ridden entrance to the port, but that was no longer my responsibility. We had a very competent Lieut. RNR as pilot.

During our first patrols, one of the major tasks was to keep trawlers out of the areas of deep anti-submarine minefields. The UK boats mostly knew about these danger areas.

The trawlers were very co-operative in taking part in our boarding exercises. In place of the usual oar-powered whaler, we had an open motor launch. On the first exercise the boat was dropped some way off from the trawler. To me, it seemed we wasted a lot time by doing this. I was surprised that neither the Skipper nor the Chief Buffer knew of the boat-handling

151

30. HMS Allington Castle, *Fishery Protection Vessel.*

routine that we had used in the B1 Escort Group. As *Allington Castle* had been in the B3 Group, and I was sure we had used the same system then, it had not occurred to me that what I was suggesting was something new.

Now that it was peacetime, we were operating with a complement of some 80 per cent of the wartime establishment. This made a great difference when it came to hoisting the launch. Even with lower deck cleared, it was a struggle to get her up. The alternative was to run the falls to the for'ard capstan. I was never very happy with this arrangement. One did not have the same control over the falls and it was easy to snag one of them on the winch drum. This was because the deck rings were not in exactly the right position to give a straight lead to the centre of the winch drums. We usually compromised by running the launch up by hand until she was clear of the water, even when we rolled, and then performing the rest of the hoist from the capstan.

We established good relations with the trawlers. To some extent this was because of the 'you-scratch-my-back-I-will-scratch-yours' routine. The scratching consisted of supplies of pusser's duty-free cigarettes on our side and a sackful of fresh fish on theirs.

Circumnavigation of Iceland

In May we headed north to make a courtesy visit to Iceland, calling first at Reykjavik. It was interesting to go through the peacetime routine of official visits and receptions. The Government did us well. The entertainments started with the officers attending an official reception, where we met Ministers of Government and members of the Diplomatic Corps. This was followed by a dinner party for the whole ship's company – that is except for a skeleton watch-keeping group and one Sub-Lieut. He had over-indulged at the earlier party and had been confined to the ship.

Before we left to cruise round the island, we were taken on a tour of the local sights. This included the Great Geyser, which, for our benefit, was stimulated with soft soap to spout on demand. We picnicked at the sight of the Althing, the oldest parliament site in the world. Martinis, for me an unfamiliar drink, were supplied in generous measure. I slept soundly all the way back to the ship. It was only later, when I had studied a bit of geology, that I realised that I had seen one of the finest examples of an exposed faultline. On the outskirts of Reykjavik I saw for the first and, so far, the only time, a goat grazing on the turf roof of a house.

Near Reykjavik we passed several substantial glasshouses heated by natural springs. I was told that the presence of the American Air Force had been an important factor in developing this horticultural trade. Iceland was looking for overseas markets. On the other hand, centrally heating the city by water piped from the nearby hot springs had been going on for a long time.

From Reykjavik we steamed round to Seydisfjord. Our reception was a little strange. On the one hand we were welcome because they thought that we were going to protect them from the Russians. It seemed that there had been a rumour around that the Russians had got their eye on Iceland. On the other hand, it was thought that we had come to tow away a whale that had become stranded along the fjord shore. There was much relief when we expressed no interest in the whale. With regard to Russia, we explained that we were solely concerned with Fishery Protection matters and believed that there was no likelihood of Russia being concerned about Iceland.

During May in the latitudes of Iceland, it is still daylight very late into the evening. When I remarked on the absence of children at around 10p.m., the Mayor told me that there is a curfew on children after 9p.m. Otherwise, with virtually no darkness at night, it is very difficult for parents to get their children to bed at a reasonable time.

Whilst steaming round the northern coast, we had the interesting experience of passing between the northern coast line and the southern edge of the pack ice. The clear passage was a matter of only a few miles wide. During the day it was so hot that many of the crew working on the upper deck dispensed with shirts

We had plenty of time in which to complete our programme. I had always wanted to see Rockall and suggested to the Skipper that we should pass close to the island on our way back to the UK, so it was arranged. A day or so later we had a signal from the Admiralty telling us that we were to participate in the Victory celebrations. We had to go to Tenby and open the ship to the public.

Open Ship at Tenby

I was not pleased. Firstly it meant that there was no time to divert to Rockall. Secondly it meant that we had to paint ship at sea so as to present a tiddly, shipshape face to the public. Rain falling on wet paint did a little damage. On the whole the ship looked pretty good.

At Tenby we anchored a short way off the town. We arranged with the civic authorities for us to ferry visitors across to the ship. Guides stood by at strategic places and sensitive parts of the ship were securely locked.

On the whole, things went quite well. There was only a slight swell running, so visitors had little difficulty in transferring from the launch to the ship's gangway. On the turning of the tide, there was more movement and visitors began to have difficulties in coming aboard. I decided that before things got any worse, we would not bring out any more visitors. Those we had on board we would get to the shore as soon as possible. There were vigorous protests from the Mayor's office. In the end we got everybody ashore without even a sprained ankle.

In Appreciation of the Navy

Shortly after this I received my demob papers and was soon on my way home in an awful demob suit. At the time I had little appreciation of the tremendous effect those six years at sea would have later on. My immediate reaction was that I was glad to get out. I felt angry with the Navy. Before I had left the *TC*, the Admiralty had called for officers to transfer to the regular Navy. I had volunteered to do so and had applied for a place in the specialist N course. I was angry when the reply came back that I was too young to take the course and would have to spend several years as a general officer before I could be considered. I had been a navigating officer for well over a year. I had drawn specialist N allowances, and for a short while had also been the Escort Group Navigating Officer. Furthermore, I held the minimum qualifying rank of Lieutenant. I felt really let down.

Having been turned down for my chosen course, I talked with my friend Dennis and his parents. For some years there had been a sort of understanding, that if I wished, I could join them on their farm after the war. They confirmed this understanding so I applied for a grant to attend an agricultural college under the Further Education and Training Scheme. Luckily for me the rules were not stringently applied and I got my grant.

Time and time again I found that the discipline and training that I had received during the War years came to my rescue. By this I do not refer to the warlike skills that one learnt. It was the discipline that one absorbed that was important: it had involved not only carrying out orders but giving them as well; that too was important. The sense that the ship or the organisation was of greater importance than the individual was also part of it, especially when living in a small expatriate community in a strange country.

A useful tip was given to me by a very senior officer. The occasion was when *Abdiel* had been subjected to an Admiral's Inspection. When the formalities were over and the officers in a relaxed mood, I found myself next to the Admiral. I ventured to ask, 'How do you assess a ship when there is no time like this for an inspection ?' He looked me in the eye and after the briefest hesitation said,' I inspect the officers' heads.'

Often I had felt irritated by the Naval bureaucratic mind. Later, I realized how important it was to have a well-established method of doing things. In some instances I adopted a modified naval way of doing or organizing things. I owe a lot to the Navy and the *Conway*.

Ship's Officers

(RN unless stated otherwise)

HMS *Canton*

Capt;	G.D. Belben DSC AM
Cmdr (G)	C.H. Lingard-Guthrie
Lieut Cmdr RNR	J.M. Park
"	J.D. Birch (N duties)
Lieut RNR	R.A. Crozier
Temp Lieut RNR	H.M. Askin
Temp Cmrd E RNR	M.R. Robson
Temp Lieut Cmdr E RNR	H. Elvins
"	L.J. Ferguson
Temp Lieut RNR	A.J. Brabban
"	W.E. Galt
"	L.R. Robertson
Surg Lieut Cmdr RNVR	C.M. Lamont
Temp Paym Cmdr RNR	J.A. Stone
Sub Lieut RNR	W.E. Evans
"	M.D. Hutley
Temp Sub Lieut RNR	F.R.M. Greasely
"	D. West
Temp Sub Lieut(E) RNR	A.J.W. Wenn
"	J.S. Shivas
"	R.W. Carson
"	C.W.A. Barnes
Temp Paym Sub Lieut RNR	H.W. Mathew
Gunner	A.R. Bradley
Mid RNR	J.P. Roberts
"	W.A. Hutchinson
Temp Mid RNR	P.T. Farrar
"	K. Robinson
"	E.J.C. Jarvis
"	F.N. Goodwin
"	J.K. Harrop
"	D.C.K. Browning

HMS *Abdiel*

Capt;	The Hon E. Pleydell–Bouverie MVO
Lieut Cmdr (T)	P.H. Chavasse Squadron T Officer
Lieut	N.H.G. Austin Executive officer
Lieut	Lapage Navigation duties
Lieut	Mc Hary(?)
Cmdr(E)	F.J.S. Fox
Temp Lieut Cmdr (E)	A.H. Brown (act)
Temp Surg Lieut RNVR	J.P. Rockford
Paym Lieut	R.H. Allen
Sub Lieut	D.L. Baxter
Temp Paym Sub Lieut RNVR	S.F. Bristow
Gunner (T)	R.J. Mullins
Gunner	A.E. Millham
Temp Mid RNR	F.N. Goodwin

HMS *Sheffield* (selected)

Capt	A.W. Clarke
Cmdr	M.W. St L Searle
Lieut Cmdr	E.F.S. Back (N)
Sub Lieut	P.E. Faquhar
Temp Sub Lieut RNVR	N.J. Feather
"	M.S. Wallace
Temp Act Sub Lieut RNVR	G.M.G. Tibbs
Act Paym Sub Lieut	D.A.P. Stephens
Temp Lieut Sp Br RNVR	T.B. Logan
Temp Sub Lieut Sp Br RNVR	C.T. Rivington
Midshipman	W.R.D. Gerrad-Pearse
	J.D. Honeywell
	R.C.H. Manson
	D.S. Mackinnon
	P.H.T. Rees
	D.A. London
Temp Mid RNR	G.D. Petrie
"	R.W. Reid
"	J.C. Lowein
"	F.N. Goodwin

HMS *King George V* (selected)

R.A.	W.W. La T Bisset (2nd i/c Force H)
Flag Captain	T.E. Halsey DSO
Cmdr	R.S. Wellby DSO
Lieut Cmdr (N)	G. Cobb
Lieut Cmdr (G)	J.C.C. Henley
Lieut (G)	J.W. Endicott
Sub Lieut	P.R. Ramsay
	P. Wareham
Temp Sub Lieut RNVR	G. Haliwell
"	H.D. Janson
"	R.J.B. Sutton
"	J.A. Ingram
Midshipman	H.T. Wilson
RCN	E.V.S. Sunderland
	T.C. Cotton
RIN	J.H. St Strange
	A. Macdonald
	D.N.A. Roberts
	R.W. Longsdale
	W.M.G. Foley
	D.S. Robertson-Macdonald
	E.G. Parker
	M.G. Le G Barnes
	D.W.S. Collins
	A. Stein
Temp Mid RNR	J.C. Lowein
"	F.N. Goodwin
RNVR	T. La F Fryett
Midshipman (E)	G.L. Coates
	A.M.J. Cummings
	D.M. Spiller

HMS *Tintagel Castle* (May 1944)

Lieut RNR	R. Atkinson DSC** Commanding Officer
Temp Lieut RNVR	A. Courtould (1st Lieut)
	R.F. Dykes (i/c Squid)
Temp Sub Lieut RNVR	J. Corlett (Communications)
Temp Act Sub Lieut RNR	F.N. Goodwin (Pilot) (Prmtd Temp Lieut RNR 1.12.45)
Temp Act Sub Lieut RNVR	T.B. Despard (A/S Officer)
Temp Mid RNVR	N.S. Kimberley (Gunnery Officer)

HMS *Allington Castle* (April 1946)

Lieut P. Aylwin Commanding Officer

Temp Lieut RNR	F.N. Goodwin (1st Lieut)
	C.P.R. Collis (Navigating Officer)
Temp Lieut RNVR	R.W. Scott
Temp Surg Lieut RNVR	R.M. Mitchell
Temp Sub Lieut RNVR	A.H. Duffy
Temp Sub Lieut (E) RNVR	G.A. Harrison
S.A.N.F(v)	L.G. O'Reilly
Temp Mid RNR	L.P.C. Crosby

HMS *Tintagel Castle*
Convoy Reports

Table II.1 HMS Tintagel Castle: Convoy Reports: Summary

Convoy No	Passage	Period	No. of Ships	Notable Events
SL159/MKS50	GIB-UK	30/05-10/06/44	No data	
OS81/KMS55	UK-GIB	23/6-4/7/44	No data	
SL163/MKS54	GIB-UK	10-21/7/44	No data	vg air cover by *Campania*
OS85/KMS59	UK-GIB	2-13/8/44	No data	*Leeds Castle's* HF/DF aerial fell down the funnel
SL167/MKS58	GIB-UK	18-30/8/44	No data	difficulties in joining on convoy from the Med
ON(S) 254	UK-HALFX	17-30/9/44	No data	
SC158	HALFX-UK	7-18/10/44	No data	
ONS35	UK-HALFX	30/10-11/11/44	No data	*TC* aiding broken down ships.
HX320	HALFX-UK	17-30/11/44	No data	*TC's* Whaler recovered wooden spar 'periscope'
ON271	UK-HALFX	09-22/12/44	No data	heavy weather spread convoy 25 miles x 35 miles
X328	HALFX-UK	28/12-8/1/45	56	Heavy weather most of the passage
ON287	UK-HALFX	25/2/-8/3/44	93	Foggy start; *TC* ships' nursemaid again
HX344	HALFX-UK	15-28/3/45	71	Ice threatened to close St John's; Group moved to Argentia.
ON295	UK-HALFX	7-20/4/45	96	U-Boat sunk by *TC*
HX352	HALFX-UK	26/4-8/5/45	No data	Foggy passage
ON303	UK-HALFX	16-30/5/45	74	Ice, Fog, 20 ships in collisions

The following notes are derived from records of the Public Records Office (PRO). These are summarized in Table 1 on page 162. Unless stated otherwise all source references are those of the PRO.

No record of HMS *Tintagel Castle*'s first voyage with a convoy could be found; thus these notes start with the homeward passage following that first convoy.

Convoy SL159/MKS50; (36 ships) 30th May–10th June '44; B3 Escort Group; HMS *Towy* (S.O.); HM Ships *Antigua, Knaresborough Castle, Leeds Castle, Anguilla, & Tintagel Castle.*

Sailed from Gibraltar at 0600 on 30th May 1944 with 5 ships in convoy. Contact to be made with SL 159 5 miles south of Europa Point and subsequently with MKS 50, 40 miles east of the Straits.

It became apparent that some ships in the convoy(s) were not aware of the intention to meet the MKS east of the Straits and return during darkness hours. Two ships went into Gib to bunker and many despairing signals were received from other ships that their destination was the UK.

At 1320 R/V was made with MKS 50 two hours ahead of its expected position. Various 90° turns enabled the convoy to mark time – although this was not easy with a newly joined convoy, which had to form a narrow front before passing through the Straits. HMS *Dart* took all the Gibraltar merchant ships and escorts astern, breaking them off on passing Europa Point.

At 0257 on 3rd June OS 78 was contacted by radar at 19 miles and HMS *Activity* joined from that convoy to provide air cover until the 10th June. Various escorts oiled from *Activity*.

Early on the 7th June in position 49° 20'N 18° 24'W HMS *Cotton* and another escort made contact with the convoy and the oiler *San Tirso* was detached with them to join convoy OS 79.

At 1200 on 9th June, in position 54° 30'N 10° 42'W the convoy split, the Loch Ewe section proceeding under escort of *Leeds Castle*. The *Towy* and the remainder of B3 group, HMS *Activity* and HM *Trawler Vizalma* proceeded independently to Greenock, reaching position A at 0630 on 10th June.

Source: ADM 217/228.

Convoy OS 81/ KMS 55 23rd June–4th July '44: B3 Group HMS *Towy* (SO) HM Ships *Antigua, Knaresborough Castle, Leeds Castle, Anguilla & Tintagel Castle* together with HMS MS *Salamis*.

The Group sailed from Moville at 1100Z 23rd June. Contact made with the convoy at the Oversay R/V where the Loch Ewe section was joining up. HMS *Inman* and her Support Group swept ahead of the convoy until 0430

24th June leaving at position 56° 02'N 10° 14'W to sweep ahead of convoy HXM 295.

The convoy was re-organized on the 23rd June leaving three short columns in the centre to give *Activity* room to operate aircraft without leaving the convoy – this was particularly desirable as there were few escorts available to screen her outside the convoy.

Whales caused numerous false alarms.

On the 23rd June *Knaresborough Castle* and *Tintagel Castle* were detached to R/V with SL 161 in order to escort the oiler *Scottish American* to join OS 81/KMS 55, the three rejoining on the 27th June in position 47° 16'N 19° 27'W

Considerable swell on the 28th prevented escorts from oiling. Four escorts oiled on the 29th and the remaining three on the 30th June.

Air cover was provided during the 30th June by two Fortresses from the Azores and a Catalina from Gibraltar. KMS 55 was handed over to the Med Escort at 0630 on 4th July off Europa Point and B3 Group proceeded to Gibraltar.

Source: ADM 217/229.

Convoy SL 163/MKS 54 (No of ships not given) 10th–21st July 1944: B3 Group; HMS Towy (SO) (Cmdr Hugh ? King); HM Ships *Antigua, Knaresborough Castle, Leeds Castle, Anguilla & Tintagel Castle*

An uneventful passage. There was some discrepancy between the sailing orders and convoy papers (20 miles) for the R/V and it was necessary to make a diversion so as to avoid a UGF convoy under escort by the 41st Group.

HMS *Athene* took station within the convoy

'Air cover was provided by the *Campania*, which also provided useful AA exercises for the escorts with drogue-towing Wildcats during the 14th-16th July inclusive. The *Campania* carried out excellent air searches; operating aircraft in the dark with a skill and speed that made it appear very easy'.

Source: ADM 217/230.

Convoy OS 85/KMS 59 2nd–13th August 1944; UK to Gibraltar.

B3 Escort Group; *Tintagel Castle* (SO) *Knaresborough Castle, Leeds Castle, Allington Castle, Hurst Castle* & HMS *Anchusa*. Also joined by H.M.N.Z. Ship *Arbutus* and H.M. Ship *Antigua*, & *Campania* (latter joined 3rd August 1330 in position 54° 51'N 11° 48'W having been delayed by defects). HMS *Bullen* joined on 5th August (51° 29'N 16° 00'W) to replace *Anguilla*, who was unable to sail from the Clyde owing to hull defects.

At 2003 on 6th August *Leeds Castle*'s H/F D/F sense aerial fell down the funnel, but was safely retrieved from its hiding place amongst the tubes of No 1 boiler and replaced.

H.M.N.Z Ship *Arbutus* detached on 8th August to proceed to Bermuda.

Source: ADM/217/564; see also ADM/199/315: Reports of Convoys UK – Mediterranean and Sierra Leone SL 143-166, MKS 35-67, OS 81-86 & KMS 55-60

Convoy SL 167/MKS 58 18th–30th August '44 Gibraltar to UK. B3 Escort Group; HM Ships *Tintagel Castle* (SO) *Antigua, Knaresborough Castle, Leeds Castle, Allington Castle* & *Hurst Castle*. HMS *Bullen*.

This was the occasion when it was necessary to join 5 ships from Gibraltar to a west-bound convoy MKS 58 when east of the Straits. The convoy was an hour late at the rendezvous and low visibility compounded the matter. Eventually it was decided to postpone the join until after the passage through the Straits. At daylight the following morning it was found that three of the Gibraltar ships had strayed during the night. Two of these were found 17 miles astern.

At 0730 on 20th Aug in position 35° 29'N. 10° 14'W R/V was made with S.L. 176. The convoy was formed with the exception of three stragglers but one of them, No 34 *Empire Planet*, continued to drop back. The convoy speed was reduced for her, but she failed to rejoin. On the 23rd she was sentenced to the Stragglers' Route. This had the desired effect and the *Empire Planet* soon began to overtake the convoy

Source: ADM 217/563.

Convoy ON(S) 254 17th–30th September '44

No details of the escorts for this convoy are given in ADM/217/325. The convoy had an uneventful passage.

In view of the fact that B1 Group escorted Convoy SC 158 from 7th to 18th October (Halifax – UK), it is probable that the Group also escorted this UK – Halifax convoy.

Convoy SC 158 07th–18th Oct '44 (No. of ships not given); Escort Group B1; HMS *Chelmer* (SO); Cmdr J.H. Elder DSC RN; Escort list not given but HMS *Tintagel Castle* included in Group.

This was an uneventful passage and the usual Narrative of Proceedings is omitted from the file. There had been some dispute at the start of the voyage between W5 and B1 as to who was i/c of the convoy, W5 maintaining that B1 was merely in support.

When approaching UK, the *Empire Mallory* developed a leak caused by heavy rolling and reported that sediment from his cargo of zinc concentrate had blocked the pump intakes. On the 17th the Master reported that the position was serious. The wind had reached gale force, but the convoy was riding comfortably with a stern sea. *Empire Mallory* reported she was listing dangerously to starboard but could maintain 10 knots for 12 hours. Eventually she passed ahead of the convoy and arrived safely at Morville.

Source: ADM 217/326.

Convoy ONS 35 UK – Halifax Oct 30th–11th Nov '44 B1 Escort Group HMS *Chelmer* (SO) Cmdr J.H. Eaden DSC RN. Details of the number of ships escorted and the names of the escorts not given. However Escorts did include *Tintagel Castle*, and two MAC ships, SS *Macoma* & SS *Adula*.

In the afternoon of the 30th Oct SS *Lombardy* had to stop to investigate engine defects. *Tintagel Castle* ordered to stand by her. Repairs were completed on the 31st and they rejoined the convoy.

Number 52, *Egton* had problems with her crankshaft. A steel dowel pin was required to effect repairs. SS *Macoma* produced a pin in record time and this was transferred to *Egton*, probably by *Tintagel Castle*, who, I believe, also transferred a second pin on the 11th. (FNG's recollection)

Source: ADM 217/328.

Convoy HX 320 NF to UK 17th–30th Nov '44 B 1 Group HMS *Chelmer* (SO) Cmdr J.H.Eaden DSC RN, HM Ships *Inman*, *Tintagel Castle* and others; Report does not include a list of escorts. HM Ships *Vimy*, *Narcissus* and H.M.C.S. *Calgary* joined on the 28th as additional escorts.

The *Abigail Gibbons* (No 83) created a diversion by reporting sighting a periscope. Three officers, including the Master and the watch on deck, had seen the periscope. Although B1 seemed to doubt the authenticity of this report, an emergency ship-shore was broadcast. In due course *Tintagel Castle* recovered an old weighted wooden spar. This was done from the whaler in quite difficult seas.

Air cover was provided by the MAC ship SS *Empire Macalpine* carrying 4 swordfish. Bad weather, Force 7 wind and confused swells prevented routine patrols. The only operational flight carried out – which was to investigate the whereabouts of the straggler SS *Drupa* – was successful, but the aircraft sustained damage to her landing gear when flying on. The aircrew suffered no casualties.

Source: ADM 217/327.

Convoy ON 271; 09th–22nd December '44; (70 ships); B1 Escort Group; HMS *Tintagel Castle* (SO) and HM Ships *Inman, Lotus, Poppy* & *Dianella*.

Proceeded 091500.A December to rendezvous with Clyde & Belfast Section of ON 271; Milford Haven section joined on 10th & Channel section on the 11th. Total ships 70. Heavy weather encountered, and on 17th convoy was spread out over a frontage of 25 miles with a depth of 35 miles. On the 20th, with a southerly gale blowing wind force 8 veering slowly and increasing in strength, one vessel with only 2.5 days fuel remaining was detached to St John's NF under escort by HMS *Poppy*.

Source: ADM 199/581. See Also ADM 217/565.

Convoy HX 328 28th Dec '44–8th January '45 Halifax to UK (56 ships)

B1 Escort Group; *Tintagel Castle* (SO) *Inman, Lotus, Dianella, Poppy*, HMCS *Cap De La Madeleine* (the latter temporally attached)

The Group left St John's N.F 28th Dec at 2000Z to R/V with HX 328 at Westomp.

Four hours after leaving harbour the weather was reported as south-westerly gale Force 8-9 and heavy snow. Homing procedures used to effect the meet of escorts and convoy. This worked well.

30th Dec 52 ships found. One of these returned to Halifax as being unable to keep up with the convoy; One of the other stragglers reported having a tank adrift in her hold.

Problems were encountered when oiling at sea in heavy weather because of the shortness of the oiling hose. Arising from this experience, General Orders were amended to the effect that Masters of Oilers should be asked by the relevant escorts to stream the additional 210ft of hose carried for oiling during rough weather.

Source: ADM 217/566.

Convoy O.N.279 UK – Halifax; 47 ships 18th–29th January 1945. B1 Escort Group. HM Ships *Tintagel Castle* (S.O.) *Dianella, Poppy, Lotus, Starwort* (*Inman* undergoing engine overhaul at Londonderry).

Junctions of the various sections of the convoy were carried out in heavy weather and in some cases hazardous conditions (eg The Mersey Section joined in severe weather on opposite courses). So as to disembark pilots, the convoy sheltered in Cardigan Bay in conditions of high wind. Eight pilots were transferred in a force 8 wind by the whaler from *Tintagel Castle, Cape Mario*'s skiff and *Kempthorn*'s motor boat. 'The boats crews exhibited good seamanship under difficult conditions.'

Early in the morning of the 20th Jan HMS *Starwort* reported an A/S contact and shortly afterwards reported 'submarine'. She was supported by HMS *Inman*. (She had joined the convoy later ?). Several attacks were carried out and after 2 1/2 hours it was concluded that these attacks were on wrecks known to be in the vicinity. It is possible that the very first contact was that of a submarine. The SO in his report raised the problems created by contacts in depths of less than 100 fathoms and the tactical importance of not allowing close escorts to be diverted by 'doubtful' contacts.

On 23rd HMS *Poppy* was stopped for eight minutes with an engine defect. The next morning she reported that the defect would restrict her speed to 10 knots. *Tintagel Castle's* second Engineer Officer was transferred to *Poppy*. He confirmed that repairs could not be carried out at sea.

The Convoy was handed over to the Canadian Escort Group on 29th January and B1 Group proceeded to St John's NF. An uneventful passage except heavy weather caused difficulties in the early stages of the voyage.

Convoy HX 336 6th Feb – 16th Feb 1945; successful passage of 48 ships Halifax to UK. B1 Escort Group. List of escorts not given.

Weather was moderate and no enemy activity encountered. Convoy discipline was good.

There were a few cases of illness on passage and the Rescue Ship did good work. In one case of peritonitis the patient's life was saved by the use of penicillin. The patient had been transferred from No 42 (R.J. Reynolds) to the Rescue Ship *Accrington*. The MO sent out an urgent request for penicillin. This was available on No 92 (*William A Carter*) and a supply was transferred to the Rescue Ship by *Dianella*.

Support was given during the north west passage through the Irish Sea by E.G. 23, E.G. 19, and E.G. 31.

The escorts suffered various breakdowns. HMS *Lotus* had a vapour valve spindle broken; this was repaired by the Chief Engineer Empire *Maccare* (Mac Ship). HMS *Dianella* had a defective feed pump, reducing her speed to a maximum of 12 knots for $1^1/2$ hours. HMS *Starwort's* telemotor system broke down for 5 hours, the ship being steered from aft by her steering engine. Three ships, *Poppy*, *Dianella* and *Tintagel Castle* had problems with RADAR. These defects began occurring during the last five days of the convoy's passage. Except for *Poppy's* problem, the affected sets were out of action for the remainder of the voyage as the necessary spares were not carried by the Group.

Source: ADM/217/567.

Convoy ON 287 25th Feb – 8th March '45 93 ships; B1 Group HMS

Chelmer (SO) Act Cmdr J.H. Eaden RN; HM Ships *Tintagel Castle, Poppy, Dianella, Starwort.* H.M.C.S. *Lindsay* sailed as additional escort. HM Ships *Inman* & *Lotus* were detached for special duties.

Tintagel Castle having proceeded to R/V with the Milford Haven Section, the remainder of the Group and *Lindsay* sailed from Morville at 2030A on 25th Feb to meet the Clyde section of ON 287 and OS 113/KMS 87. The Section was found in some disorder because the position of the acting Commodore was not known. H.M.C.S. *Port Arthur,* bound for Halifax joined the convoy off Mew Island.

There was considerable congestion of traffic in the St George's Channel and south Irish Sea because of a combination of ON, OS, and KMS convoy(s) and relevant sections and escorts meeting at junction points; superimposed on this were the various changing Support Groups as one passes through the Support Force area. On one occasion there were no less than 17 escorts present not to mention a Sunderland and a Swordfish aircraft.

With this background, it was not surprising that a total of 645 signals were handled by *Chelmer* from 2030 on February 25th, the time of sailing, to 2000 on February 28th, the time at which the channel section detached.

The 'meet' with the Barry Roads and Milford Haven Sections of the combined convoys during the afternoon of the 27th Feb was delayed due to persistent fog, which had been present since daylight. Fortunately the visibility improved just prior to the actual junction and the two sections escorted by HM Ships *Tintagel Castle, Helir II, Huddersfield Town, Southern Wave* and *Southern Breeze* and supported by E.G 21 – HM Ships *Conn* (SO) *Deane, Fitzroy, Rupert* and *Bryon* – formed up the main section without incident.

Force 37 (*Berkeley Castle, Lancaster Castle, Dumbarton Castle* & *Carisbrook Castle*) joined at 0530A; detaching at 1545A 26th Feb.

Persistent fog delayed the meet with the Barry Roads and Milford Haven section of the combined convoys. However visibility improved and the junction was formed without incident. OS 113/KMS 87 detached at 2030A 26th. The Channel Section joined at 1245A on 28th Feb. EG 21 detached at 1123 28th.

Tintagel Castle remained in close support of *Nicholas Gilman,* who had broken down on Feb 28th. She rejoined the convoy 2130Z on March 1st. At 2316A 28th Feb *Tintagel Castle* signalled that she had intercepted *Ostlav* 24 miles astern of the convoy. *Ostlav* was stopped with engine trouble and expected to resume steaming at midnight. *Tintagel Castle* proceeded to rejoin the convoy.

On 4th March the MAC Ship *Alexia* developed engine trouble and had to stop. *Tintagel Castle* was ordered to stand by her. Convoy speed was reduced to 8 knots. Later *Alexia* was able to proceed and she attached herself to the rear of the convoy before dark.

The convoy was handed over to W.5 on March 8th in severe weather. The Group arrived at St John's on March 9th at 1330Z

Source: ADM 217/330.

Convoy HX 344 Halifax – UK: 15th–28th March (71 ships) B1 Group HMS *Chelmer* (SO) Cmdr J.H. Eaden; HM Ships *Tintagel Castle, Poppy, Dianella, & Starwort*. The MAC Ship *Empire MacDermott* provide air cover.

The Group sailed from St John's, NF on March 15th. The presence of pack ice and 'growlers' in the approaches to St John's Harbour, combined with an easterly wind, had threatened to close the port. The Group arrived at Argentia at 0820 local time on 16th March. The US Authorities placed the facilities of the base at the Group's disposal. *Tintagel Castle* experienced some difficulty with fragments of ice entering the condenser intake whilst on passage through the thin ice (FNG's recollection)

The Group left Argentia at 0700 local time on 18th March to R/V with HX 344 at Westomp. *Tintagel Castle* was detached to escort the *Johnan Printz*, who had been intercepted and to shepherd the stray back to the convoy. The vessel had become lost in the fog and was on her way to St John's.

Visibility had improved by noon and B1 took over the escort from W.2 Group who remained with the convoy as additional escorts until 20th March.

On 23rd March the convoy was joined by *Clan Urquhart* and HMS *066* escorted by HMC Ships *Prescott & Edmonston* who joined the screen.

The English Channel Section was detached in thick fog on 27th March. Fog persisted throughout the passage of the Irish Sea.

Source: ADM 217/329.

Convoy ON 295 7th–20th April '45 (96 ships); B1 Escort Group HMS *Chelmer* (S.O). Details of escorts not given.

Attack by *Vanquisher* and *Tintagel Castle* 47° 36'N 10° 35'W on 10/04/45.

B1 Escort Group sailed from Morville, less *Tintagel Castle* and *Poppy* 0900B on Saturday 7th April 1945. *Poppy & Tintagel Castle* had been detached to act as escort for HM Submarine *Sidon* and the joiners from Milford Haven.

The 23rd Escort Group provided support until 0630B 8th April; The 22nd Escort Group provided support from 1500B 8th April until 0520B 9th April.

The Milford Haven Section with *Tintagel Castle* joined at 0100B 9th April.

By 1500B 10th April the OS/KMS Section had broken off with HM Ships *Abellia* (S.O), *Clover*, *Oxford Castle* and Channel section of ON 295 with HM Ships *Vanquisher*, *Sunflower* and *Alisma* had joined.

Various Non-Sub contacts were made during the passage of the Irish Sea. On the 9th April the convoy was diverted to avoid a 'smoke contact' reported by a shore-based aircraft. An aircraft flown off the MAC Ship *Gadila* failed to find anything and the convoy resumed course at 2000B.

At 0145B 10th April HMS *Poppy* in 49° 34'N 08° 07'W at position D gained an asdic contact and reported it as 'probable'; HMS *Chelmer* joined her from position A and the convoy was turned to port to make room. After attacking, the contact disappeared. An 'Observant' was carried out by both ships until the convoy was clear when station was resumed, it having been decided that the contact was 'non-sub' and did not justify further attention once the convoy was clear. Nor was it considered to warrant any action on the part of E.G. 32, who had intercepted the reports on TSB from some thirty miles away and asked if he should join in.

HMS *Tintagel Castle*, Asdic contact at 40ft depth

At 2025B in 47° 50'N 09° 49'W HMS *Tintagel Castle* in position X gained contact and carried out two squid attacks on an object at a depth of 40ft. As there was no movement, she thought it might be a submerged wreck. At 2129 *Inman* was told to join her from position S in case it might be a U-Boat but at 2148, *Tintagel Castle* was getting a number of echoes and, deciding it was definitely non-sub, started to rejoin from 10 miles astern.

U-Boat sighted by HMS *Vanquisher*.

(See Appendix II.B for a detailed account)

The convoy of 96 ships was in 14 columns, 8 ships deep except for the box for the 2 MAC ships. Convoy position course and speed was 47° 37'N 10° 40'W, 255°, 9.5 knots. Weather; sea slight; wind 4-5; visibility 5 miles.

The escorts were disposed as follows:-

Chelmer	A	*Tintagel Castle*	X
Dianella	B	*Sunflower*	P
Poppy	D	*Alisma*	N
Starwort	F	*Vanquisher*	L
Inman	I		

At 2350B *Vanquisher* reported U-Boat in sight on the Port Side and opened fire. It was reported to me (S.O) that rockets had been fired and an underwater explosion heard (this must have been pom pom tracer or pom pom star shell, and depth charges, from *Vanquisher*) which led the SO to

believe that the convoy had been attacked and this was reported in his
102358B.

At 2355 *Chelmer* illuminated the area ahead of *Vanquisher* and while doing
so, the U-Boat was reported to have dived. A report from *Vanquisher* that the
U-Boat was 'Snorting' was not heard on the bridge during the noise of the
illumination.

At 2359 an XX position was established; at 2400 *Alisma* was ordered to
support *Vanquisher*, and at 0004 was ordered, when joining, to pass between
Vanquisher and the convoy.

Inman was ordered to report if there was a wreck and if so to direct the
rescue ship. She reported that there was no wreck and that there were no
stragglers. By this time enquiries on the bridge had led the SO to doubt the
report of rockets.

At 0009, *Vanquisher* was ordered to establish a datum and control an
Observant with *Alisma*. Shortly afterwards they gained contact and *Tintagel
Castle*, who was returning from her previous contact, reported being within
two miles. She was ordered to join in and a deliberate hunt was started.
Vanquisher having been told to take his time and kill him.

Approval was given for *Sunflower* to remain with *Vanquisher* and the screen
was re-disposed as follows:-

Chelmer	A	Starwort	R
Dianella	D	*Inman*	N
Poppy	H		

At 0215B it was appreciated from intercepted signals that contact had
faded and that the U-Boat was probably badly damaged if not sunk, So
Tintagel Castle was told to leave not later than 0400B. *Tintagel Castle* rejoined
at 1445B

It would appear that *Vanquisher* trod on the U-Boat and took him
completely by surprise and that while 'snorting' he had been quite unaware
of the approach of a convoy of 96 ships.

On the 19th April the Swordfish from the MAC *Miralda* flew off at dawn
on a search ahead and gave no less than two Tantivies. These proved to be
Icebergs and Growlers, through which the convoy passed later on.

The convoy was handed over to S.O.W 2 at Westomp (43° 59'N 47°
12'W) at 1530P 19th April. *Poppy* and *Dianella* remained with S.O.W. 2
detaching with the St Lawrence Section during the night and subsequently
proceeding to St John's.

Chelmer with *Inman* and *Tintagel Castle* proceeded to St John's arriving at
1900Z 20th April.

Commodore D Western Approaches, Londonderry, referring to the attack on the U-Boat, minuted as follows: 'This action illustrates several points of good drill – notably admirable co-operation and thoroughness and a sound appreciation of the value of modern anti U-Boat equipment. It is thought that this U-Boat was probably sunk.

'It is pleasing to note that a very keen ship of a keen, hard working Group has had at last a chance to display her worth'

Source: ADM 217/331; ADM 199/895 (last report in the volume).

Convoy HX 352 26th April–8th May '45 B1 Group HMS *Chelmer* (SO) Commander R. Thomson DSC RD RN. HM Ships include *Tintagel Castle*, *Inman*, *Dianella*, Starwort, *Poppy* (no detailed list of escorts given in the report, thus this list may not be complete)

The group sailed from St John's at 0945 local time 27th April to join HX 352 at Westomp (43° 59'N 49° 50'W). The convoy was about 2 hours ahead of schedule. Dense fog was encountered shortly after leaving harbour. Icebergs and growlers were known to be in the area. The Group was formed in divisions in line ahead disposed 2 miles abeam apart, the distance apart of ships in column being one mile. The meet took place in a comparatively clear patch.

This passage was (FNG's recollection) undertaken almost entirely in fog or low cloud making sun or star sights almost impossible.

The report states that *Tintagel Castle* with the Bristol Channel Section was detached in dense fog on 6th May.

Source: ADM 217/332.

Convoy O.N. 303, B1 Escort Group HMS *Chelmer* Commander R Thompson, DSC RD, RN. 16th May–30th May 1945. (74 ships) and HM Ships *Tintagel Castle*, *Lotus*, *Poppy*, and *Inman*.

The Escort Group sailed from Londonderry at various times on May 16th and 17th 1945; *Lotus* to Milford Haven whilst *Poppy* and *Tintagel Castle* proceeded to the Clyde; *Inman* to Belfast. *Chelmer* was delayed in sailing by a defect but sailed to the Clyde early on May 17th. The OS 129/KMS 303 and its escorts joined the convoy from Liverpool and was detached on the 19th in position 51° 30'N 07° 47'W. Although the passage through the Irish Sea passed off without incident, the Milford Haven Section of the Convoy was joined successfully in dense fog. Dense fog and low visibility was the weather theme for the remainder of the passage. The Channel Section of ON 303 joined in position 49° 58'N 10° 04'W at midday on the 19th. The convoy was supported by the Escort Group 19 (Loch Shin (S.O), *Cotton* and *Antigua* from early on the 19th to the evening of the 20th.

On the 20th *Vesper*, who had been escorting the Channel Section, reported having sighted a possible schnorkel, dropped astern and dropped a pattern of depth charges by eye. The convoy was turned away to starboard and Observant carried out by *Chelmer* and *Clematis* (escort with *Vesper* of the Channel Section). Smoke only had been seen, and as the MAC Ship's aircraft was known to have earlier dropped a marker in the vicinity, *Vesper's* sighting was considered doubtful from the outset. An hour after the initial sighting the convoy resumed its original course.

Vesper and consorts were detached at noon on the 21st May to join HX 355. On the 23rd and 24th May two ships were detached to proceed independently to their respective destinations. This left some 72 ships in the convoy. On the 26th May the *Hadley F Brown* reported that she had 10ft of water in the No 1 hold. The Master was concerned lest the bulkhead should not stand up, due to the movement of the ship and asked to be allowed to proceed to St John's. In view of the ice reports it was decided that he should remain with the convoy and detach with the ships bound for Newfoundland ports. In the meantime *Chelmer* transferred two 20-ton hand-worked pumps, there being no suitable 110 Volt pumps available.

Encounter with icebergs in fog

The convoy had been in thick fog, visibility zero almost continuously for four days since 23rd May when on the 27th May at 1602 in position 43° 08'N 49° 18'W course 233° 9.5 knots, *Chelmer* ahead of the convoy (position AL) obtained a RADAR contact at 3 miles ahead eight degree on the starboard bow. A number of confused echoes were reported. While investigating and with visibility down to about 50 yards, the SO found himself in close proximity to a very large iceberg, the full length of which could not be seen but which was thought to have been up to .75 miles. There was also another berg to the northward as well as growlers.

It was inevitable that collisions would occur. Either the convoy would hit the ice at 9.5 knots or turn 90° together, in which case a number of ships would collide with each other. The SO chose the second alternative and asked the Commodore to do a 'Double Item' turn (90° to Port together). This turn was executed 20 minutes after the first RADAR report. Almost immediately the Commodore's ship *Villanger* was reported in collision. The convoy was ordered to stop. For some time the R/T AND W/T channels were flooded with reports of collisions and damage. A signal was despatched for tugs to be sent out.

Both the Commodore's and Vice Commodore's ships had been in collision and the *Empire Stewart* was ordered to take over the duties of

Commodore and the main body of the convoy was handed over to HMS *Inman*. By this time the convoy ships were considered to have lost way and *Chelmer*, *Poppy*, *Tintagel Castle* and *Lotus* were closing ships with a view to rendering assistance where necessary and to find the Commodore. He was transferred to *Tintagel Castle* and embarked on *Chelmer* the next morning.

In the meantime the SO had devized a plan to withdraw the convoy from the danger of the ice. All ships were ordered to proceed on a course of 090°. Then to stop again and turn together to 180° and proceed on this course until well clear of the area before resuming a westerly course. This was successfully accomplished and at 1930 the turn to the south was carried out without further collisions.

By the time darkness fell (not that it made any difference to the visibility) *Inman* with the main body of the convoy was well clear whilst *Poppy* and *Lotus* were shepherding stragglers. *Chelmer* and *Tintagel Castle* remained in the vicinity of the icebergs looking for seriously damaged ships.

By 2230 it was apparent that 20 ships had been damaged and only one had actually hit the ice (See Table II.2). In only three cases did the damage sound dangerous. There had been reports of ships being holed and compartments filling up but no SOS had been made nor was there any reason to expect one. All ships appeared to be able to proceed and *Chelmer* and *Tintagel Castle* moved on with the rear ships.

A signal from C in C N.A indicated clear weather to the south. *Inman* went on ahead and found the Meteorological report to be very good. The *Empire Stewart* led the main body of the convoy out into the clear and by 1527/28th had formed up the convoy and set a course 300° at 7.5 knots. *Poppy* and *Lotus* acted as goal keepers at the turning point. *Chelmer* and *Tintagel Castle* brought up the extreme rear on an intercepting course at 10 knots. An hour and a half later *Inman* reported 68 ships present in the main body and that one ship (*Ovbula*) had been detached in accordance with previous orders. This return to normal was emphasized at 1830 when Commodore White had disembarked from *Chelmer* and was again in charge of the convoy on board the *Samthar*. Later that night a U.S. Ship with call sign P4EJ reported that he had three ships from ON 303 in company still in fog. He was asked to help them to rendezvous with the convoy in the afternoon of the next day in a new rendezvous position which had been broadcast on BAMS.

The tugs *Tenacity*, *Chippawa* and *Commanche* had been sailed from New-foundland with orders to proceed to the scene of the collisions. It did not seem that they would be required but it was arranged for them to meet the convoy on its new route in case any ship should be found to want a tug to stand by.

The relief Escort Group joined the convoy at 2130/28th and *Inman*, *Poppy* and *Lotus* were detached to proceed to St John's. The relief Escort Group (E.G.W.8) took over the convoy at 0730/29th. The convoy now consisted of 72 ships. The whereabouts of all but two of those not in company was known and there was reason to believe that these two were proceeding ahead independently. *Chelmer* and *Tintagel Castle* proceeded to St John's New-foundland arriving there at 1000/30th.

In his concluding remarks in his report, the S.O. B1 wrote 'I think one of the outstanding features of this episode was the splendid way in which the Master of the *Empire Stuart* immediately took charge of the convoy when the Commodore and Vice Commodore's ships had been too badly damaged to enable them to carry on.

'The manner in which he controlled the scattered ships, led them out of the danger area and formed up the convoy was a fine example of skill and leadership'.

Other Comments

When forwarding the Escort Group Commander's report to C in C Western Approaches, the Commodore (D) Western Approaches, included the following comments in his covering minute; '. . . At 1602 on the 27th May, with visibility about 50 yards, HMS *Chelmer* obtained Radar contact ahead at 6,000 yards and whilst investigating this, found it to be a particularly large iceberg, estimated by Senior Officer B.1 Group, to be more than a mile in breadth. It was directly in the path of the convoy. Commander Thomson immediately decided that the convoy must be diverted rather than stopped and ordered the convoy to turn 90° to port together. This resulted in a total of ten collisions affecting twenty ships and causing damage of varying degree, though in no instance was there any loss of life nor any ship lost. This difficult situation and subsequent happenings are fully described in the Narrative. I consider that Commander Thomson acted with commendable promptness and took the only possible course'.

'The Commodore's ship (SS *Valange* [sic]) was damaged; also the Vice Commodore's, but the Master of the *Empire Stewart* took over the duties of Commodore in a particularly commendable manner (see paragraph 41 of the Narrative). A brief summary of the damage done was assessed by 2230 that night – twenty ships damaged in varying degree but only seriously damaged in three cases, whilst all were able to proceed unassisted. Only one ship hit the ice.'

The Director of Anti-U-Boat Division (C.D. Howard-Johnston) commented: 'I do not think it is being wise after the event to state that the implication of A.C.I 412, paragraph 3, was relevant, (Extract – 'One or more escorts detached ahead have proved successful in locating icebergs which may be indicated to the Convoy...').

...I think it is important to find out:-

(a) How is it that *Chelmer* did not get a longer range contact from such a large object;

(b) Why *Poppy*, also stationed in a van position, did not locate the ice at long range;

(c) What objections there were to complying with the sense of A.C.I. 412, paragraph 3.

'...it is suggested that it be made clear to Western Approaches at this stage that the Admiralty takes a serious view of the matter, which it is expected will have been fully enquired into in the usual Service manner'.

The Director of Trade Division (W.A.Stephens) on 24th June 1945 submitted the chart showing how the convoy had already been diverted to the southward to pass through a position about 120 miles south of a known area of ice on the Eastern edge of the Grand Banks north of 44° 30'N. At the day of the encounter the convoy was some 80 miles south of the southernmost reported ice position. He continues to explain that:-

'Owing to escort considerations it was necessary for the ON/HX traffic to be routed reasonably near to Halifax and St John's for ships joining and leaving. In the ice season C. in C. C.N.A. had always therefore to keep these convoys as far to the northward as appeared safe. The situation shown on the 'chartlet' does not suggest any failure on his part to route the convoy reasonably clear of known dangers.

'As regards the actual encounter with the ice, it will be seen from the copy of the Commodore's report enclosed that the circumstances were very difficult indeed with fog and rain making the visibility practically nil at a time when immediate and wide avoiding action was imperative.

On the whole I think the Commodore and the merchant ships did pretty well to avoid any more serious consequences. All the ships got in under their own power and no lives were lost. *Empire Stuart*'s performance was particularly meritorious and the sense of the Commodore's and S.O. Escort's remarks on this has been conveyed to her owners'.

Sir Robert Atkinson (then Lieut Atkinson RNR) the Commanding Officer of *Tintagel Castle* during her first commission, commenting on the above account, also expressed surprise that *Chelmer* did not detect the ice at a longer range. He continued: 'On one occasion *TC* did precisely that – illuminated the huge iceberg by starshell since we couldn't contact the Commodore. The convoy turned immediately, there were no collisions' (personal communication).

Table II.2 Convoy ON 303; Collision Reports

A.1 Form No.	Name of Ship	Damage Report
131	*Fort Columbia*	Port Bow damaged above water-line not making water.
81	*Paine Weigate*	Holed in No 3 Hold – depth of water not known – maximum speed 4 knots.
71	*Villanger*	No 5 Hold full of water.
105	*John Henry or Patrick Mahoney*	Rammed Forepeak – reported filling up at 1730 (This report was made by a ship using Pendants 105. *John Henry* was number 105 on the A.1 Form but there is reason to believe that the report was originated by *Patrick Mahoney* Number 115).
28	*Alexander Bell*	Reported by *Inman* to be in collision with 52 – nothing further heard.
41	*Samaustral*	Hit iceberg – no serious damage.
114	*William Mulholland*	No serious damage.
145	*Fort Perrot*	No serious damage.
123	*Empire Ray*	Starboard Bow and anchor, starboard boats smashed; can do full speed.
64	*Empire McMahon*	Only slight damage
103	*Pennsylvania*	Holed
54	*Diplodon*	No serious damage – can do full speed.
52	*Ovula*	Slight damage.
111	*Empire Yukon*	Damaged Port bow and quarter
56	*John B. Hood*	Holed 15 feet above water-line – no serious damage.
107	*James Walker*	In collision; doing 6 knots quite happily
93	*Joseph H. Hollister*	Bow holed 15 feet from water-line.
55	*Jonathan Trumball*	Slight damage; can do full speed.
63	*Harrison Smith*	Suspected to be in collision with 56
72	*Skotaas*	Collision with 81 – bow damage.

178

APPENDIX IIB

The Sinking of U 878 by
HM Ships *Tintagel Castle* and *Vanquisher*

THE *TINTAGEL CASTLE* WAS re-joining the convoy after investigating a non–sub contact. At approximately 2145Z on the night of the 10th April 1945, when the *Tintagel Castle* was some 13 miles astern of the convoy, HMS *Vanquisher* reported sighting the schnorkel and periscope of a submarine. The *Vanquisher* opened fire on the submarine, which dived. *Vanquisher* soon made contact and attacked with depth charges and followed this up by carrying out the standard Observant Operation. *Tintagel Castle* was ordered to join the *Vanquisher* and reached her within forty minutes. At that time *Vanquisher* had already re-gained contact with the U-Boat and assumed the duties of directing ship, passing ranges and bearings.

Tintagel Castle obtained a non-sub contact within ten minutes, and *Vanquisher* still in contact and directing operations, enabled the *Tintagel Castle* to make a firm contact at 2317Z on a bearing of 050° at 1,300 yards. Speed was reduced to 6 knots and at 1,000 yards a slow deliberate attack was started with the U-Boat moving slowly to the right. All instruments were carefully checked and lined up.

With the range closed to about 800 yards and contact obtained by the 147B the depth of the U-Boat was estimated at 700ft. At 600 yards a firm contact was made with Q and the depth accurately observed to be stable at 600ft. Nine and a half minutes after contact had been made the centre bearing was 088° at 400 yards and the U-Boats' course and speed plotted as 100° − 3 knots. The Squid was fired at 2327Z, exactly 10 minutes after contact had been made. The bombs exploded 28 seconds later and a minute later a loud muffled explosion was heard followed 20 seconds later by an even louder second explosion. This was felt by HMS *Inman*, who at that time was five miles away. *Vanquisher* was questioned and confirmed that she had not fired depth charges.

Five minutes after the first attack, contact was re-gained at a distance of 500 yards and on a bearing of 290° and the range was opened in preparation for a second attack. During the run out, rattle and whistle effects were heard and the target appeared to be stopped. The second attack was made five minutes after the first with the target at 300 ft depth. Three minutes after this

179

attack the target was reported to be stopped. Two small underwater explosions were heard between eight and ten minutes after the second attack. The contact slowly faded.

At about an hour after the first attack another small underwater explosion was heard and a squid attack started; abandoned a minute later because the contact was not good enough for attack purposes. A search was organized by *Vanquisher*. The Escort Group Senior Officer, concluding that the submarine was probably sunk or severely damaged, ordered that the *Tintagel Castle* should not remain in the vicinity of the attack beyond 0200Z. After a long stern chase the *Tintagel Castle* resumed her station on the Convoy at 1255Z on the 11th April. This was some thirteen and a half hours after the start of the attack and eighteen and a half hours since *Tintagel Castle* had first left her screening position to investigate and attack what was eventually classified as a non-sub contact. This serves to emphasize the tactical dilemma of Escort Group Commanders in balancing the need to conserve a secure A/S Screen around the convoy and the eagerness of his CO's to press home and bring all attacks to a successful conclusion.

Appendix III

Ship's Movement Orders

HMS *Abdiel*

Date of Arrival	Place	Date of Departure	Remarks
11.4	Greenock	?	D of D 18.4 Taken in hand 15.4 Docking for examination of propellers. Completed 18.4
24.4	Gibraltar	?	
28.4	Malta	28.4	
30.4	Alexandria	2.5	
3.5	Haifa	4.5	
5.5	Alexandria	6.5	
12.5	Haifa	13.5	
14.5	Alexandria	17.5	St 1851/17.5 From C. in C. Med As soon as mines are embarked return to Alexandria at high speed. ST1241C/M.5 From C. in C. Med; A is expected to arrive Haifa about 001/18 mines are to embarked immediately on arrival
18.5	Haifa	18.5	
19.5	Alexandria	19.5	
22.5	Alexandria	26.5	ST2305/25.5 From C. in C. Med A has returned from landing stores & ammunition at Suda Bay & is re-embarking SS Troops who could not be landed from destroyers due to weather. A sails again tonight 25/26 with 2 destroyers carrying remainder of personnel
27.5	Alexandria	31.5	

Date of Arrival	Place	Date of Departure	Remarks
1.6	Alexandria	17.6	ST 0127c/6.6 from C. in C. Med Cretan Evacuation (1) 24/25.5 64 disembarked from Suda Bay (2) 26/27.5 A 2 Destroyers 930 disembarked from Suda (3) 312/5-1/6 Phoebe, A & 3 destroyers 3634 disembarked from Sphakia. ST1152c/16.6 from ?? A is to embark 12 A?C torpedoes. Sail 16/6 with all convenient despatch for Famagusta disembark torpedoes & return to Alexandria on completion. Passengers or equipment for Cyprus may be embarked if required
6.6	Alexandria	26.6	ST1112/18.7 From RA Alexandria to VALF Request A may enter harbour passing the boom by 18/7 if possible. ST1834c/18.7 From RA Alex:- A loaded 100 tons 200 men with DECOY leaves Alex 1000 19th passing through A about 1630. By 1930 W 2110 to arr Tobruk Boom 0001, B 0530, thence with DECOY through A abt 0830 to arr Alex 140020th.
27.6	Alexandria	19.7	
20.7	Tobruk	20.7	
20.7	Alexandria	22.7	
25.7	Famagusta	ST26.7	
26.7	?	ST27.7	
26.7	Famagusta	27.7	
27.7	Haifa	28.7	
29.7	Alexandria	4.8	
5.8	Port Said	7.8	
8.8	Famagusta	8.8	
?	Haifa	12.8	
13.8	Port Said	23.8	

Date of Arrival	Place	Date of Departure	Remarks
14.8	Famagusta	14.8	
14.8	Port Said	15.8	
16.8	Famagusta	16.8	
16.8	Alexandria	20.8	
22.8	Tobruk	23.8	
23.8	Alexandria	?	
25.8	Tobruk	25.8	
26.8	Alex	26.8	
?	Alexandria	27.8	
27.8	Tobruk	28.8	
28.8	Alex	9.9	
10.9	Alex	17.9	
17.9	Tobruk	18.9	
18.9	Alex	20.9	
20.9	Tobruk	20.9	
21.9	Alex	22.9	
22.9	Tobruk	23.9	
23.9	Alex	24.9	
24.9	Tobruk	25.9	
25.9	Alex	27.9	
27.9	Tobruk	28.9	
?	Alex	12.10	
13.10	Alex	18.10	
18.10	Tobruk	19.10	
19.10	Alex	21.10	
21.10	Tobruk	22.10	

Date of Arrival	Place	Date of Departure	Remarks
22.10	Alex	24.10	
24.10	Tobruk	24.10	
25.10	Alex	26.10	
?	Tobruk	25.10	
3.11	Famagusta	3.11	
–	Alex	4.11	
4/5.11	Famagusta	4/5.11	
6/7.11	Famagusta	6/7.11	
7/8.11	Famagusta	7/8.11	
9.11	Alex	14.11	
14.11	Tobruk	14.11	
15.11	Alex	26.11	
27.11	Haifa	?	C. in C. Med 1148°/14.12 Operation ME9 postponed A return to Haifa
14.12	Haifa	14.12	
?	Haifa	17.12	
30.12	Alex	29.12	
30.12	Haifa	29.12	
1.1/42	Suez	1.1	
1.1	Port Said	1.1	
4.1	ADEN	4.1	
25.1	Trincomalee	25.1	D of D 16.2 taken in hand Colombo 13.2 for docking for grounding damage: Completion DU
27.1	Port Blair	28.1	
3.2	Trincomalee	4.2	
5.2	Colombo	10.3	

185

Date of Arrival	Place	Date of Departure	Remarks
11.3	Addu Atoll	?	
16.3	Mombasa	16.3	
20.3	Durban	5.6	
ST20.3	?		Capt Supt Durban 1903z/23.3 taken in hand 21.3du CinC SA Durban 1821Z/14.4 DC will be delayed. AM 1229B/12.5 Request A be sailed for Clyde as soon as ready she will probably be taken in hand by Messrs Wallesend Shipping co. D of D 18.5 Ready to sail 5.6.42 A's 1500B/30.5 Leaves Durban 5.6 Capetown 7.6 Pointe Noire 12.6; Freetown 16.6 Gibraltar 20-21.6 and Greenock 25.6 with two officers, 14 lascars, 3 passengers survivors of British Ship *ELYSIA*
7.6	Durban	7.6	
9.6	Simonstown	?	*Abdiel* 2024A/15.6 Am proceeding Takoradi to repair defective evaporator-Expected time of arrival 0500Z/17 Requirements 600 tons oil fuel
14.6	Pointe Noire	14.6	
17.6	Takoradi	17.6	
20.6	Bathurst	26.6	had dept Freetown 19.6
25.6	Gibraltar	26.6	
29.6	Greenock	30.6	
1.7	Tyne	17.11	

HMS *Tintagel Castle*

Arrive	Port	Depart	Notes
1944			
20.4	Tobermory	7.5	Working up
7.5	Greenock	13.5	
13.5	Londonderry	14.5	
25.5	Gibraltar		Capt D Greenock. 09.1710/6 Request arrangements to take *TC* in hand on return from escort duty 10/6
10.6	Clyde	19.6	
23.6	Londonderry	23.6	
4.7	Gibraltar	10.7	
21.7	Clyde	1.8	
1.8	Londonderry	2.8	
13.8	Gibraltar	18.8	MKS 58
30.8	Clyde	7.9	
?	Larne	14.9	
?	Loch Ewe	16.9	
?	Londonderry	16.9	
16.9	Londonderry	17.9	
29.9	St John's NF	6.10	
19.10	Oban	?	
19.10	Londonderry	27.10	
?	Londonderry	29.10	
5.11	Londonderry	?	
13.11	St John's NF	?	
30.11	Londonderry	?	
?	Belfast	9.12	
?	Londonderry	11.12	
22.12	St John's NF	28.12	
1945			
08.01	Londonderry	?	
30.01	St John's NF	5.2	
?	St John's NF	6.2	
16.2	Londonderry	25.2	
?	Milford Haven	27.2	
9.3	St John's NF	15.3	
?	Argentia NF	18.3	
29.3	Londonderry	6.4	
7.4	Cardiff	8.4	

21.4	St John's NF	27.4
8.5	Londonderry	17.5
30.5	St John's NF	4.6
?	Londonderry	23.6
25.6	Rosyth	27.7
28.7	Humber	28.7
29.7	Rosyth	?
?	Granton	19.8
21.8	Oslo	25.8
?	Christiansands	3.9
7.9	Sheerness	26.1
27.1	Portland	Record ends

The following additional notes were found:-

AM 141741/10 *TC* is allocated to C. in C. Rosyth for air sea rescue duties in place of *Leeds Castle*.

AM 102257/11 TC is re-allocated to F.O.G.M.A. for air seas rescue duties.

1946 C in C Nore (7) 231145/1 (St)? end sailing 26/1 to Portland 27/1.

Source: Ship Movement Orders; Royal Navy Museum Library, Portsmouth.

HMS *Allington Castle*

Arrive 1946	Port	Depart	Notes
20.01			C. in C. Nore AC sail at 0900/18.1 to Dover
24.1	Swansea		
28.1	Pembroke Dock		
2.02	Fleetwood		
15.02	Fleetwood		
20.02	Belfast		
27.02	Pembroke Dock		

Remarks

S.O.F.P. STORK 241121Z/1 intend AC to arrive Chatham March 1st.

AC 270950/1. Intend proceeding to Milford Haven 28/2 eta 28/1.

AC 300945Z/1 Intend proceeding 30/1 to patrol outer Fastnet fishing ground thence to Fleetwood eta 3/2.

AC 010928/2 ETA Fleetwood 1002/2.

AC 091800/2 Intend sailing 0600/2.2 to patrol N Irish Sea Area ETA Fleetwood 1000 15.2

Capt Supt Pembroke Dock. 12/605Z AC should arrive 27.2 at Pembroke Dock.

S.O.M.P.[1] 170941/Z Intend AC to arrive Belfast 19.2 returning Fleetwood 22.2 arr Pembroke Dock 27.2

AC 181330Z/2 Proceeding on patrol ETA Belfast now 21.2 AC ETA Pike Lighthouse 1130/20.2

AC 22 1111/Z Intend proceed 2100/23.2 to Fleetwood ETA 1600 24.2

AC 25 0921/25(?) Intend proceeding 0600/26.2 to Milford Haven ETA 0900/27.2

Record Ends.Source: Ship Movement orders; Royal Navy Museum Library.

Note: This record refers to the time when the *Allington Castle* was operating as a Fishery protection vessel. Her sphere of operations extended from the South Western Approaches to the UK northwards to include Iceland. She reported directly to the Senior Officer Fishery Protection [SOFP] and acted independently of other Naval Commands.

Source: Personal recollection of F.N. Goodwin who was AC's 1st Lieut. at that time.

---

1. The original was hand written. For 'M' one should probably read 'F'.

Index